Old Testament Int

THEOLOGY OF THE OLD TESTAMENT

SPCK INTERNATIONAL STUDY GUIDES

The SPCK International Study Guides incorporate the much loved and respected TEF series. Written by scholars with experience of the worldwide Church, they combine good scholarship with clarity, simplicity and non-technical language. Ecumenical in authorship and outlook, the Guides are ideal for first-year theology students, Bible study groups, multi-cultural classes, people for whom English is a second language, and anyone who needs a sound but accessible guide to the Bible and theology.

SPCK INTERNATIONAL STUDY GUIDE 15

Old Testament Introduction 3

THEOLOGY OF THE
OLD TESTAMENT

DAVID F. HINSON

Published in Great Britain in 2001 by
Society for Promoting Christian Knowledge
Holy Trinity Church
Marylebone Road
London
NW1 4DU

First published in 1976
Revised edition 2001

Scripture quotations are from
THE REVISED STANDARD VERSION COMMON BIBLE
© 1946, 1952 and 1971 by the Division of Christian Education
of the National Council of the Churches of Christ in the USA.
Used by permission. All rights reserved.

British Library Cataloguing-in-Publication Data

A catalogue record for this book is available from
the British Library

ISBN 0–281–05384–7

Typeset by WestKey Ltd., Falmouth, Cornwall.
Printed in Great Britain at the
University Press, Cambridge, England

Contents

Illustrations and Charts

Preface

The publishing of this revised edition of *Theology of the Old Testament* brings to an end my involvement in producing the Old Testament Introduction for what was originally the TEF Study Guide series and is now the International Study Guide series, published by SPCK in London. I have found joy in the work I have been given to do in connection with my three books, and I have been amazed by the widespread use of them. SPCK has greatly increased the frequency of reprints by giving them away as part of their Books for Life scheme, for the benefit of students studying to become ministers of their churches in many parts of the world.

But of course I have had much assistance and support in the work I have done. So let me express my thanks to all who have helped me. First, as always, to Daphne Terry, who has been the mastermind through which the whole series of TEF Guides were produced. She has proved to be an excellent editor, returning each chapter of the manuscripts with detailed comments on aspects of what her authors had written, which have led the writers to make suitable improvements. I have had three editors in succession during the three years I have been working on this volume. These include Lucy Glasson and Robin Keeley. I am particularly indebted to Robin for his guidance as I settled to the work of completing the manuscript. He suggested a number of changes to the first edition concerning the format of the book. My present editor is Kate Hughes who has been helpful in many ways as the book has reached the editorial stage of production, and Mary Matthews has seen it through to printing. There have been others behind the scenes who have worked to ensure the book is well presented, such as the producer of the Subject Index which was beyond my ability because of the complex content of the book. To these too I am grateful. Locally, I have very good reason to thank my wife and family for their support throughout the years, and even in my retirement when more leisurely pursuits have often had to give way to my writing.

Robin Keeley arranged for Mike Butterworth, whom I had met on earlier occasions, to provide me with detailed comments on the first edition of *Theology of the Old Testament*. These were a very valuable aid to my work. I also benefited from advice provided by two Indian cannot be blamed for any faults in what I have written.

Many people have read my books, but I know that most readers have had to make allowances for the fact that I have written as a European, with all the background of English thought. The time must surely come when scholars and teachers of each different culture will write such books looking at the Old Testament from their African, Indian or other point of view according to their own background and circumstances. This will help the Old Testament speak in its own way to each culture, and enable ministers to guide their people in appropriate ways to understand what is written in it.

A professor has been reported as telling his students at the start of his course with them that one-tenth of everything he taught them would be wrong, but he was unable to tell them which one-tenth it was! This expresses the due humility of those who teach, because none of us are likely to be perfect in what we say, and this leaves room for discussion. So please accept my apologies if you discover anything that is mistaken in what I have written.

DAVID F. HINSON

Using this Book

This book is the third of a group of three volumes on the Old Testament. The first was about the history of Israel and the development of Jewish religious practices. The second was about the books of the Old Testament: the people involved and how the books developed as scriptures. You need to be aware of current ideas about these earlier subject before you can fully understand the subject of this book. You will benefit most if you use the earlier books of this group to gain this knowledge, but provided that you have studied these subjects in some other way, you will be able to begin work on the theology of the Old Testament.

What is Old Testament Theology?

Many twentieth-century Christian writers have produced books with the title *Old Testament Theology.* Each of these books is its author's attempt to discover and set down in writing what people of Old Testament times believed and taught. Our Old Testament scholars attempt to describe what God revealed to the people of Israel about himself, about humankind, and about the world. At the end of this book you will find fuller information about the variety of interpretations people have produced. But for the present you will find it helpful to begin with the study of this book, especially if you have never studied Old Testament theology before.

You will discover that the writers of Old Testament times present ideas which are sometimes in step with New Testament theology, and sometimes quite different from what Christians have believed and do believe. The difference between the two types of theology is that the writers and editors of the Old Testament lived before God's Son came to live on earth, and were without the help of the revelation he brought. They were in fact helping to prepare for his coming, by stimulating their fellow Jews to think about God and his purposes, and by calling them to share in their nation's experience of his presence among them. As a result the Jewish people and those who had accepted Judaism's faith had some understanding of God's purposes. So they were more able to appreciate the significance of the life and teachings of Jesus, and what he was doing for humankind, than any who had missed out on such guidance.

Why Do We Need to Study Old Testament Theology?

Some people say that because Christ did come we have the full revelation of God in the writings of the New Testament and can go straight to them without any need to study the Old Testament. Some people say that the things their own tribe or nation had discovered about God prepared them for the gospel, as it is taught in the traditional religion of their people. They say that the Old Testament was a preparation for the coming of Christ in Israel, but that Animism, Hinduism, Buddhism, or whatever other religion is practised in their country, is the preparation for Christ among their own people. This sort of attitude draws our attention to the fact that God has always been working to make himself known to all people in every place. We can understand some of the insights and understanding of the non-biblical religions as the result of God's inspiration. Paul recognized this fact in Romans 1.19, and John wrote about it in the prologue to his Gospel: John 1.9. Let us take an example: many of the tribes of Africa already had a belief in one God long before Christian missionaries brought the gospel to them. Their beliefs often included the idea that God was remote, perhaps because he reacted to their wrong doing and withdrew from them. They believed that the only direct contact they could have was with the multitude of spirits who inhabited the world they lived in. David Livingstone discovered this during his time among the Ba-Ila in Central Africa, and he was able to explain that God had come close through the work of his Son on earth.

All of us, as we develop our thinking about Christian teachings, have to weigh and consider the thoughts about God taught to us from childhood, or that are offered to us now as adults. We need to do so to discover whether these teachings give us an adequate basis for faith and life. We will quickly appreciate those parts of the Bible which deal with matters we have already given thought to, especially if they seem to provide us with a similar or better understanding of the issues involved. Since Christ is right at the centre of the revelation of God, most of us will have appreciated the appeal of the Gospels before we have come to understand other parts of the Bible. We can see in Jesus the riches of revelation which are available to us as we go on learning about life.

But we need to recognize that there is much more to God's revelation than the things we have found to be immediately helpful for our own understanding of life. We have a responsibility to search out the fullest details of the revelation that the New Testament contains, and so to know Christ in all his glory. But when we begin to study the New Testament with a determination to understand it fully, we quickly discover that we need to know what preceded it in the life of the people of Israel. The men and women who were involved in the Gospels already held the understanding that the Old Testament had given them when they met Jesus and used it as a basis for understanding his revelation. The writers of the Gospels tell us about the way in which people responded to Jesus. They assumed that their readers would understand the significance of the way in which they related to Jesus, without providing any detailed explanation of what they said and did. For example, in the conversation between Martha and Jesus in John 11.20–27, she makes use of the idea that the dead will rise at the end of the world, just as we can see prophesied in Daniel 12.2. But Jesus is concerned to share with her the news that the facts are even better than that. He says that a living relationship with him leads now to eternal life, and this continues in the life beyond this. Physical death is unable to destroy the spiritual life of the person concerned.

Bible Version

I based the first edition of this book on the Revised Standard Version (RSV) which scholars widely accepted as suitable for detailed study by those who lack adequate knowledge of the original languages of the Bible, which includes the majority of Christians. Although there is now a New Revised Standard Version, the United Bible Societies have decided to keep the original version in print because of the massive demand for this edition which has come from many parts of Africa. So we are able to continue to use this version in this book. Many scholars believe that it is still the best translation, presenting the contents in as accurate a fashion as possible compared with the original Hebrew, Aramaic and Greek. Too many recent versions deliberately alter the meaning of the original to meet changes in the way in which people use words today. The most obvious example is the widespread desire to avoid the fact that in Hebrew 'man' is used to speak of either sex (Genesis 1.27). Because English lacks a singular pronoun which covers both sexes, translators now change singulars into the plural, because 'they', 'them' and 'their' apply to both male and female. This change causes alterations in meaning as a result. This is all right for popular versions which are written for those who can only accept current usage, and lack any interest in what was actually written in the Hebrew. But this way fails to provide an accurate translation of the original languages.

Using Bible References

In this volume there are a large number of Bible references drawn
from many parts of the Old Testament. You will find it helpful to
read each section of the guide straight through once, to get the
general sense, and then to read sentence by sentence looking up all
the references. Notice especially how we find the same or similar
ideas in different parts of the Old Testament. Try to remember the
period of Israelite history which each book represents, and the time
at which the original writers or editors prepared the book as a record
of God's revelation. Notice especially what is said in the Torah, the
Prophets and the Writings, which are the major divisions in the
Hebrew scriptures.

   A recent editor of this series has asked writers to give the full form
of the titles of the books of the Bible, whenever quotations are provided. He has found in the past that abbreviations can cause problems for people who speak English as a second language. So I have
accepted this change from the way I gave quotations in the original
edition, and the earlier revised editions of the first two volumes in
this group. Some readers will without doubt be glad to have this
assistance.

Problems in Translation

The study of Old Testament theology involves a close look at the
meaning of the technical terms we find in that part of the Bible.
Because the original language was normally Hebrew, and occasionally Aramaic, the Bibles we read are all translations. They have
involved scholars in many parts of the world in the difficult work of
translating from Hebrew into English, or else into an appropriate
vernacular for their own people. The basic problem is that words in
any language possess different meanings according to the sense of
the sentences in which they occur. For example, people often use the
word *'book'* as a noun to refer to any of the following kinds of literature: *an album, a diary, a jotter, a manual, a notebook, a pad, a tract, a
volume.* People sometimes use the word *'book'* as a verb meaning such
things as *to arrange for a meeting,* or *to enter up a bill,* or *to reserve a seat*
or *to organize a programme.* Anybody who translates this word *'book'*
into another language needs to know in what sense it was originally
used in the document they are translating. They must then find a
word in the new language which carries the same or a very similar
meaning. So they have first to decide what they think the original
writers and later editors meant by the words they have used, and
then to decide which word in the language of the people they are
serving will most accurately express the same meaning. You will find

this easy to understand if you have ever been asked to act as an interpreter. If so, you too will have needed to try to understand what the speaker meant, and then to decide how to express the idea clearly in the language of the hearers. Two problems arise.

1 *Understanding the words we wish to translate*
   Old Testament scholars are at times uncertain what the original writer meant in using the words they are translating. In some cases the differences in meaning that the words can hold are so important that the translators feel they must list alternative meanings as footnotes, at the bottom of the page. Then readers know about the other meanings which the author or editors of the Hebrew text may have intended. For example, the Hebrew word used for *Spirit* in Genesis 1.2 can also mean *wind*, so those who prepared the RSV added a footnote 'b Or *wind*'. In this example the New English Bible translators actually wrote 'a mighty wind' in the main text, and 'the spirit of God' as a footnote. Sometimes scholars are unable to translate Hebrew sentences because the verses fail to provide any clear meaning. Perhaps they include a word which is so rare that scholars lack knowledge of what it means. Or the handwritten early copies of the scriptures that still exist are damaged or are in some places illegible. So the translators have to make an honest guess. In the RSV you will find footnotes which begin with *Cn*, which is short for *conjecture* which is another word for an honest guess. Sometimes the verses they are translating have ordinary words, which fail to give a clear meaning. See, for example, Genesis 16.13 and footnote *u*. The probable reason for such confused sentences is that people originally wrote and copied the Hebrew texts by hand. Those who prepared the copies sometimes failed to make an accurate copy. Sometimes later copiers tried to correct what they believed were mistakes in the text they were copying. So scholars have to compare the various early copies of these scriptures available to them before deciding what they think will be the best translation.

2 *Finding the right words in the new language*
   Because Hebrew words can often be used in various ways, the translators have to choose the English words which are appropriate in each use of each word. So they may translate the same Hebrew word in many different ways in various parts of the Old Testament according to the way the word is used in each sentence. For example, the Hebrew word usually translated as *justice* is also translated in more than 35 other ways. The word 'justice' also appears as 'appointment' in 2 Chronicles 31.13, as 'crime' in Ezekiel 7.23, and as 'specification' in 1 Kings 6.38 in the RSV. Unless we have a thorough knowledge of Hebrew we are unable to understand what problems scholars have faced in making their

choice of possible translations, so sharing in creating the contrasting versions of the English scriptures. We should, however, accept
that each of the groups of scholars who prepared the different
translations had real reasons for the choices they made about the
words to be used in their version of the scriptures. If you have ever
sat listening to interpreters at work, when you yourself know both
languages involved, you will remember the times when you felt
you could have provided a better translation of what was being
said. You will know that the interpreters have usually had good
reason for the words they have chosen, even though you would
have chosen other ways of expressing what had been said. We
should feel deeply indebted to scholars who have produced the
various English versions, and also those who have prepared adequate vernacular versions for the tribes and peoples they are serving. Without them we would be unable to study the Bible, and to
know for ourselves the importance of what is written in it.

Study Suggestions

Those who read the International Study Guides do so under varying
circumstances. Some people have these books as a class reader shared
with other students under the guidance of a tutor. Some use them as
books borrowed from the college library to supplement what they
have been taught in class. Others use them for home studies as part
of a programme of Theological Education by Extension, normally
referred to as TEE. Students learning by this method will use the
books as a basic source of information, and will be asked to write
essays or do other exercises relating to what they have read. These
they will send to their tutor who will mark what they have written,
and provide helpful comments to correct misunderstandings and
help deepen their understanding of important subjects. Yet others
will read the books as members of a congregation's study group, and
share in discussion with their pastor and other Christians. Maybe
some will read them out of personal interest, simply having an
enquiring mind, but without sharing with others and so unable to
discuss the issues raised. So writers of the Study Guides try to provide
all that is necessary to serve the whole range of readers.

We hope that you will feel happy to use the Study Suggestions in
whatever ways help you most. In recent years an important question
has been asked: how can readers be confident that they have understood what they have read? If a tutor or pastor is present when
students are reading a book, they can ask him or her questions about
anything which they find difficult to understand. The teachers can
ask questions to make sure everybody in the group does understand.
But those who study at home lack this advantage, and yet do need

some way of checking their own understanding of what they have read. This revised edition of *Theology of the Old Testament* contains questions at the end of each section of a chapter by which you can check your own ideas about what you have read. These are headed Check Your Understanding '1', '. . . 2', and so on. Write the answers on a piece of paper or in an exercise book as soon as you have finished reading the section concerned. Then turn to the back of the book and check your answers against those given under the heading 'Answers to Check Your Understanding Questions'. If you have the right answers you can go on safely to the next section of the chapter. If you have got the wrong answers reread the same section and ask yourself why the answer you have now been given is correct.

There are Subjects for Discussion or Essay Writing at the end of each chapter. These are suggestions that will help you think further about the significance of what you have read, and how it relates to daily life. If you have a tutor or pastor to guide you, they will tell you which exercises to tackle, or else provide you with other exercises that they have chosen. If you are studying alone and without such help you should try to find somebody willing to share in the same studies, so that you can discuss issues with them, and compare your ideas. If this is impossible, you may be able to find a friend who would enjoy discussing the issues raised by the questions, without doing the studies involved, and he or she will perhaps learn more about the Old Testament in the process.

The questions set under the heading 'Work with the Bible and a concordance' are set to enable you to do some research into the ideas of the Old Testament beyond what this book provides. You must have a concordance in order to tackle the exercises which are set. This is a book which lists all the references in the Bible to each of the words in the English version of the Old and New Testament used in the concordance. So it is a large book and expensive. Perhaps you can borrow a concordance from a friend who has one. If you are studying at college the library may contain a concordance that you can borrow or use in the library. Remember that other students will also need to use the concordance. If you have any knowledge of the Hebrew language you will find an analytical concordance particularly helpful because it tells you which Hebrew word lies behind the English translation that is the basis of the concordance.

The Illustrations

In this revised edition of *Theology of the Old Testament*, you will find one page of illustrations for each chapter, placed as close as possible to the part of the chapter which it supports. These illustrations serve two separate purposes. Most of them illustrate the ideas that were current among other peoples in the times of the Old Testament, and compare or contrast them with what Jews believed. The picture in Chapter 3 relates Old Testament ideas to the world of today, and encourages us to recognize the relevance of what we read.

The Indexes

There are two indexes at the back of the book. The Subject Index includes all the major subjects mentioned in this Guide; but it lists only the major references to each subject, so that the Index is a guide to the most important thoughts on each subject. The Bible Reference Index is much fuller and longer than in the earlier volumes of this *Introduction to the Old Testament* because we are unable to group the references to a particular book of the Old Testament according to the chapter where most of its references occur. References to some of the books are scattered widely throughout the Guide, indicating the breadth of the theological teaching they contain.

The Word of God

1

The word of our God will stand for ever
(Isaiah 40.8b)

The Old Testament as the Word of God

Some people read the Old Testament because it contains beautiful poetry and exciting stories. Others read it because the Old Testament helps to complete their knowledge of the history of the world's peoples. But most people who read it do so because they believe the Old Testament is part of the Word of God. Jews read it as their only scripture. They believe that in the Old Testament God made his covenant with the Jews. They say that he only expects the Jews to obey his laws given in its first five books, using them as their guide for life as God's people. They believe that by their own faithfulness and their suffering they can bring God's blessing to other people, who are also part of God's creation but exist outside the covenant. Muslims regard the Old Testament and the New Testament as parts of God's revelation, but claim that in the Qur'an they have God's full and final revelation. As Christians we believe that the Old Testament records the early revelations of God by which he prepared the way for the Jews to understand and accept the coming of Christ. We find that the Old Testament is so closely related to the New Testament that we need to read both. Together they help us to understand the character and purposes of God, and the nature and destiny of humankind.

This third volume in our course on the Old Testament is concerned with this understanding of God and people. This has been the purpose of our study of the history of Israel, and the origin and contents of the books of the Old Testament. We shall now study what the Old Testament has to teach us, and how it helps us to have a living relationship with God and to share in the fulfilment of his purposes for us.

We must begin, however, by being clear in our own minds what we mean when we say that the Old Testament is the Word of God. We shall only understand what the Old Testament teaches, if we first consider how it presents its message to us.

Christians have different ideas about the meaning of the phrase 'the Word of God'. Part of the problem is a grammatical difficulty. The little word *of* can carry more than one meaning. Think about the following sentences: 'You can trust the word of an honest person.' Here we could replace the word *of* by the phrase 'spoken by' without changing the meaning of the sentence. 'You can trust the word spoken by an honest man.' But now notice this sentence: 'Have you had word of Mr Smith since we last met?' Here we could replace *of* by *about*. The questioner wants to know if there is any news *about* Mr Smith. Which meaning for the word *of* is the correct one in the phrase 'the Word of God'? Some Christians take it to mean 'the Word spoken by God'; and others prefer to interpret the phrase as 'the Word about God'. We shall see later that there is another interpretation which is probably more helpful than either of these, but let us now consider these two ideas about the Old Testament.

The Word Spoken by God

We would find it very easy to understand and accept the teaching of the Old Testament if scholars could assure us that the whole of Scripture is a record of 'the Word spoken by God'. We believe that God is always honest; so we could turn to any chapter and any verse and find something that God said, which we would accept as true. Some Christians use the Old Testament in this way. They accept without question everything that they read in it. If anything they read seems puzzling to understand, or difficult to accept, they blame themselves for failing to appreciate what is written. They feel distrustful of any attempts to explain the difficulties as arising from the misunderstanding and inaccuracies of human authors and copyists. Conservative scholars and some thinking Christians recognize the difference between the words as originally given and the multitude of varied texts which have come to us. But this leaves most people with uncertainty about what we read today in the Old Testament. We have no fully effective way to get back to the things which were written at first.

The fact is that as we turn the pages of the Old Testament we do find words which the writers record as having been spoken by God. In Genesis 1 the clause 'God said "Let . . ."' occurs eight times, each time describing a further stage in the creation of the world. Again, one of the most frequent phrases in the prophetic books is 'Thus says the LORD' (Amos 1.3, 6, 9). But we can be sure that human writers have recorded these things, and have produced the books we read in the Old Testament.

Many of the words and sentences in the Old Testament are spoken or written by people, rather than by God. Sometimes we know who spoke what we read, especially in the legends and history recorded in the Old Testament. We can read the words of Abraham (Genesis 13.8, 9 etc.), Moses (Exodus 4.1, etc.), and David (1 Samuel 20.1). But we are ignorant of the names of the writers who recorded the stories about these men, and we are unable to say whether they were recording remembered sayings, or inventing suitable sayings to complete the stories they were telling. Sometimes we are unaware of who first used the words we read, but we can see that they express the thoughts of some ancient writer about God, for example Psalms 92, 121. Sometimes the thoughts are clearly human, and fail to express God's will or purpose, for example Psalm 137, and especially verses 8–9.

This is in great contrast to the Islamic idea of Scripture. The Muslims believe that the angel Gabriel gave Muhammad a vision of a sacred book in heaven which was written by God, and ordered him to recite its contents to his people. If you could read the Qur'an you would find that it presents itself throughout as containing the messages of God, which Muhammad taught to his followers. Sometimes the Qur'an describes Allah as correcting mistaken ideas about important biblical leaders, and especially about Mary and Jesus, but it lacks stories about other people told by men or women of the Arabic world. The Muslims claim that the Qur'an is the final and complete Word of God for all people.

But to Christians the full revelation of God is to be seen in the person of Christ, and experienced through our relationship with him. He is the Word of God, being himself divine. The Old Testament is a human record of the way in which God prepared the people of Israel for the coming of Christ. We shall see that their understanding developed over the centuries of their history. The New Testament is a record of what people remembered Jesus doing and saying during his earthly ministry, and how people responded to Jesus. It records the beginning of the Church, which is the company of those who in every generation believe in and trust our Saviour and Lord. It also tells of the activities of the Holy Spirit among those who believed in New Testament times, and the help he provided, and does provide for those who serve the LORD. We shall return to the significance of Christ himself as the Word of God in the section of Chapter 3 headed 'The Eternal Trinity' (pages 48–50).

The Word about God

Anybody who turns the pages of the Old Testament will quickly realize that in the Bible there is much that people have written about God. Even if such a reader denies that God exists, he or she is unable to deny that the Old Testament is *about* God. The reader has to admit that those who helped to write the Old Testament believed in God, and tried to explain life and history by using the idea of God. Such a person will deny that the writers have given an accurate account of events, because he or she rejects belief in God and is unable to accept this presentation of history which is based on belief in God.

We must realize that the people who wrote the Old Testament did so because they had shared in some experience of life which convinced them that God was a living reality. They felt that they must pass on to others the things which had convinced them of his reality. For some of them it was the whole history of their people up to their own day which convinced them that God had a plan of salvation for Israel. For others it was the wisdom and the justice of the laws handed down to them from earlier generations which convinced them of the rule of God. For the prophets, a more personal experience drove them to try to interpret the events of their own day in the light of God's rule, and of his purpose for his people. For the Psalmists, it was the sense of God's presence and power in the midst of a worshipping congregation which inspired them to write about the glories of God. They were also realistic about their sufferings and at times demanded to know why God had allowed such troubles. For the wise men of Old Testament days it was the intellectual struggles and the sudden gleams of new light on their problems which led them to record the truth about life as they saw it. They were all writing about God, convinced of the truth of what they wrote.

Anybody who reads the Bible must come to a decision about the value of these writings. As we have seen, people who deny the existence of God will treat the Old Testament as at best an interesting record of the ideas of the people of ancient Israel. They will reject the belief that these ideas are true. But those who have some experience of God and believe that he does reveal himself to people will be glad to read of the experiences of others, and will compare their own discoveries in the spiritual world with those of the people of ancient Israel. They will find much which matches their own experience of God, but some of the ideas expressed in the Old Testament will seem to conflict with their own experience of God. They will want to understand why the people of Israel believed as they did in these matters, but will probably prefer to read and re-read those parts of the Old Testament which confirm their own experiences.

But this is an inadequate answer to our question about the way in which the Old Testament is part of 'The Word of God', because it leaves us to judge for ourselves what is true and what is less than true. It suggests that a person's own judgement of spiritual reality is the best guide to eternal truth. But the Church has always recognized that the Bible has an authority for Christians, and that truth comes to us from the Bible in fresh and convincing ways. Does the phrase 'the Word of God' then mean more than 'the Word about God'?

The Word that Belongs to God

The word *of* has as its simplest meaning: 'belonging to', that is, a phrase containing *of* expresses the idea that a thing is used by, and under the control of, its owner. The flag *of* Zambia, for example, is for use by the people of Zambia and is under their control. Nobody else can use it properly unless with the permission and by the direction of the government and people of Zambia. Let us explore this idea as it relates to the Old Testament, which is the word *of* God.

The Old Testament is for God's use, and he controls its right use. We shall understand its proper value and significance as we come to understand God's way and God's purposes in our own lives. We shall fail to understand the Old Testament aright if we forget that God was involved in its preparation, and that the human experience which it expresses springs from God's activity among men and women. The basic truth is that from the very beginning God planned and worked for the day when people would have a personal living relationship with him, through which they would come to understand his greatness and his glory. The Bible came into being as a human response to this divine activity. It was preserved as a means by which people could share together the knowledge of God that came from this activity of his.

So the Bible has come into being as a result of the meeting of God with people, and people with God. The ways in which this meeting happens are usually described by two related words, *inspiration* and *revelation*. These words refer to different aspects of God's relationship with people. I find the distinction between them best described as follows:

Inspiration is the process by which God stimulates people to think fresh thoughts, and to seek new understanding. He does this in many different ways, but always people must be willing to respond and to search out the significance of their new experience of God. Otherwise they fail to gain the full benefit of his activity.

Revelation is the process by which God actually gives people new knowledge and new understanding. It is the proper result of inspiration. People must be willing to grasp and accept and use the new knowledge, if the process of revelation is to reach its fulfilment. They must make their new knowledge a real foundation for life and activity, and especially for their relationship with God himself.

We can recognize these two processes of inspiration and revelation in all the events and experiences described in the Old Testament. Those who wrote the Old Testament were expressing their own individual response to the activity of God. They were experiencing the prompting of God's spirit in the inspiration which made them search out new truth from all that was happening to them and to their nation. They were grappling with the truth which God was revealing, and they were seeking to express it in ways which their fellow Israelites would understand and appreciate.

Each generation of writers were people of their own time, who had shared in the benefits of God's work among his people in earlier periods. God was able to lead them on to fresh discoveries and new understanding, which they in turn shared with those who came after them. So, as the centuries passed, there grew up a great fund of knowledge of God and of his purposes. And this provided the opportunity for deeper understanding and richer experience of fellowship with God for succeeding generations.

Eventually, among the Jews the time was right for the coming of Christ. Those who accepted and lived by the truth which men in earlier centuries had recorded for the people of their time were able to share in the new revelation which came into the world full and complete in Jesus Christ. All that the Old Testament recorded was a necessary preparation to enable men and women to respond to the grace and truth that was in him (John 1.17; see also Hebrews 1.1–3, and our Lord's own words in John 5.39).

In a similar way, the Old Testament can prepare us today, by helping to deepen and enrich our spiritual understanding. It can enable us to appreciate more fully the person and work of Christ, and make us alert to, and ready for, God's presence and activity in our own lives, and in our communities. The Old Testament is the Word of God because it enables us to draw close to God and know his living presence, and to share fellowship with him in common with other believers. This is the purpose for which it was written: that we and all generations might be inspired and led into a personal relationship with, and knowledge of, God.

📖 Check Your Understanding 1

This is the first of the self-test exercises in this book. They are designed to help you check that you have properly understood what you have read in the section before each one. Write down your own answers on a piece of paper and then compare them with the answers given at the back of this book. If you find you have a different answer think carefully about the reason for your suggestion, and see if it agrees with the information you have been given. To do this you will need to read the section again.

1 People can use the term *word* in several different ways. Which two of the following terms come nearest to the meaning of *word* in the phrase 'Word of God'?

COMMAND   COMMUNICATION   DISCLOSURE

INFORMATION   PROMISE   PROVERB

REPORT   STATEMENT   VOW

2 When the prophets use the words 'the LORD says' what do they mean by them?

Which of the following alternatives expresses most clearly the truth about their experiences?

(a) I have heard the voice of God and now pass on his exact words to you.

(b) Because I have clear ideas of what God is like, I think that this is what he would say to you.

(c) God has given me insight into his purposes and I am now trying to share this insight with you.

The Methods of Inspiration Used by God

We have seen that, according to the writers of the Old Testament, God has always been at work in people's lives in order to establish a personal fellowship, a living relationship. This new life that he has been offering involves people in new thoughts, new feelings and new activities. 'Inspiration' is the name we give to the process by which God stimulates us towards these new ways of living. By inspiration he challenges us to live the sort of life which is a freely chosen response to him, and to his plans and purposes for humankind.

We need now to take a closer look at the ways in which God inspired people in Old Testament times to live as his servants and to do his will. The writers of the Old Testament describe many of the experiences which made people of those days think and feel and act as they did. These descriptions help us to see God at work inspiring people to find new life.

It will help us to understand our own experiences of God if we examine the means of inspiration described in the Old Testament. We should not expect to share in every one of these sorts of experience. They are tools for God's work, and are under his control. He knows how best to bring inspiration to each of us, and to the Christians communities to which we belong. We need only to be alert to the ways in which God approaches people, so that we may recognize the times when he draws near to us. Personally I believe that God is willing to use any means which we put at his disposal, but that he prefers to use those methods which best express the personal relationship he wishes to share with each of us.

Dreams

Dreams were widely accepted in ancient times as carrying significant messages. Many of the great people of Old Testament times are described as receiving inspiration through dreams. Jacob knew through dreams that God would be with him in his travels (Genesis

28.12, 15). Joseph learnt through his dreams that he was to be a leader of people (Genesis 37.5–11). Solomon was promised wisdom in a dream (1 Kings 3.5–15). In the Gospels Joseph and the wise men received warnings of danger through dreams (Matthew 2.12–13). The gift of the Holy Spirit at the time of the new age would result in further significant dreams (Joel 2.28; and compare Acts 2.17). But God was and is concerned for the welfare of all people as is shown by the fact that he gave Pharaoh warning of the coming famine, and when necessary provided an interpreter (Genesis 41.1–7; 14–16).

However, there are clear warnings in the Old Testament about false dreams, and about people who tell others of false dreams as though they had genuine messages from God (Deuteronomy 13.1–5; Jeremiah 23.32; Zechariah 10.2). God alone can provide the right interpretation for dreams and those who live in close fellowship with him can discern the truth (Genesis 40.8). We certainly need to distinguish between the many dreams which we experience from night to night and the special dreams which carry a message for us. Often we can relate the various aspects of these idle dreams to people, events, or feelings that have occurred during our daily life.

Visions

A vision is similar in many ways to a dream, except that it comes to people when they are awake and alert, rather than when they are asleep. Moses probably saw a vision when 'the angel of the Lord appeared to him in a flame of fire out of the midst of a bush' (Exodus 3.2). The disciple of Elisha saw a vision of 'horses and chariots of fire' protecting the prophet from his enemies (2 Kings 6.17). Isaiah saw a vision of Seraphim, and one of them touching his lips with a burning coal (Isaiah 6.6–7). Ezekiel saw a vision of God as a human figure surrounded by fire (Ezekiel 1.26–28).

The Old Testament also contains warnings about paying attention to false visions. Some people are said to describe 'visions of their own minds, not from the mouth of the LORD' (Jeremiah 23.16). Some priests and prophets 'err in vision, they stumble in giving judgment' (Isaiah 28.7). But when the Holy Spirit is poured out on all people, 'young men shall see visions' (Joel 2.28).

Signs

Often in giving visions God took up and used natural and ordinary things, including them in the mysterious experience. There was a bush that was the starting-point of the vision of Moses. The temple and the smoke of sacrifices helped provide the material for Isaiah's vision. Amos saw signs about the LORD's intention to judge Israel (Amos 7.7–9). The plumb line became a sign for him, and later he

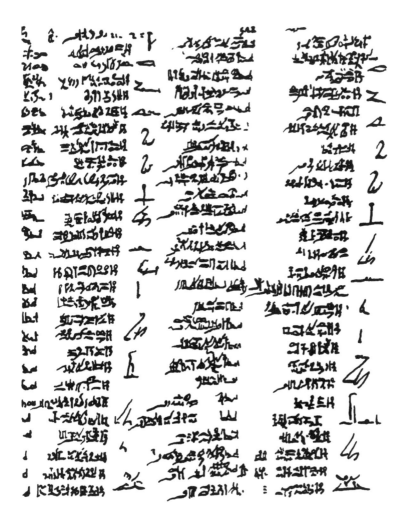

Figure 1. Throughout human history people have been interested in dreams, and have wanted to interpret them. This is part of an Egyptian papyrus from about 1300 BC which suggests explanations for some of the things seen in dreams, for example: 'If a man sees himself in a dream (a) plunging into the river – good: it means cleansing from all evils (b) seeing his face in a mirror – bad: it means another wife'!

Biblical writers believed that 'God alone can provide the right interpretation for dreams' (page 8). What do your own people think about dreams? What do *you* think?

described its effect upon him, as he preached to others. Jeremiah saw a boiling pot tilting over, and it became a sign to him of God's judgement of Judah (Jeremiah 1.13–14).

Sometimes the priests or prophets felt led by God to set up particular objects as permanent reminders to the people of what God had done. Such reminders could challenge those who saw them not only to remember but to open their hearts afresh to God. Joshua set up an altar near the Jordan as a sign (Joshua 4.6–7). The altar served to remind the people of God's ways with Israel, and so challenged them to obedience to the LORD who had given them their homeland. Sometimes a future event was promised in God's name, and the fulfilment of the promise would be a sign of his power and mercy (1 Samuel 10.2–10; 2 Kings 19.29–30, etc.).

Miracles

The Hebrew word for *miracles* seldom appears in the Old Testament. People preferred to use a word which is best translated *wonder*. This term expresses the special character of a miracle: something which makes people wonder. This word stands for an event or an experience which puzzles people, lacks any normal explanation, but has important significance.

Usually Old Testament writers describe such things as being the direct result of God's activity in the world. Perhaps some of them used this interpretation too quickly and too easily, without considering the possibility of a natural explanation. When we read what they wrote, we may feel compelled to question their judgement of an event, and to suggest some other cause for it, as we have done sometimes in Volume 1 of this course, *History of Israel*. Even so, unexpected, apparently unnatural, and unexplained events and experiences gave people a lively sense of God's presence and power, and this was a starting-point for a deepening relationship with him. For example, when the Israelites followed a pillar of cloud by day, and a pillar of fire by night, it may have been an erupting volcano which they could see far to the east (Exodus 13.21). If so, the miraculous element in this story would then be the timing of the eruption coinciding with the Israelites' need for guidance. God was using this event for his own purposes, and the Israelites were right to believe that he wanted them to regard it as a sign to guide their travels. By this event God was preparing them for their experiences at Mount Sinai. (See pages 37–38 for a further study of the nature of miracles.)

People God Called to Speak

The Old Testament describes many occasions when God challenged and inspired people most clearly and directly through the words of their leaders. For example, the LORD called Moses to lead his people out of Egypt (Exodus 3.7–8a, 10) and called Samuel to be his messenger to Eli and to the Israelites. Samuel was personally alert and aware of the presence of God, and so he was able to express to others God's purposes for his people (1 Samuel 3.10–14). Jeremiah experienced God's call (Jeremiah 1.4–10). He had the harshest of messages, that the Babylonians would defeat God's people. The law-givers, the kings, the priests, the prophets, and the collectors of wisdom all served at one time or another as messengers for God. Their words challenged individuals or the whole community to seek new ways of life which would bring them nearer to God. These people were a source of inspiration to their nation, opening up the way to fellowship with God. Yet these leaders failed to escape entirely from the accusation of their contemporaries that they were using their authority in false and misleading ways. Notice especially Amos 7.10–17 and Jeremiah 36.5–6.

These experiences, by which God made people alive to a sense of his presence and power, were all inadequate on their own to provide a full and complete guide to the religious life. Each could be misunderstood by people who resisted the truth that God wanted them to learn. Leaders who wanted to hinder the people from hearing what God was saying could misinterpret them. Yet through these varied sorts of experience God could and did draw near to people, and offer them a living fellowship with himself. His ultimate purpose was that they should know him for themselves:

> No longer shall each man teach his neighbour and each his brother, saying 'Know the LORD,' for they shall all know me, from the least of them to the greatest, says the LORD; for I will forgive their iniquity, and I will remember their sin no more. (Jeremiah 31.34)

God is available to us all through the work of the Holy Spirit, but sadly even yet many people do not want to hear what God says, or they are content with something less than a personal relationship with him.

 Check Your Understanding 2

Remember to write your answers on a piece of paper, to see what you think is right, before looking at the given answers.

1 Which three of the following words are nearest in meaning to the word 'inspiration', as we have used it in this section of the book?

DISCERNMENT DRAMATIZATION ENCOURAGEMENT ORIGINALITY PROMPTING SENSATION STIMULUS

2 Which offices held by leaders of Israel involved them in being spokesmen for God? Did those who held these offices always serve God well as spokesmen?

Now check your answers against those given at the back of this book.

God's Work of Revelation

We have seen that inspiration is the process by which God draws near to people, and calls them into fellowship with himself. Through the experience of God we gain new knowledge about his character and purposes, and the possibility of new ways of life. The processes of giving and receiving this new knowledge are both part of what we call 'revelation'. God gives and human beings receive, and both these activities must take place before revelation is complete. As Christians we shall need to see how what God taught in Old Testament times helped towards the development of Christian doctrine. Throughout the Old Testament there is evidence of God teaching his people through his acts of inspiration and revelation. Abraham learnt to serve the one God. The people of Israel in slavery in Egypt learnt that God had power to release them from slavery. When they first settled in Palestine they learnt that God could give them leaders to resist the attacks of many enemies. David learnt that he could not commit adultery without challenge. Isaiah learnt that the sins of the people were bringing danger to the nation, through the activities of the Assyrians. The people of the Exile learnt that God was with them even in Babylon, and could challenge and encourage them in the face of their despair. The many spokesmen and writers of Old Testament times brought fresh insights and understanding to the people. Sometimes fresh revelation challenged and rejected widely-held beliefs. For example, many writers believed that those who faced disasters and ill health did so because God was punishing them for their sin. But the writers who between them produced the book of Job struggled with the fact that a righteous man could and did suffer severe hardships. The reassurance they needed could not come from human knowledge and wisdom but only through the presence of God in the life of the ones who suffer.

All these experiences and many others helped the People of Israel to learn little by little more of the truth about God, his will and his purposes for his people and for all humans. As the writer to the Hebrews says, 'In many and various ways God spoke of old to our fathers by the prophets' (Hebrews 1.1). He sees all this leading forward to the coming of Jesus, who 'reflects the glory of God and bears the very stamp of his nature, upholding the universe by his word of power' (Hebrews 1.3). Many times Old Testament ideas are confirmed and strengthened by the writers of the New Testament who had committed themselves to the service of Jesus Christ. Malachi tells us: 'For I the LORD do not change' (Malachi 3.6). The writer to the Hebrews says: 'Jesus Christ is the same yesterday and today and for ever' (Hebrews 13.8). God's character is forever perfect (2 Samuel 22.31a, compare Matthew 5.48). His purposes remain the same (Psalm 18.30; Ephesians 3.11). God's activities in relationship with people only change according to the needs of the situation, in order to meet his eternal purposes (Jeremiah 18.5–11; Mark 11.25). What God has revealed through all the ages is truth about himself and his purposes – the same truth which God seeks to make known to every human being (Isaiah 45.19; John 14.6). This truth can be expressed in many different ways in many different situations. But, rightly understood, all that we know about God and his purposes fits together as one pattern of truth, to be distinguished from all that is false (Psalm 119.29; Romans 9.2).

But nobody can claim to have a mastery of the whole truth about God. Each receives some part of the truth through his or her own experience of God. We each benefit by sharing in the experience and knowledge of others who also serve the LORD. As we share our knowledge together, we come nearer to appreciating the whole truth which is in the heart and mind of God. The books of the Old Testament themselves were written as a way for people to share together their knowledge of God. We reach out towards the truth as we share and appreciate the experiences of those who wrote and edited the books of the Bible.

God responds to our search for the truth by leading us into deeper understanding. He is the perfect teacher: he knows best what we need to learn, and he knows best the ways in which we can learn. God shuns teaching us by dictating to humans factual statements of the realities he wants us to know. Statements are easily misunderstood, so we would be wrong to think that the truth can be confined to a few words. Statements and words always have associations with the experiences and the understanding of the people of any particular generation. They are seldom adequate to pass on what is important to later generations for whom the words may come to mean something very different. For example, the word 'missionary' was once used to describe people prepared to give up the ease and comfort of home life to travel to foreign lands to spread the gospel, without knowledge of what they would face, and prepared to die if needs be. Today in Britain it tends to be used in harsh, unfair criticism to describe people who wanted to have power and authority over the indigenous people of a foreign country. But the circumstances have completely changed for those who go to serve the Church overseas. Many people today travel around the world for a wide variety of reasons, so that those invited by the Churches to work abroad often have contact with people of their own nationality as well as friends of the country in which they serve. The local people have rightly gained a new way of life which enables them to take authority in national, social and religious activities. The expatriates often go for a brief time to meet a need that the local people are unable at present to meet, and to train others to take over from them when they leave. It is also becoming more common for there to be two-way traffic, with people going from traditional 'receiving' countries to work in 'sending' ones. So new terms are needed. For example 'Mission Partner' expresses the fact that we are all equal in the sight of God, and need to love and respect one another.

This is an example of the way in which God encourages each generation to think for itself. He gradually opens up the way for us through new experiences towards deeper appreciation and a fuller knowledge of his truth. Any teacher knows that this is the creative and effective way to get students to tackle their responsibilities. God is the great example on which teachers should model their work.

We can see evidence of God's work in the experiences which are described in the Old Testament. We need to be aware of the pattern of his work, in order to understand for ourselves the truth that is in the Old Testament. Let us take notice of some of the things which every good teacher knows to be important, and see how the Bible shows us God using these methods.

Start From Where the Students Are: Build New Knowledge on What They Know Already

There is evidence in the stories of the Patriarchs that they often worshipped God in places which could inspire a sense of wonder and a desire to respond to the beauty or strength of some natural object. Trees (Genesis 18.1), stones (Genesis 28.10–22), streams (Genesis 32.22–32) and mountains (Exodus 19.16–17) all provided them with places where God could be worshipped. Nothing in Genesis suggests that they regarded these as objects to be worshipped, or as inhabited by spirits that demanded their service. Their devotions were directed to the God who had first appeared to Abraham and called him into his service. However, Abraham was the one whom God called to a new commitment and way of life from that of his ancestors. Probably he grew up in a society that did worship such things, or the spirits they thought inhabited them. If so, Abraham was familiar with the belief that these objects marked places for worship. God met him there and led him to a deeper and richer experience of worship, and an awareness of his need to serve the true God. Those who followed him would then have made use of such places, knowing that they were meeting Abraham's God.

Work in a Well-Planned Order: Some Things Must be Learnt Before Others Can be Understood

Christians are often puzzled by the fact that the writers of the Old Testament seem to have very little idea of the Trinity of God: Father, Son and Holy Spirit. But the Israelites lived at a time when most of their neighbouring nations believed in many different gods. The most important idea in the religious education of the Jews was that God is One. It was only when they had fully grasped the idea of the Unity of God, with all it implies, that they were ready to receive the truth of the Trinity: the Three-in-One. Jesus came, and people learnt this truth out of their experience of him. The Old Testament shows how people's understanding of other truths about God also developed slowly, a little at a time. For example, the knowledge of God's justice was necessary before people could fully understand his mercy. The Exodus saw the beginnings of a new community life, with the need for rules to govern the tribes and later the Israelite nation. Only when people had firmly grasped the need for just dealings could they fully recognize their need for God's mercy. Otherwise they could make the mistake of thinking that God is easy-going with sinners. His mercy provided them with the opportunity to start a new life in which they could learn to live justly, caring for others as well as themselves. Mercy was the only way forward towards the completion of God's plans for his people, and for all humanity.

Take Account of Varying Ability in the Class

In any class some students will understand more quickly than others. They will make progress at different speeds. The wise teacher is able to stimulate and inspire the brightest student, and at the same time encourage the slowest. At any time in the history of Israel there were a few people who were outstanding in their spiritual understanding. They were far ahead of their own generation. Others held on to outworn ideas, and failed to appreciate the new measure of truth available at their time.

Some scholars have tended to see in the Old Testament a clear pattern of development in understanding, and have assumed that all the Israelites developed in understanding at the same speed. Such people deny, for example, that Moses could have received and passed on the Ten Commandments because they imply a settled lifestyle with houses, servants and agriculture. They see the Ten Commandments as having a later origin, but being attributed to Moses to give them prestige. But this is to neglect the deep understanding that God gave to Moses, as compared with the people of his time. It is probably true that some of the people to whom the Commandments were presented misinterpreted the first commandment 'You shall have no other gods before me' (Exodus 20.3, and notice the RSV footnote which offers the alternative translation 'besides' me). This could be taken to mean that God was supreme and others gods of less importance. But we can be confident that Moses took the words to mean that the LORD was unique: the true, living God. Especially if we remember Moses' experience of settled life in Egypt.

Teach by Putting Students into Situations Where the New Knowledge They Need to Receive is Seen to be Important

The practical use of theoretical knowledge is the best way to master a new truth. For example, if you want to learn a new language, the best way is to go where you will need to use it in order to be understood. Then your knowledge will be important to you and will become more firmly fixed in your mind through use. The Bible shows God using this method. He refused to lead his people away from places of conflict and trouble in order to leave them free to think and to study as the way to master new truth. Instead, he brought them to a land which has been a centre of conflict all through the centuries. They had to learn from that experience that God controls all history, and they had to struggle with this truth in the middle of international conflict. As a result, they came to a new appreciation of what it means to be God's people, and of how God works his purposes out among humans. They reached a new understanding of the meaning and purpose of suffering, first as a refining fire, and later as a means for the redemption of sinners.

Perhaps the best example of this process for us to think about is the Exile in Babylon. The people of Judah had developed particular social and religious patterns of behaviour, and felt secure because they had adopted them. The land of Palestine was theirs because God had given it to Abraham. The line of David was promised security and well-being. Jerusalem was the only centre for public worship. Their sacrifices provided for penitence, leading to God's forgiveness and blessing. They believed that God would one day rule the world from Jerusalem, so they believed it would never fall to their enemies. They felt content in themselves, and they failed to remain committed in their service of God. They failed to seek God's further acts of revelation. Their exile in Babylon came as a great shock to them because they lost the very things they cherished so much: their life in Palestine, their rule by David's line, their opportunity for sacrifice, their security from conquest, their hope for God's reign from Jerusalem. They needed to learn that God was with them in the Exile, even without these things in which they had put their trust. Probably at this time the priests began their important work of recording past history and traditions, and established meeting places for prayer and praise and reading these new scriptures: the first synagogues.

The Theology of the Old Testament

The importance of the Old Testament is that it is a record of God's work of revelation, making himself known to the people of Israel so that they could be ready to receive Jesus Christ as the One sent by God to fulfil his purposes on earth and among human beings. When we ask: 'What did God teach his people in Old Testament times?' we are asking to know what is contained in the theology of the Old Testament. This whole volume is written to help you discover the answers to this question.

Our present purpose is different from that of trying to discover what the Patriarchs believed – or the people of David's time, or those who lived in exile. That is the study of Old Testament religion. We have spent some time thinking about that in Volume 1 of this course, *History of Israel*, in the third section of each chapter under such headings as 'The God of Abraham', 'The God of Moses' and 'The LORD of Hosts'.

Our aim also differs from noticing the beliefs and understanding about God held by each of the various writers of the Old Testament, though we shall only understand what they wrote as we consider the whole pattern of their thought by studying all that they wrote. We tried to do this in Volume 2, *The Books of the Old Testament* – see especially those sections of each chapter headed 'Message'.

We are now involved in the much more difficult task of discovering the truth about God and his purposes which underlies the whole Old Testament. We shall try to answer such questions as:

- What is God like?
- What was his purpose in creating human beings?
- How shall we serve him?

We shall draw on the insights of people from various ages in order to reach our answers. We shall compare and contrast what they have to say in order to get as full an answer as we can. We shall feel free to do so, believing that God himself was at work in the hearts and minds of people in every period of Israelite history, and that each writer was led to some appreciation of the truth. We shall keep alert to the fact that it is possible to trace growing and deepening appreciation of the truth among the writers of the Old Testament; this was the result of God's work among his people through the centuries. We shall remember that, even so, at the time of Christ there were many among God's people who still failed to appreciate the corporate knowledge of God which had been built up over the centuries. Such people rejected Christ when he came. We shall only avoid their terrible mistake as we seek the help of God in understanding all that we read.

Students learning at or near a college may have the opportunity to read books by other authors under the same title, *Theology of the Old Testament*. If you have this opportunity, please first read the Postscript to this book on pages 185–90. This will help you to understand the major differences in what the various authors write.

📖 **Check Your Understanding 3**

By now you should have discovered the value of these tests to help you check for yourself whether you have understood what you have read in the previous section. If you miss them out, you will remain uncertain whether you have properly understood what you have studied. The correct answers are, as usual, at the back of the book. If you have given a wrong answer go back over the previous sections to discover why.

1 Revelation is the giving and receiving of truth. Which of the following words has the same or a similar meaning to 'truth' as we have used it in this chapter?

INFORMATION   KNOWLEDGE   LAW

PRINCIPLE   RELATIONSHIP   THEORIES

UNDERSTANDING

2 People can use each of the following words to express part of the meaning of the word 'revelation'. Which of the words would apply to the activity of God, and which to the activity of human beings?

DISCOVER   LEARN   MAKE KNOWN

RECOGNIZE   TEACH   UNCOVER

📖 Study Suggestions

1 When we read the Old Testament, what should we expect to find:
   (a) Precise theological statements about God and his purposes?
   (b) Human attempts to express what they have experienced of God in their daily lives?
   (c) Promises and prophecies made by God, recorded word for word by people, most of which have subsequently been fulfilled?

2 Miracles are described in this chapter as 'unexpected, apparently unnatural, and unexplained events and experiences' (page 10).
   (a) Do you think this is an adequate description, or would you want to qualify it in any way?
   (b) What difference, if any, does it make that we are sometimes able to give natural explanations of what happened?

3 A church leader once told a village congregation that God is bored by religion. What do you think he meant? Was he right?

4 How would you answer somebody who says to you, 'The Old Testament belongs to many centuries ago, and records the beliefs and practices of people who lived in a primitive and superstitious time. Why should we imagine that it contains anything of importance for today?'?

5 Think about the following statement: 'The Old Testament fails to provide the total guidance we need.' Can you, from your knowledge of the ministry of Jesus, suggest three areas of religious thought in which Jewish ideas were inadequate, and where Jesus had to share new insights?

6 Each of the ways in which God could inspire people could be misinterpreted by 'leaders who wanted to hinder the people from hearing what God was saying' (page 11). In what ways if any, could the people of Israel recognize those who were truly inspired, and distinguish them from those who were trying to mislead them?

7 The Hebrew language of the Bible lacks a word which normally means 'inspiration'. Instead, the idea is expressed by describing the activity of the Spirit of the LORD. Use a concordance to study the verses in Ezekiel which say that the Spirit

influenced the prophet, and then make a written report on the leading ideas involved.

8 Use a concordance to study the way in which the writers of the New Testament use the words 'reveal' and 'revelation'.

   (a) Do they give most emphasis to past experiences of divine revelation, or do they mainly understand revelation as a present or future experience?

   (b) How does the way they use these words affect our understanding of the nature and significance of revelation?

9 'God's character is forever perfect. His purposes remain the same' (page 13). Some of the Old Testament writers call God 'the Rock' to express this idea. Study Deuteronomy 32.1–43, and make a list of the things about the character of God which the passage says are unchanging.

The Nature of God

2

The Unity of God

'Hear, O Israel: The LORD our God is one LORD.'
(Deuteronomy 6.4)

Jews give these words a central place in their worship, and allow them to influence all their thoughts about religious matters. They are the first words of the *Shema*, or Confession of Faith, which the Jews use regularly in worship in their synagogues. These words are also among the verses of Scripture that Jews put in their 'phylacteries' (Matthew 23.5). Phylacteries are small leather boxes which strict Jews wear, tied to their left upper arm and to their forehead, in their daily private devotions (Deuteronomy 6.8). Because the Jews give these words a central place in their religion, they must be important for our own understanding of the Old Testament. Jesus himself used these same words to explain to a scribe how he should serve God (Mark 12.29). So we should study them with care.

This brief statement contains three important ideas:

1 God is identified by the special name LORD.
2 God is said to be *one*.
3 When the Jews use these words they find it necessary to describe the LORD by saying he is *one LORD*. God is unique, and there are no words which can truly describe him other than this special name. A prayer-book produced by liberal Jews attempts to put the divine name into plain English by using the words 'the Eternal One', naming one of the unique qualities of God.

Together these ideas form a basis for our whole understanding of God revealed in the Old Testament.

The LORD

According to Exodus 6.2–3, God revealed his name to Moses at Sinai as 'LORD'. These verses also tell us that the name had been unknown among the Israelites prior to that time. Yet the book of Genesis does use this name in almost every chapter. At first story-tellers used the title in passing on the stories about God's activities in the world: what he said, and what he did. But as soon as God called Abraham to serve him, Genesis tells us that Abraham began to call on the name of the LORD (Genesis 12.8). Soon afterwards we find that Abraham told the king of Sodom that he now served the LORD (Genesis 14.22). We can only understand this contradiction of verses between Exodus 6.2–3 and Genesis if we accept that the Torah consists of material from many different sources put together during or after the Exile in Babylon. One of these sources knew about the experience of Moses, and rightly recorded that he was the first to know the name. Another source was ignorant about the first revelation to Moses, and believed that the name had always been used among the Israelites. So they used the name LORD both in recording what God did and what people said about him. The editors who produced the book of Genesis knew both traditions, and combined them without making any effort to remove the conflict of ideas involved. Perhaps they found it necessary because there were many people who knew and cherished each of the traditions. If Abraham, in actual fact, lacked knowledge of the name LORD, how did he identify God? Exodus tells us that he used the Hebrew name *El Shaddai*, which means 'God Almighty' (Exodus 6.3). Later people continued to use this name, and it appears in several places elsewhere in the Old Testament, especially in Job. Often the texts present this name simply as 'Almighty'.

Following the compilation of the Torah and its wide availability in one form or another during and after the Exile in Babylon, the Jews came to believe that the Hebrew name for God was so sacred that it should never be spoken by humans. So whenever the Hebrew Scriptures were heard or are read, they replace the divine name with a word of respect often used of human leaders (Genesis 27.29; Numbers 12.11) or human masters (Exodus 21.4–6; Isaiah 1.3). This had an unfortunate effect. Nobody ever spoke the divine name, and Hebrew manuscripts originally only recorded the consonants of words. Nobody ever heard the divine name spoken, and the manuscripts failed to provide any clue as to the vowels originally used. So when later manuscript writers wanted to add vowels to the divine name in their manuscripts they decided to set down the vowels belonging to the ordinary word for a human lord. Jewish readers understood the significance of this combination of consonants from one word and vowels from another, but early Christian translators of Old Testament scriptures into their own languages failed to do so. So they tried to combine the vowels and consonants and produced the name *Jehovah*. In Hebrew that makes complete nonsense! However, many modern English translations of the Bible print the divine name as LORD to distinguish it from the ordinary Hebrew word for Lord, which they print as *lord*, and in capitals as *LORD*.

It is possible to turn the Hebrew consonants into Roman letters by writing YHWH. Scholars have made this pronounceable by writing YAHWEH. The group of Hebrew consonants does give some clue to the name's origin. They suggest some form of the Hebrew verb for 'to be'. We can find evidence for this in Exodus 3.14. A footnote in the RSV gives us a total choice of three ways of explaining the name LORD: 'I am who I am', 'I am what I am' or 'I will be what I will be'. The Hebrew language works without any distinct system for past, present or future among its verb forms. Instead they have forms which express things completed, and things still happening, and both forms can refer to any particular time past, present or future. This makes translation difficult, and scholars who prepare translations have to consider what time the writer was thinking about when he first wrote what we want to read. The three suggestions about the Divine name offer us alternative meanings. *I am who I am* stresses the idea that God is a person, who behaves according to his true nature. *I am what I am* suggests that he is free to be himself, and without any pressure on him to behave otherwise. *I will be what I will be* suggests that Moses and those who came after him will learn more about the LORD over the centuries ahead as they learn to serve him and to know his will for them. I rather like another idea: *I am what I will be*, always the same and yet always making fuller revelation of his eternal nature and purposes.

For the Jews YHWH stood, and still stands, as the name of the God who was known to Abraham and to Moses, and who chose the Israelites to be his special people. They know that he has been active throughout their history, and they believe that he still has an important part for them to play in the history of the world.

 Check Your Understanding 4

1 In a single sentence for each, write what you think the connection is between the following words and the title YHWH

JEHOVAH   LORD   YAHWEH

2 'this contradiction of verses between Exodus 6.2–3 and Genesis' (page 22). Which of the following words best explains why there is 'this contradiction'?

CARELESSNESS   DECEPTION   EDITING
MISUNDERSTANDING

One

The Hebrew word that English versions of the Old Testament translate as *one* is the ordinary word used in counting, and fails to provide any single explanation of what the Jews meant when they said that 'the LORD our God is **one** LORD'. The word can suggest three different ideas about God.

Many people may have interpreted it: 'Yahweh is one, but there are others we should please.'

Some Jews believed: 'Yahweh is the only God for Israel, but there are other gods for other peoples.' The other nations worshipped many gods whom they thought had power and influence in their lives, but Yahweh's power was to be supreme in Israel.

Quite certainly *The LORD is One* came eventually to mean that 'Yahweh, the God of Israel, is the only God; all others are mere idols without any real existence or power.'

Probably the great leaders in Israel, throughout the period covered by the Old Testament, understood more fully than other people of their time that Yahweh is the only God. The mass of people, like the people of neighbouring lands, went on speaking about other gods as though they had power and importance for them, and only gradually came to understand the fuller truth that God is One. Even the Jewish leaders may have failed to understand the full significance of what they believed about the LORD. Perhaps they acted upon their faith without being able to say clearly what they believed. Let us look briefly at the way in which belief in the unity of God affected the lives of some of the outstanding characters of the Old Testament.

We will start with the Patriarchs. Their stories are legends. Existing documents for other nations of their time provide evidence that other peoples observed similar customs. Later writers and editors of the Old Testament take the stories seriously. Their evidence comes from traditions preserved by people whose ability to remember things was far greater than ours, who depend on written or computerized storage of information. What we learn from the Exodus about the people of Israel clearly indicates circumstances that relate closely to the life and faith of the Patriarchs as Genesis describes them. The fact that the people who took part in the Exodus recognized the authority of the LORD must mean that God had been active among them at an earlier time. The presence of God's people as settlers in Egypt at the beginning of Exodus suggests circumstances brought about by the things Genesis records about Joseph. So we can draw acceptable conclusions about the development of faith among them from the book of Genesis.

Abraham was the first to become aware of the LORD, even though he probably knew him as *El Shaddai* (God Almighty) (Exodus 6.2, 3). He was so deeply influenced by the experience that he committed himself to the service of the LORD, believing that through doing so he would have a part in events which would eventually bring blessing to all peoples (Genesis 12.3). Yet the fear he expressed about going into Egypt in a time of famine suggests that he was unaware of the fact that God's

Fig. 2.   Fig. 3.

Figure 2. 'Probably the great leaders in Israel . . . understood more fully than other people of their time that Yahweh is the only God.' (page 24). But most nations in Old Testament times believed in many gods. This carved stone was used in Babylonia to mark a boundary, and shows pictures of the gods whose protection the owner wanted.

Figure 3. 'Phylacteries are small leather boxes which strict Jews wear, tied to their left upper arm and to their forehead, in their daily private devotions.' (page 21). Do you remember why they do this? Can you think of signs and symbols that Christians use in their public worship? Do you use such things in your private devotions?

authority and support would be with him there as it had been ever since he left Haran to settle in Palestine (Genesis 12.10–20). Perhaps he learnt the major lesson that wherever he went God was with him.

The Israelites who took part in the Exodus showed both recognition of the LORD and uncertainty about how much they could rely on him in their travels. Moses came to them as a messenger from 'the LORD, the God of your fathers' (Exodus 3.15), and called on them to gain freedom from slavery away from Egypt. The story totally lacks any evidence that they feared the gods of the Egyptians. After crossing the Red Sea, they celebrated the LORD's victory over the Egyptians, but without describing it as a victory over the gods of Egypt (Exodus 15.21). The later victory song of Exodus 15.1–18 does mention other gods, but never suggests they were in conflict with the LORD. The poet simply describes how powerless they were compared with the LORD, who 'will reign for ever and ever' (v. 8).

The Ten Commandments express the idea that the Israelites have a duty to worship and serve the LORD, and that they must avoid serving other gods (Exodus 20.2–3). Moses probably recognized the supremacy of the LORD so completely that for him other gods were without existence. But some of the Israelites failed fully to understand these commandments. They knew they themselves should only serve the LORD, but they recognized the power of other gods served by other nations.

Later, in the time of the Judges and the Kings of united Israel, many Israelites accepted the authority of the LORD in Israel, but also believed that other gods had their own areas of power and importance (Judges 11.24; 1 Samuel 26.19, 20). Some of their stories suggest that the LORD was in conflict with other gods, and could defeat them (1 Samuel 5.1–5). Other stories say that the LORD had given authority to lesser gods, 'sons of god', enabling them to rule other nations, but leaving them responsible to the LORD for what they did (Deuteronomy 32.8; Psalm 82.1–4). A similar idea is expressed in other psalms (Psalms 96.4; 135.5). But the emphasis here is on the idea that the LORD is supreme, and there is nobody to challenge his authority (Psalms 86.8; 89.6; 95.3). The LORD is 'God of gods' (Psalm 136.2). All these verses show how the Israelites gradually came to understand the idea that God is fully in control of history, both in Israel and beyond in the whole creation.

In conflict with these ideas, there was a continuing widespread belief among the Israelites that, although the LORD was their God who helped them in battle, they also needed to worship the fertility gods of Palestine, the Baalim and the Ashtaroth, to ensure good crops and large families. The idea may have persisted especially among the descendants of other peoples who were already settled in Palestine when the Israelites arrived. Some of these people came to be integrated into the people of God, but brought their pagan beliefs with them. By the time of David they accepted him as their king, and thought of themselves as Israelites. In the Northern Kingdom Jezebel, wife of King Ahab, encouraged the worship of the fertility gods, because Baal had an important place in the religion of her own people, the Phoenicians. Elijah challenged this idea, and his own attitude is clear from these words spoken at Mount Carmel: 'How long will you go limping with two different opinions? If the LORD is God follow him; but if Baal, then follow him' (1 Kings 18.21).

Yet the worship of the Baalim remained a source of conflict in Israel, right up to the time of their exile. Manasseh encouraged the people in this practice, which led to the reformation under Josiah. Jeremiah condemned the common practice in the Southern Kingdom of burning incense to the Baalim (Jeremiah 7.9; 11.13). To him this practice was as bad as murder or adultery: they were all abominations. He warned the people that the Babylonians would conquer them.

One LORD

The unknown writer of the Exile, the writer of Isaiah 40—55, was the first who expressed quite clearly the idea that the gods served by other nations were imaginary, lacking any real existence, and that the LORD is God of all nations (Isaiah 44.6; 45.22; 46.9). This prophet explained carefully what is involved in the belief that 'the LORD our God is one LORD'. He saw that, if this is true, then the LORD must be the Creator (Isaiah 40.12, 22), and must have control of all past history (Isaiah 40.23–24; 41.2–4); and all future developments (Isaiah 40.8–11; 42.8–9; 43.13). The LORD is the one whom all people must serve (Isaiah 45.8, 22–23). These ideas need careful study, and we shall look closely at them later in this book.

We should remember that from this source sprang the three great religions whose members worship the one true God. Judaism itself is still based essentially on the Torah, but has additional beliefs and practices provided by rabbis in the centuries following the time of Christ. They prefer to call what we call the Old Testament the Jewish Scriptures, because they deny that there is a new covenant which has replaced the covenant provided at Sinai. Christianity is the fulfilment of everything that God was revealing to the Jews in Old Testament times. Christianity is distinctive because we know Christ, and have the witness of the writers of the New Testament as a guide to our experience and understanding of God the Father, God the Son and God the Holy Spirit. We speak of the Unity of the three in their purposes and activities. The Islamic peoples believe that Muhammad brought further revelation from God by reciting the Qur'an between AD 610 and 630. This encourages its readers to respect others who share in the use of the Scriptures, which they see as a forerunner to the Qur'an, needing correction and improvement in the light of their new beliefs.

📖 Check Your Understanding 5

1 Which three of the following words can we rightly use of the LORD?

IDENTIFIABLE   ISOLATED   LONELY

OUTSTANDING   SELF-CENTRED   SOLITARY   UNIQUE

2 Use a dictionary to discover which of the following words describe the behaviour of the Israelites who served both the LORD and the Baalim.

ANIMISM   MONOTHEISM   POLYTHEISM   SYNCRETISM

Our Mysterious God

> One called to another and said:
> 'Holy, holy, holy is the LORD of hosts;
> the whole earth is full of his glory'.
> (Isaiah 6.3)

The words of the Seraphim at the time of Isaiah's call to be God's messenger lead us into the next part of our study. Most of this book is a study of the nature of God in his relationship with the created world, and with humans. The term immanence is used to describe God's nearness to us, his intention to share a living active fellowship with humankind, who can become his people. But before we turn to all that can be said about that, we must think about his *transcendence* (see later Ch. 4, page 61). That term refers to all about God that is strange to us and beyond our human understanding (Deuteronomy 29.29). We shall now study a series of words which highlight the problems Old Testament writers faced when they wanted to describe the mysterious aspects of God's nature. We, too, can experience his mystifying nature, and speak only of the awareness we have of aspects of God's nature that we can never fully describe or explain. Let us begin with the words of the Seraphim.

Holy

An authoritative Hebrew–English Dictionary says the word for *holy* is derived from a root word meaning *separation, withdrawal*, and the main form of the word itself means *apartness, sacredness*. When the Old Testament people used the word to speak of God they were expressing everything that makes God different from human beings and from other spiritual beings, everything which demands faith rather than complete knowledge and understanding.

The great difference between the Israelites and God made them very uneasy. God's holiness called out in them a sense of awe and unworthiness. We can best understand this if we remember that we ourselves are most at peace with people and experiences which are familiar to us. Our companions share some of our ideas, habits and customs. Sometimes, as humans, we feel anxious if we meet people who seem totally different from ourselves. How will they react to us, whether in their attitude and behaviour when they meet us, or in the secret thoughts of their hearts about us? How should we behave to gain their approval? How can we build a good relationship with them? The LORD is unique, and thinks and acts in ways quite different from our own (Isaiah 55.8–9). Our own thoughts and behaviour, and those of our friends, fail to provide us with a basis for understanding God. Any form of comparison is impossible (Exodus 15.11; 1 Samuel 2.2; Isaiah 40.25). So the Israelites felt great fear when God entered their lives. God needed to reassure Abraham when he showed anxiety (Genesis 15.1). Jacob became aware of God's presence through a dream, and recognized the *awesomeness* of the place where he slept (Genesis 28.10–17). Moses was *afraid* when he met God at the burning bush (Exodus 3.6b). The people he led out of Egypt were *afraid* when they faced great noise and saw lightning at Sinai signifying God's presence (Exodus 20.18–19). They refused to allow God to make himself known directly to them, and preferred that Moses should act as an intermediary.

Fear of the LORD remained a real problem among God's people, but gradually over the years, as they came to know more about God's activities among them, they began to recognize God's righteousness, and his demand that his people should be righteous (Isaiah 5.16). This explains the reason for Isaiah's fear at the time when the Seraphim sang about God's holiness. He recognized that he himself, and the people among whom he lived, had failed to serve God and that judgement should follow. We shall return to this subject when we study our relationship with God in Chapter 8, pages 134–5.

Glory

In English this word can mean things about the nature of individuals which cause people to marvel at them, or things that they do which make them famous. But the word can also mean praise given to such individuals by other people because of their character or their achievements. The two meanings belong together. For example, when someone says 'She has an amazing mastery of the use of computers', they are giving her honour because she has achieved a special knowledge and ability in the use of computers that few people do. The speaker is giving glory (honour) to the woman, but it is a response to what she has achieved. The speaker could also call her achievement her crowning glory. The speaker's approval gives her glory for all she has done. The same is true in Hebrew, where God is glorious, but he also receives glory from those who worship him.

If the Old Testament spoke only of God's holiness, it could leave people with an unrelieved feeling of fear, because we would be unable to get to know this strange being who lives a life hidden from us. But God's holiness is such that it becomes known to us through revelations of God's glory. The Psalmists in particular make this clear (Psalms 19.1; 72.18–19; 97.6; 138.4–6). The Psalmists call on worshippers to give glory to God, to exult and rejoice in him and the benefits which come from him (Psalms 24.7–9; 64.10; 96.1–4). Those who praise God, who exalt his name, provide witness to others of God's glory (Psalms 113.1–4; 145.10–13).

We are not to treat God's glory lightly, as though it removes our need to respect and obey God. He revealed his glory in and through the gloom of clouds (Exodus 19.16), and it was like a devouring fire (Exodus 24.16–17; Leviticus 9.23–24). When Moses asked to see God's glory, God told him that he could know his righteousness, but if he saw his face he would die (Exodus 33.18–23). We see evidence of this need for reverence for God again in the account of the tent of meeting, which the Israelites erected outside the camp (Exodus 33.7–11). The writer of Exodus 40.34 pictures a cloud covering the tabernacle because the glory of God filled it. The writer of 1 Kings 8.10–11 gives the same picture of the Temple built by Solomon in Jerusalem. Ezekiel's majestic visions of the LORD, which came first to him in exile (Ezekiel 1.26–28), saw his glory as being over the Temple in Jerusalem (Ezekiel 9.3–4; 10.3–5). In Ezekiel 11.22–23 the LORD departed from Jerusalem, but eventually Ezekiel saw in a vision that the LORD returned to the city (Ezekiel 43.2–5; 44.4).

Holiness and glory are like the two sides of a coin, which we cannot separate from each other if we are to grasp something of the mystery of God. But over the years the people of God received further insights into the nature of our mysterious God, so we shall turn now to examine some of these insights. They are by their very nature difficult for us fully to understand, and often scripture expresses the ideas by saying how God is different from human beings.

God is Eternal

Humans are born and die. We have a beginning at conception, and end our life on earth when we die. But God has always been, without a beginning and without an ending: he is for ever. The Hebrew word used most often to express *for ever* is often misunderstood by people today. Basically it means *for a long time*, and can refer to the whole of a human's earthly life. So when Psalm 23 ends 'and I shall dwell in the house of the LORD for ever', the RSV properly gives as a footnote, 'As long as I live'. At the time the psalm was written the people of God lacked any idea of a life after death. So, for humans, *for ever* was limited in meaning to our physical life on earth, but for God there is life without any ending (Psalm 102.12). We can say of God that *he is for ever, eternal,* or *everlasting*. The people who translated the RSV use all three English terms to translate the same Hebrew word. The writers are grappling with a difficult idea, because for humans time with beginning and ending is an essential part of our experience of life here. The writer of Ecclesiastes takes note of this difficulty (Ecclesiastes 3.11).

What does God's eternal nature involve? He existed before creation (Psalms 90.2; 93.2), and before anything else (Isaiah 41.4). He created wisdom as the basis for all that he made (Proverbs 8.22). He was responsible for the world's existence (Isaiah 40.28). He has control over creation (Psalm 93.1–2). He lives outside the controls of time (Psalms 90.4; 102.2). His rule is eternal (Exodus 15.18; Psalms 145.13; 146.10). He lives for ever (Deuteronomy 32.40). He is king for ever (Psalms 9.7; 10.16; 29.1). His purposes remain the same for ever (Psalm 33.11). As I have said, *ever* means *as long as I live*, and for God this is always, without any end.

God is Everywhere

Humans are limited to being in one place at a time and can only pay attention to a few things at any one time, or share conversation with a few people at a time. God is very different. He is as much where you are as where I am, even though we are far apart. He hears your prayer and responds to it, while answering mine, giving full attention to each of us (Jeremiah 23.23–24). At first the belief that God is everywhere took the form among the Israelites of a belief that God was with them wherever they went. In Genesis we have the story of God calling Abraham to go to the promised land. But he seems to have been slow to recognize that God had authority outside that land. When he went into Egypt to find food, he seems to have feared that the LORD was unable to protect him in this foreign land. In fact God saved Abraham from the results of his own attempt to protect himself (Genesis 12.10–19). So Abraham learnt an important lesson. Among the Israelites there was a fear of coming face to face with God, but at the same time they were aware that God was nearby, waiting to make his will known to them (Exodus 20.19). God's presence during the Exodus was made clear because of the signs of his presence in the tent of meeting (Exodus 33.9–11), and in their victories over foreign nations (Numbers 21.31–35). The LORD promised to be near to Joshua as he led God's people into the promised land (Joshua 1.5, 9). The people accepted Joshua as leader because God made his purposes known through him (Joshua 1.16–17). The people recognized that they had a privileged position in their relationship with God (Deuteronomy 4.7–8; Psalm 148.14). The prophets proclaimed God's authority over foreign nations, and his power to punish them (Amos 1.1–2.3; Isaiah 19.1–4, 18–20). They believed that eventually the foreign nations would come to them to learn about the LORD (Isaiah 2.2–4; 42.6–9). Psalm 139.7–12 gives us the clearest expression of God's presence being everywhere. We must guard against the error of thinking that if God is everywhere, then he must be in all things. We are wrong if we listen to those who say that all things and all beings have a part in the nature of God himself. The Old Testament never supposes that the Creator is also by creation developing and extending his own personal nature. It always pictures the LORD in relationship with his people, but we should avoid thinking that in some sense he includes his people within himself. He has authority over creation which the Old Testament always sees as distinct from him.

God is All Powerful

According to Exodus 6.3, the Patriarchs called God *God Almighty*. The RSV gives as a footnote *El Shaddai*, which is the Hebrew on which we base the English form of the name. *El* is the name for any god, and it probably expresses thoughts about a being who is more powerful and has more authority than others. The Old Testament writers often use a special plural form, *Elohim*. They use it in several ways:

- to speak of the LORD, when the plural expresses honour and respect
- to speak of other gods, distinct from the LORD (Exodus 15.11, 20.3; Psalm 16.4; Isaiah 21.9)
- to describe a human being as *mighty* (Genesis 23.6) or even to describe mighty mountains (Psalm 68.15) and mighty vegetation (Psalm 80.10).

This wide variation of meaning explains the different ways in which the various English versions translate the first clause of Psalm 8.5. The writer of Hebrews 2.7 quotes this verse as referring to Jesus being 'for a little while lower than the angels'.

The origin of the word *Shaddai* is uncertain, but in use it came to emphasize that God is more than mighty, being supreme in his authority. The combined name *El Shaddai* is used several times in Genesis, as Exodus 6.3 suggests. But in most of the other places in the Old Testament where *Shaddai* appears, it stands alone, or the writer uses it as an alternative for *God* rather than repeat the word God twice in the same verse. The mystery we face in the use of this name for God is to understand how God uses his power without destroying our free will. His patience with wilful human beings is marvellous, but we are unable to understand fully how he will eventually bring all things into harmony, and overcome evil through the free choice of all his people (Nehemiah 9.17; Psalm 103.8; Joel 2.13).

God Knows and Understands All Things

Because God lives without being limited to one time or one place, but is always present in every place, he possesses a unique ability to know and understand all things. Because God is creator he has a unique knowledge of the universe he has created. This contrasts greatly with our knowledge and understanding. We can never in our present state, controlled by time and space, have equal knowledge with God. Even our deepest-held convictions about God and his creation are inadequate, and can involve us in misunderstanding. Total knowledge and total understanding belong to God alone. The finest scholars with long experience of study are limited in their understanding of their own subject, and often ignorant of matters which are outside their own field of study.

What evidence is there that people of Old Testament times recognized these facts? God knows all things (Isaiah 40.28; Job 11.7–8; 38.1–7; 42.3b, 5–6). God knows the secrets of people's hearts (Psalm 139.1–6; Jeremiah 11.20; 17.9–10). He knows the foolishness of much of our thinking (Proverbs 16.2; 21.2; 24.12). Some people believed that the work of the prophets was to proclaim to people their future, but scholars have recognized that their real work was to proclaim what God was doing. Sometimes prophets offered humans two alternative futures according to whether they went on in their sin or repented (Isaiah 1.19–20; Jeremiah 17.24–27; Ezekiel 18.5–24). At other times they told the people what God would do to bless them if they repented (Isaiah 58.9b–14; Jeremiah 4.1–2; Ezekiel 43.10–12). This change in interpretation takes account of the fact that God has given people free will, and that they have a genuine choice. God can have a shrewd idea of what we will do, because he has complete knowledge of us. But he is unable to say with absolute certainty whether we will respond to his purposes, or reject them. In fact, warnings in the Old Testament leave the way open for God's people to change their ways and find his blessing. There are times when the prophets used words which express God's uncertainty in their reports of his revelation ('may be', Jeremiah 26.1–3; 'perhaps', Ezekiel 12.1–3). They even suggest the idea that God had expected that his people would behave in one way, but found that they did the reverse ('I thought', Jeremiah 3.6–7, 19–20).

📖 Check Your Understanding 6

1 Which three of the following words seem best to describe God's eternal nature?

AGELESS CONSTANT EVERLASTING INTERMINABLE

UNREMITTING

2 There are technical words that scholars use to describe the mysterious aspects of God's nature. Use a dictionary to discover which of the following words express the ideas we discuss in this chapter under the headings 'God is everywhere', 'God is all powerful', and 'God knows and understands all things'. Then write them down on a piece of paper to show the true connections.

OMNIPOTENT OMNIPRESENT OMNISCIENT

📖 **Study Suggestions**

FOR GROUP DISCUSSION

1 Could Christians use the Jewish Confession of Faith? If so, how would their understanding of its words differ from that of Jewish people at worship?
2 Which of the possible translations of the name Yahweh seems best to express the truth about the LORD?
3 Why do you think it is that the section dealing with 'Our Mysterious God' so often tells us about human relationships with the LORD, and contrasts his nature with our own?

FOR ESSAY WRITING

4 The Jews became reluctant to speak the name Yahweh. What difficulties did the fact that they refused to use it create? How did they cope with these problems?
5 'Holiness and glory are like the two sides of a coin' (page 30). Explain what this sentence means, and the difference between 'holiness' and 'glory'.
6 If the LORD is almighty, is there anything that he will refuse to do? Use illustrations to explain your answer.

WORK WITH THE BIBLE AND A CONCORDANCE

7 All other gods 'are mere idols' (page 24). Use a concordance to help you study the references to idols in Isaiah 40—66. What reasons does Deutero-Isaiah give for scorning idols?
8 Examine the use of the word 'everlasting' in the Psalms. Who and what are the things they describe as everlasting? Do any of the verses describe humans as everlasting?
9 Which two books of the Old Testament use the title 'Almighty' (*Shaddai*) most often to describe God? Can you suggest a reason for each of these books using this title when other books seldom use it?

Our God Is with Us

3

Be strong and of good courage;
be not frightened, neither be dismayed;
for the LORD your God is with you
wherever you go.

(Joshua 1.9)

We have studied 'our mysterious God' and recognized that some of his qualities and abilities are beyond our full understanding. Now we must look more closely at the ways in which God is involved in the world and in our lives, which can provide us with insights into his nature. I suggested earlier that faith in the Unity of God brings much fuller understanding of creation, history and morality than was possible for people who believed in many gods. Such people fail to understand how these subjects can provide deep understanding for them. They tend to think that they can only glimpse how the gods relate to each other, in conflict or co-operation with each other. They tend to feel that they are caught up in the disputes and conflicts of gods who are remote from them. Let us turn to look at these three subjects. After that we will study the fact that the Old Testament fails to provide clear teaching that God is a Trinity of Father, Son and Holy Spirit.

The LORD and Creation

Have you not known? Have you not heard?
The LORD is the everlasting God,
the Creator of the ends of the earth.

(Isaiah 40.28)

The Babylonians believed that the creation of the world was a result of conflict between gods and goddesses: Marduk was victorious over Tiamat and created the sky and earth from her body (see Volume 1: first edition page 134, revised edition page 145, for fuller details).

The Persians believed that the world was the battlefield for a continuing conflict between Ormazd and Ahriman. They expected Ormazd, the god of goodness, to be victorious, but the battle was still to be won; the struggle between these gods continued (see

Volume 1: first edition page 150, revised edition page 162, for fuller details).

The Israelites took a totally different view of creation. Because they learnt that the LORD is the only God, they came to believe that creation is entirely his activity. 'In the beginning God created the heavens and the earth . . . And God saw everything that he had made, and behold, it was very good' (Genesis 1.1, 31. Compare Isaiah 41.4; 43.10; 44.6).

We should notice that these verses which illustrate God's part in creation as the one God, without hindrance or help from others, come from the later periods of Old Testament thought. Deutero-Isaiah belonged to the time of the Exile, and Genesis I comes from the P-tradition which editors incorporated in the Torah during or after the Exile. But we can find similar and related ideas in earlier writings. The second account of creation (Genesis 2.4–25) comes from the J-tradition, which editors may have gathered in the time of Solomon. Two of the psalms which express praise to the LORD for his activity in creation also imply that it was all his doing (Psalms 8 and 104). No one knows their exact dates, but Psalm 8 comes from a collection of psalms which editors perhaps gathered between 1000 and 900 BC (see Volume 2: first edition page 100, revised edition page 108, for fuller details).

Several important ideas follow from the belief that 'God created the heavens and the earth'.

The LORD is Almighty

We have already studied this idea under 'Our Mysterious God', sub-section 'God is All Powerful'. But it is important to remember that his supremacy is part of his essential nature, and we should avoid thinking that it was the result of victory over other gods. He is without rivals. All things owe their origin to him, and none of them can finally prevent him fulfilling his purposes (Isaiah 43.13; Job 9.2–4, 10). We can find belief in the Almighty in Old Testament writings from the time of the Patriarchs and the Kings (Genesis 35.11; Isaiah 13.6–7) as well as the Exile and the Return (Ezekiel 1.24; Job 40.2; Joel 1.15).

The LORD Controls Nature

God exercises his power over the natural world in two separate ways:

1 He has set the natural order of things in motion. By his authority day follows night, harvest follows seedtime (Genesis 8.22; Jeremiah 31.35–36; 33.20–21). In our own time, science is the study of this natural order. Scientists today experiment in order to discover in detail just how the world works, and to use this knowledge for the benefit of the human race. They know far more than

people did in Old Testament times about the world we live in. But they share the belief that there is order and regularity in nature. The Israelites believed that the regular patterns of the natural world come from God's design and activities.

2 The Israelites also believed that God continues to be active in and through his creation (Amos 5.8; Psalm 145.15–16). They believed that the world is secure because the LORD reigns over it (1 Chronicles 16.29; Psalms 93.1; 96.10; 119.90). The regular patterns of nature depend upon God for their continuity (Job 9.5–10; Isaiah 30.23). Even human life depends on the LORD (Nehemiah 9.21; Psalm 3.5; Malachi 2.15).

The LORD Works Miracles Through Nature

The Israelites' belief that God is active in the normal sequence of nature gives us a clue to their attitude to miracles. Two ideas which are common today fail to find support in the Old Testament:

1 The idea that God sometimes breaks into nature and history by sudden action conflicts with Old Testament thought, because it denies the reality of his *continuing* presence and activity.
2 The idea that God has to overcome and redirect the forces of nature in order to achieve his purposes falsely suggests that nature is in some sense separate from and even contrary to his will. This idea would suggest that God showed very poor efficiency as a designer and creator because what he made failed to meet his requirements, and nature failed to respond to his purposes.

The Old Testament holds together the idea that creation is well-designed and properly ordered, with the idea that God is able to work in and through nature. In order to understand Old Testament ideas about miracles, we need to see them as illustrating how God uses the forces of nature, rather than as showing his conquest and disturbance of the normal activities of nature.

Sometimes the writers of the Old Testament emphasize strange and unusual happenings as evidence of God's activity, but more often they describe God using ordinary natural events to achieve his purposes. The plagues in Egypt were probably all normal events in the climate and conditions of that country. For example, the rivers running blood-red could simply be a tradition passed down the generation about the red soil carried down by the Nile at flood time. If so, the writers of the Old Testament saw the timing of the plagues and their severity as evidence of God at work. They fitted in so well with Moses' need to illustrate to Pharaoh God's authority and power. The drought in Elijah's time, and the lightning which burnt up his offering, were perhaps natural events, but even so they were under the LORD's control. Why should we suppose that God is less able to make use of the properties of nature than we are, who continually use inventions based on natural realities of the created world?

If God both controls and uses nature, does this mean that we must blame him for such events as droughts, famine, or hurricanes? For a long time Old Testament prophets tended to suggest such things were God's punishment for the sins of his people. But the book of Job challenges this idea. It contains a long debate in which a rich man, Job, loses all his possessions, his children are all killed, and he himself is seriously diseased. Three friends come to console him, but believe that he must have done some great evil to be punished so severely; he denies it. In the end God himself comes to answer his complaints, pointing to the fact that as a human being he is unable to know everything about creation (Job 38 and 39). Job recognizes the compassion of God in coming to him, and accepts that he is ignorant (Job 40.4–5; 42.2, 3b, 5–6). Notice that verses 42.3a and 4 probably show God interrupting Job's confession of faith. God then declares that Job is righteous and has remained faithful (Job 42.7–8). The book probably dates from towards the end of the Exile, but before the preaching of Deutero-Isaiah. The book makes a bold stand against traditional ideas about human suffering, and prepares the way for the idea of God's Servant who suffers to redeem Israel (Isaiah 53). We should always remember that God is our support and friend in times of suffering, and enables us to face and endure suffering. God can bring joy out of sorrow (Isaiah 61.3).

The LORD is God of Wisdom

We have already studied the wisdom of God under 'Our Mysterious God', subsection 'God Knows and Understands All Things' (pages 32–33). But we can add here that true wisdom comes from God and enables humans to reach a deeper appreciation of reality than they could have without his help. He is the Good Teacher we thought about under the heading 'God's Work of Revelation' (pages 12–17). He possesses complete knowledge of creation (Psalm 147.4–6). The writer of Job presents us with a contrast between the LORD and Job in the knowledge they possess. Job 28.20–28 describes God as the sole person who possesses complete wisdom. For humans, 'The fear of the LORD is the beginning of wisdom' (Psalm 111.10; compare Proverbs 1.7; 9.10; 15.33). Many biblical writers tell of people who had wisdom because the LORD had given it to them (Genesis 41.39; Exodus 35.30–33; 1 Kings 3.12).

The LORD Has a Purpose for His Creation

The two stories of creation in Genesis both give central place to the making of human beings. In Genesis 1 men and women are the climax of creation. 'So God created man in his own image, . . . male and female he created them' (Genesis 1.27). In Genesis 2 God prepares a garden for the man and then creates a mate for him. God gives humankind responsibility to use the world wisely and with good purpose (Genesis 1.28; 2.15). Throughout the history of Israel we read of people whom God called to help fulfil his purposes. Israel itself had a special place in God's plans as the means of bringing his blessing to all humankind. He chose the Israelites to discover his plan of salvation, and to make it known to all peoples (Genesis 12.1–3; Exodus 19.5–6). But God did not base his choice on the fact that they were outstanding among the many peoples of the world. More likely the opposite was true: they were the most insignificant (Deuteronomy 7.6–8). But the writer of Deuteronomy says it was because God loved them. Here there lies a very important point: nobody is too insignificant to have a part in God's plans. God's choice lay on a people who frequently needed reminding about their responsibilities as God's chosen people (Deuteronomy 4.35–40; Amos 3.1–2; Ezekiel 20.5–7). We shall study the nature of God's purposes more fully in the later sections of this book, but it is important to remember that humankind has a central place in God's plans.

Evil Fails to Stop the LORD's Work

We have already seen that the Old Testament writers rejected the idea that there is a power of evil which existed alongside the LORD from eternity. They recognized that there is evil in the world, but saw it as a result of corruption. People can choose good, but they often choose evil instead. The story of the Fall in Genesis 3 expresses this idea, as do such verses as Genesis 6.12 and Exodus 32.7. We shall study in Chapter 4 the question raised in the Old Testament about the existence of other corruptible beings. Here it is sufficient to notice that the Old Testament always describes the powers of evil as being less than God. God's power is supreme, and he will fulfil his purposes.

📖 Check Your Understanding 7

1 Which two of the following verbs are nearest in meaning to the verb *to create* as we have used it in this section?

TO BUILD   TO CONSTRUCT   TO ERECT   TO GENERATE
TO INVENT   TO MANUFACTURE   TO PRODUCE

2 Which two of the following statements best describes the origin of human suffering?

(a) God's punishment for our sins

(b) The outcome of our sinful behaviour
(c) The trouble caused by an evil god
(d) A mysterious source we are unable to understand

The LORD and History

Thus says the LORD . . .
Who is like me? Let him proclaim it,
Let him declare and set it forth before me.
Who has announced from of old the things to come?
Let them tell us what is yet to be.
Fear not, nor be afraid;
have I not told you from of old and declared it?
And you are my witnesses!
Is there a God besides me!
There is no Rock; I know not any.

(Isaiah 44.6–8)

The Israelites were the first of all the peoples of ancient South West
Asia to write connected accounts of their history. Other nations built
monuments to celebrate their victories, but they had nothing to say
about their defeats. They were unable to see any organized pattern of
events which could encourage them to write history books.

The reason for this is easy to see. Most nations believed in many
gods, and that each god showed his power when his own people
were victorious. But when they were defeated, they believed that this
was because their god had been defeated too. For them, any connected account of history would need to explain the rise and fall of
the gods that they served. Some of them composed myths about the
relationships between the gods and regarded human history as the
accidental result of conflicts between the gods. This was especially
true of the Greeks.

Those who accepted dualism shared much the same view of history. They saw the whole of history as the outcome of conflict
between the forces of good and the forces of evil. Human beings were
involved in the conflict, but they could only guess at the underlying
course of events. The real battle, they believed, was between the
gods.

The Israelites, on the other hand, believed in *one LORD*, and they
saw history as the result of relationships between the LORD and
humankind. This was part of human experience, and those who
looked for the ways of the LORD in all that happened could interpret
and understand it. The J-tradition provided the basis for the first
connected account of history among the Israelites. The editors of
this tradition related the whole of history to the LORD's call of Abraham. God had promised that certain things would happen as part of
his plan for the salvation of humankind.

Abraham's obedience was vital if God was to achieve this universal purpose (Genesis 12.1–3). In the course of time God fulfilled the promises that he made to Abraham. The same belief is the basis of all the later historical records in the Old Testament: history is the result of the LORD's initiative and the response of humans.

The LORD's Initiative

The Old Testament describes all the major events of Israelite history as the result of the LORD's activities among his people and in the world. It was the LORD who took the first step, and his people followed or else refused to do so. We have already noticed the LORD's call of Abraham. The LORD brought Joseph and his brothers into Egypt (Genesis 45.6–8). The LORD rescued his people from Egypt (Exodus 3.7–8). The LORD enabled Joshua to lead the people into the promised land (Joshua 1.1–9). The LORD raised up judges to rescue his people from their enemies (Judges 2.18). Samuel doubted the wisdom of appointing kings in Israel, but in the end the LORD chose Saul to be king (1 Samuel 9.15–16). The LORD raised up prophets to guide the kings and their people (2 Samuel 7.4–12), The LORD even raised up foreign nations to punish his people for their disobedience (Amos 6.14), and a foreign ruler, Cyrus, to set them free from their exile (Isaiah 44.28).

All through the Old Testament we find the writers describing the LORD at work. They were chiefly interested in his activities among his own people, the Israelites. But many of the prophets spoke also of God's judgement on other nations (for example, Amos 1.3—2.3; Isaiah 13—23; Jeremiah 46—51; Ezekiel 25—32). From Genesis 12.3 onwards, the writers see the future of all nations as tied up with the LORD's activities in Israel. Many of the prophets give Jerusalem an important place in their visions of the future (for example, Isaiah 2.1–4; Jeremiah 3.17; Joel 3.1–2; Zechariah 2.11–12).

Humanity's Response

God's initiative in history is always through his relationship with humans: Abraham and Sarah, Moses and Miriam, Hannah and Samuel, David. Every one of these possessed their own faults, but through their response to the LORD's call they all influenced the course of Israelite history. God was able to use them for his purposes.

But the writers of the Old Testament were realistic; they recognized that such people were rare, and that for every one devoted servant of the LORD there were many disobedient people, both among the Israelites and from other nations. How could the LORD influence history when so few were responsive to his will? The Old Testament writers gave several different answers to this question. We can summarize them under four headings:

The influence of one obedient person is more far-reaching that that of many disobedient people.

For example, Joseph was badly treated by his brothers and by Potiphar's wife, but because he remained faithful to the LORD, he lived to save the Egyptians from the worst effects of a severe famine, and also provide a new home for his relatives. Pharaoh said of him, 'There is none so discreet and wise as you are' (Genesis 41.39).

Many of those who were obedient to the LORD were unpopular in their own life-time, and were only later recognized as people who had known the ways of the LORD. Isaiah of Jerusalem was disappointed that the people of his time failed to listen to him, but he believed that later they would see he had been right, and would be influenced by his teaching and example (Isaiah 30.8–11). Similarly the people of Jerusalem despised Jeremiah, but after the destruction of Jerusalem those who wrote Lamentations were able to recognize that events were a fulfilment of what he had said (see Volume 2: first edition page 120, revised edition page 148, for fuller details). The written records of the words and actions of such people were appreciated and recorded for the benefit of future generations. We too can benefit from their influence.

Even those who are completely unaware of the LORD's call may serve his purposes nonetheless.

The Assyrians were unaware that they were serving the LORD when they attacked Jerusalem. Their Rabshakeh urged the people to ignore the king of Judah if he said 'The LORD will deliver us.' Every god served by other nations had been powerless to save any of their peoples from the Assyrians (Isaiah 36.18–20, and compare Isaiah 10.5–11). Yet Isaiah believed that the LORD was using the Assyrians to punish Judah (Isaiah 7.18–20). Similarly, at the end of the Exile the LORD raised up Cyrus to set his people free, even though Cyrus himself failed to recognize that he was serving the LORD (Isaiah 45.1, 4–5).

But the writers also came to realize that such people may either (a) come to know that they are serving the LORD, as Deutero-Isaiah hoped in the case of Cyrus (Isaiah 45.3); or (b) go on doing things contrary to the will of the LORD, and so come under judgement, as in the case of the Assyrians (Isaiah 10.12–19).

Even those who disobey the LORD are in their own way responding to him.

According to Old Testament writers, we only fully understand people's actions if we see them as the result of their relationship to the LORD: either accepting or rejecting his will. Pharaoh's refusal to let

Figure 4. A South African congregation gives thanks to God for the overthrow of Apartheid, confident that God worked in the hearts of people to bring a change of understanding about human relationships.

the Israelites leave Egypt is described in this way: 'the LORD said ... I will harden his heart so that he will not let the people go' (Exodus 4.21). This implies that the LORD had given Pharaoh a fair opportunity to do his will. When Pharaoh refused to respond, he came under God's judgement and God punished him. If the LORD had failed to give Pharaoh the opportunity to know his will he would have been without guilt and would simply have misunderstood the situation and caused trouble. The same idea is found in the account of Isaiah's call. God had chosen Isaiah to be his messenger to Judah. The LORD warned Isaiah that even though Judah would have the opportunity to respond to the LORD, the likelihood was that they would refuse to repent and so would come under God's judgement (Isaiah 6.9, 10)

The LORD will bring an end to evil, and will establish righteousness on his Day.

The Israelites believed that history was leading somewhere, that all the LORD's activities among humans would eventually bring a time when all people would serve the LORD (Isaiah 65.17). There would then be peace and justice on earth (Isaiah 65.21; Micah 4.4). Those who rejected the way of the LORD would be unable to disturb the life of society, and incapable of bringing suffering and injustice. Instead they would face judgement (Zephaniah 1.15), while the righteous would share the new order on earth under God's rule.

📖 **Check Your Understanding 8**

1 'The LORD's initiative'. Which one of the following words best expresses the same idea as *initiative*?

LOVING   ORIGINATING

PLANNING   PROMPTING   TEACHING

2 'Abraham and Sarah, Moses and Miriam, Hannah and Samuel, David . . . all influenced the course of Israelite history' (page 41). Which two of the following words best express the same ideas as the word *course* in this statement?

DIRECTION   DURATION   ORDERLINESS

OUTCOME   SYLLABUS

The LORD and Morality

> He has showed you, O man, what is good;
> and what does the LORD require of you
> but to do justice, and to love kindness,
> and to walk humbly with your God?
>
> (Micah 6.8)

Every human society develops its own pattern of accepted forms of behaviour, in order to restrict causes of conflict and to enable people to live together in peace. Such a pattern of accepted behaviour we call 'morality', and it is a code of ethics. By regular use the pattern becomes part of the customs of the people who use it, though many other sorts of activity may also be called customs.

Usually communities build up their systems of morality over long periods of time, and many different things affect the particular form the tribe or people accept. For example:

1 A great leader from the past may have set a standard of behaviour which his or her people admire, and therefore continue to copy.
2 People find that they depend on each other for the necessities of life, and this affects their relationships. Their need for such things as food, shelter and protection from enemies affects their customary behaviour as a group, and so helps to form the pattern of their morality.
3 The group's experience of life together shows them that certain ways of behaving have creative results in their relationships, and other ways prove to be destructive. These experiences affect what the group as a whole accepts as moral behaviour.
4 Relationships with more powerful tribes and nations will lead a group to act in ways which will bring harmony and avoid conflict.

In ways like these a morality develops which controls the behaviour of the group, and its members will disapprove of and even punish any individual who acts against the best interests of the group. Through the years people find need for changes in their patterns of behaviour, and these can lead to better community life. For example, at one time people in Britain believed in using slaves brought from Africa. Some owners took good care of their slaves, and believed that they were providing a better way of life for them than their tribal life in Africa. But later many Europeans came to recognize that they were robbing their slaves of their human right to freedom, and slaves had to be set free. They made the trade illegal, so that people were no longer brought away from their home environment and tribal life. Sadly, many people today find themselves oppressed in ways close to slavery.

Besides all these ways in which tribal and national morality develop, we need to recognize that all people have an innate sense of right and wrong which helps to mould their pattern of morality. The Old Testament gives us no clue as to how this occurs, because the chief interest of the writers was the way in which God made himself known to the Jews. They felt that they should treat most foreigners with caution as sources of evil influence. The Jews believed that foreigners could benefit from God's blessings if they accepted belief in the LORD (Isaiah 2.1–4). But Paul tells his readers that God has been active in revealing his nature to all people through creation itself from the very beginning. He says that all peoples have the opportunity to recognize what is good even if they do not have an awareness of God as creator and LORD (Romans 1.19–23). Methodists hold dear the doctrine of Prevenient Grace, which teaches that the Holy Spirit is at work in the hearts and minds of all people, working to bring them to a true knowledge of God.

Our interest now is to consider whether a people's religious understanding and experiences affect the development of their pattern of morality. This depends on how far people believe that their religion concerns human relationships, as well as relationships with the divine. The answer varies, in fact, with the sort of religion that people follow. Let us consider the probable influence of polytheism, dualism and monotheism.

Polytheism

This is the belief in many different gods, among whom there is conflict and trouble. The worshippers' main concern is to persuade each of their gods to treat them with favour. Usually a worshipper does this by offering sacrifices and performing rituals, and sometimes by behaving in particular ways towards other people.

But each different god requires different responses, so anyone who worships more than one god is likely to be faced with conflicting loyalties. Each person may behave in a particular way to please their chosen god, but their religion may teach that another god will be displeased by this behaviour. No single pattern of behaviour will enable such worshippers to please all the gods at once. Their religion is unable to give them a sure guide for their behaviour, but will drive them to act first in one way and then in an opposite way. Thus we see that polytheism is the form of religion least likely to have deep influence on the development of an accepted pattern of morality. Such a religion is more likely to give people the feeling that they can never really know the difference between right and wrong. Instead, they will be taught to do what other people expect them to do. In India, for example, the Hindu caste system places each family in a particular role in society, and they are expected to fulfil the responsibilities of their own caste. Members of each caste are denied the possibility of choosing a different role and following a different career. Some people are placed outside the caste system and regarded as having no role and no status in society.

Dualism

In its simplest form, dualism is the belief that there are two gods who are in conflict with each other, both fighting for supreme power. Holders of such a religion believe that one of the gods is the god of goodness and the other the god of evil. According to this belief, human beings have a choice; they can serve one god or the other, but they cannot serve both. But they cannot base the standard of judgement on the will of either god, because each could claim that his or her way was best. In fact the choice is based on the patterns of behaviour which a human society favours. It regards the god which supports these as good and the god which does not as bad. Naturally the people expect that the god they have chosen will eventually reign supreme when the battle is over. Dualism, as such, is unable to create, or even to help create, a new pattern of morality. The Zoroastrianism of Persia in Old Testament times seems to have led to the finest example of tolerance with regard to other peoples and their gods. Cyrus encouraged each nation to follow their own religion, and helped them to do so. Perhaps underlying this was the recognition that the Persians themselves had chosen the god they served on the basis of their own understanding of right and wrong. (see Volume 1: first edition pages 150–2, revised edition pages 162–4, for fuller details).

Monotheism

Monotheism is the belief in one God. In ancient times some Greeks believed in one god, but supposed that he was so perfect that he had no interest or involvement with people, because he had no needs which they could meet. So there was no purpose in worshipping him, or trying to serve him. This sounds to us as though their god was utterly selfish! But what if God did need humans for his own benefit? We could find little hope of being blessed and our service would probably be slavery. But for the people of Israel these problems did not exist. God had revealed himself from the time of Abraham, as desiring to have fellowship with humankind and working for the blessing of every nation through the witness of the Israelites (Genesis 12.1–3). They came to know that God is the creator and sustainer of all life and being. Today Jews, Christians and Muslims all recognize that God is active and purposeful to bless us. People can respond to God, either by accepting and living by God's purposes as we become aware of them, or else rejecting his purposes and disobeying him. So for all three monotheistic religions good is seen to be everything that is in tune with God's purposes, and evil to be everything that is contrary.

The people of Israel developed a pattern of morality which they believed was in tune with the purposes of the LORD. The more closely they came to understand God, the nearer they came to developing an ideal morality. The more they were aware of God's purposes, the more clearly they recognized their responsibility to serve him, and the possibility of judgement if they did not.

The Ten Commandments provided the basis for all later development of Israelite morality. They were the essential guidelines for a way of life which was entirely acceptable to the LORD. 'You shall therefore keep my statutes, and my ordinances, by doing which a man shall live: I am the LORD' (Leviticus 18.5).

In their later codes of law, the Israelites attempted to interpret the basic guidelines in the light of the circumstances of a particular time. What was right for nomads was ill suited for a settled agricultural people. What was right for a tribe of Israel in the time of the Judges was ill suited for people living under the rule of David. What was right for life in Palestine was ill suited for life in exile in Babylon. But always the guide to what was right was the will of the LORD. What he wanted from his people, they accepted as the way of righteousness. The Ten Commandments remained as a basic pattern for obedience which they could not change, though they expressed it in different ways at different times.

The prophets were continually challenging the Israelites to live according to the patterns of morality which they had received from the LORD. Often the prophets had to deal with situations which arose

because many of the Israelites did not understand the special importance of morality in their religion. Continually they were tempted to
follow the pattern of other religions, and to suppose that what the
LORD chiefly required from his people was worship and sacrifice.
They found it difficult to understand that even though they took
part in the sacrifices and feast days, the LORD was displeased with
their service. The prophets had to repeat again and again that, 'to
obey is better than sacrifice' (1 Samuel 15.22; Isaiah 1.12–17; Proverbs 21.3, etc.). They accepted that under the right circumstances
worship was important, but declared that worship and morality
belong together in the service of the LORD.

 Check Your Understanding 9

1 Which of the following definitions most fully describes the
  Old Testament idea of morality at its best?
   (a) A way of life that will win the approval of the group to
       which individuals belong.
   (b) A way of life that is appropriate to the purpose of life
       both for the individual and the individual's group.
   (c) A way of life that will bring material prosperity to the
       individual and the individual's group.
2 The Ten Commandments 'were the essential guidelines for a
  way of life which was entirely acceptable to the LORD' (page
  47). Which one of the following words best expresses the
  meaning of *guidelines* in that sentence?

DESIGNS   DIRECTIONS

PLANS   SCHEMES   SUGGESTIONS

The Eternal Trinity

We have seen that the most distinctive idea of the Jewish faith is the
Unity of God: 'Hear, O Israel: The LORD our God is one LORD' (Deuteronomy 6.4). This idea was very different from the ideas held by
people of other nations of South West Asia. At first, it was an idea
that seemed strange to the Israelites themselves and was difficult to
grasp and to understand. But gradually, through the centuries, as the
LORD worked among his people in the varying situations of their history, more and more of them came to appreciate the importance of
this belief in the Unity of God.

   We have seen that the idea affected their understanding of such
important matters as creation, history and morality. It transformed
their whole understanding of human life, and presented them with
new responsibilities as they tried to live out their lives in the light of
this faith.

In the New Testament we see the beginnings of a new idea about God – the idea which eventually found expression as the doctrine of the Trinity: Father, Son and Holy Spirit. New Testament writers described the Son as being in existence, and at work, from the beginning of creation (Colossians 1.16). He who came to live a human life was God from the beginning (Philippians 2.6). Similarly, they described the Holy Spirit as *eternal* (Hebrews 9.14). The same Spirit of God that enabled them to preach the gospel had been given to Abraham through faith (Galatians 3.14) and had inspired the prophets of the Old Testament (1 Peter 1.10–12; 1 Corinthians 2.11).

Some readers may ask why God's revelation of himself in Old Testament times omitted the idea of the Trinity. The answer seems to be that the Jews needed first to grasp the truth about the Unity of God. The true nature of God is difficult for people to grasp at any time. The Jews needed first to learn that God is One, the idea central to their beliefs today. Only so could they reach the truth about creation, history and morality. Without this knowledge, in a time when all other nations believed in many gods the ordinary Jews might have been liable to misunderstand the nature of Father, Son and Holy Spirit. They could have assumed that they were to worship three Gods. Often in their history many of them also worshipped the Baalim, the local fertility gods, despite the fact that they had the guidance of the Ten Commandments and the *Shema* in Deuteronomy 6.4–9.

We too, who are Christians today, need to recognize the Unity of God and to be aware of the difference this makes for us in our understanding of creation, history and morality. However great the importance of our belief in Father, Son and Holy Spirit, we must remember the fact that the three Persons are one Godhead. Whatever is true about the Unity of God is also true of the Trinity. Our response to God's single purpose for us in creation and history is the true basis for Christian morality.

But belief in the Trinity is more than a useful theory, or a carefully devised scheme of thought which satisfies our desire for an understanding of God. This belief is the only way we have in human thought and language to express a mystery. Perhaps the centrality of love in all God's purposes provides an important clue to the nature of the unity of the three Persons. Any close fellowship among humans depends on a level of agreement and an understanding of and respect for each other where we differ. The deeper our commitment to each other the more we are in harmony in what we think and do. For the Trinity this is taken to perfection: in total knowledge and wisdom the three act in total unity.

According to the New Testament, the God who revealed himself to the Israelites in Old Testament times *was* always Father, Son and Holy Spirit, even though the Jews were only aware of him as the one LORD, and lacked understanding of his Triune (Three-in-One) nature. But is there any evidence that people of Old Testament times began to share in thoughts which would gradually lead to the New Testament doctrine of the Trinity? Did God provide them with experiences which would prepare the way for belief in the Trinity? Were they, without full realization, experiencing God the Trinity?

Having put the question in this particular way, we find that a number of Old Testament ideas were eventually taken up and used by New Testament writers in order to express what they needed to say about the Trinity. These ideas related to God's activity within creation and in relationship with humankind. The writers who spoke of *Wisdom, the Word of God* and *the Spirit of the LORD* were struggling to express ideas which find fullest expression in the New Testament use of these ideas.

As we shall see in the following paragraphs, early writers used each of these terms as a way of talking about the LORD. But later writers used them to describe separate impersonal forces under the LORD's control. Then poetic literature used them to describe independent beings believed to be active in their own ways, though responsive to the LORD. Slowly and cautiously people were learning to have a fuller vision of God, which would only find true expression when the Son became Jesus Christ, living among people for their salvation and making the Godhead known. Sadly, Jews today utterly reject such an interpretation of their scriptures, and insist that these terms represent the one and only God, who made covenant with them for the blessing of all humankind.

Wisdom

In Old Testament times the people of several different countries produced what we call Wisdom Literature. We know that such books of wisdom existed in both Mesopotamia and Egypt long before the Israelites settled in Palestine. Scholars believe that professional groups of scribes provided them, each in their own country. These scribes probably intended their writings to give guidance for the officials of the royal courts in handling political matters. Such literature was influenced by the culture of the area in which it was produced. In Egypt the scribes described *wisdom* as existing in the world but needing to be discovered by humankind. The Egyptians used the term *maat*, which we can translate as 'world order' or 'truth'. They believed that Maat was a goddess, beloved by her creator. The Israelites were unlikely to have accepted this idea because they were called to serve the LORD under the guidance of the Ten Commandments. Instead, the Israelites recognized God as the source of wisdom (Proverbs 9.10).

For them, wisdom was a spiritual gift, a source of good decisions and appropriate actions. God's own activities show his wisdom (Psalm 104.24; Isaiah 28.29; Jeremiah 10.12). People possess wisdom as a gift from the LORD (Deuteronomy 4.6; 1 Kings 3.12; Proverbs 2.6). In Job, the writer describes wisdom as something that God possesses and understands (Job 28.23–24). He alone can search it out, and he alone can make use of it (Job 28.27–28).

But in Proverbs 1—8, the writer describes wisdom as a woman. She is active and alive, and does what she thinks right. She offers understanding to all who will listen to her. In most of these chapters we may regard this way of describing wisdom as simply picture language – a device of poetry, a way of expressing a difficult idea in words which people would quickly understand.

But in Proverbs 8.22–36 we find new ideas about wisdom, describing it in different ways. For example, the LORD created wisdom at the beginning of his work (verse 22). Wisdom was 'like a master workman' (verse 30). Wisdom found delight in all that the LORD made (verses 30–31). Wisdom provides life to all who find her (verse 35). We may think that these expressions too are poetic forms, but they do provide a starting place for ideas which were developed further in the books which now form the Apocrypha.

There, in the book called *The Wisdom of Solomon* we find the following words:

> Wisdom, the fashioner of all things, taught me.
> For in her there is a spirit that is intelligent, holy,
> unique, manifold, subtle,
> mobile, clear, unpolluted,
> distinct, invulnerable, loving the good, keen,
> irresistible, beneficent, humane,
> steadfast, sure, free from anxiety,
> all-powerful, overseeing all,
> and penetrating through all spirits
> that are intelligent and pure and most subtle.
> For wisdom is more mobile than any motion;
> because of her pureness she pervades and penetrates all
>   things.
> For she is a breath of the power of God,
> and a pure emanation of the glory of the Almighty;
> therefore nothing defiled gains entrance into her.
> For she is a reflection of eternal light,
> a spotless mirror of the working of God,
> and an image of his goodness.
> Though she is but one, she can do all things,
> and while remaining in herself, she renews all things:
> in every generation she passes into holy souls

and makes them friends of God, and prophets;
for God loves nothing so much as the man who lives
with wisdom.
(Wisdom 7.22–28)

In the New Testament both Paul and the writer to the Hebrews used
similar terms to describe Christ, the Son of God (Colossians 1.15–17,
Hebrews 1.2–3). We need to remember that Greek-speaking Jews who
lived outside Palestine treated the books of the Apocrypha as Scripture. Paul would have read this passage with interest and have been
willing to learn from it. He would know that those to whom he wrote
would know this book. So he would find it natural to draw on such
words to express the glory of Jesus Christ. So what started out as a
poetical description of the wisdom of God became an expression of
something far more significant than the writers of the Old Testament
or the Apocrypha could imagine. The way was open for discussion of
the Person of Christ – who he was.

The Word of God

We have already studied what Christians mean when we describe
the Bible as the Word of God (pages 5–6). When we read the Bible
we learn that at times God made himself known to people in a personal way. We, too, can discover that God makes himself known to
us in similar ways, Spirit to spirit. In this way God brings us the
blessing of fellowship with himself, offering us a place and part in
his kingdom. Christians can use the term 'Word of God' to refer to
God's disclosure of himself and his purposes to believers. In New
Testament times Jesus was God's full revelation, bringing us much
fresh understanding of his nature and intentions through his life,
death, resurrection and ascension. So John is able to describe Jesus
as 'the Word' (John 1.1–5, 14–17).

But how did people of Old Testament times use the term *Word
of God*? Did the Israelites, and later the Jews, gain a deepening
understanding of the significance of God's Word? Can we say that
this process prepared the way for humans to understand that Jesus
is the supreme Word of God? Before we can answer this question
we need to think about the significance of words in ordinary use.
British people sometimes say: 'Sticks and stones may break my
bones, but words will never hurt me.' But they have learnt that
this saying is false. It is not true that words have no effect. We
know that words can harm, and words can bless. Human disagree-
ments are made worse by harsh, angry, assertive words, but can be
resolved by humble, patient and, if necessary, penitent words.
Caring words can deepen and enrich human relationships. We
often need words of encouragement when we are facing suffering,

tackling some difficult opportunity, or accepting great responsibility. So words can be powerful in many different ways.

From the beginning of the Bible words spoken by God play an important part in creation, and in the lives of people. By God's commands the world came into being. 'Let there be light', 'Let there be a firmament', etc. The one great distinction between humans and other living creatures is that God speaks to them (Genesis 1.28–30; 2.16–17; 3.9–13, etc.). They have the ability to listen to and understand him. His speech to the serpent in Genesis 3.14 is set in poetic language, and is really an explanation to humans of the ability of snakes to cause us fear. When Samuel began his work for God, 'the word of the LORD was rare . . . there was no frequent vision' (1 Samuel 3.1). At that time God's people had little time for God, and many people behaved immorally. God gave Samuel responsibility as a judge and a guide for his people. He spoke in God's name (1 Samuel 16.6–13). When the prophets came in the time of the kings they often spoke in the name of God, adding 'Thus says the LORD' (Isaiah 10.24; Amos 1.3, 6, 9; Micah 2.3). This phrase occurs 242 times in the Old Testament. The prophets also spoke of their meetings with God, and how he gave them warnings or encouragement to pass on to the people of their times (Jeremiah 1.4–10). Sometimes the prophets spoke of eating God's word (Isaiah 55.1–2; Jeremiah 15.16; Ezekiel 3.1–3). As food provides strength for strenuous activities, so God's word provides the power to speak with authority in his name. A prophet's declarations of God's warnings provides the means by which things happen. The prophets were servants of God, but they needed the help of God's word to present a powerful message. The word of God is powerful (Isaiah 55.11). So people mocked the prophets if their words failed to find fulfilment (Jeremiah 17.14–16). Jeremiah at times felt that God had given him false messages (Jeremiah 20.7–10), because the fulfilment was delayed for many years. Sometimes the prophets felt compelled to pass on messages which they were reluctant to give (Amos 3.8).

The Hebrew term for *word* can be used about a live action, rather than simply a message about needed action: see, for example, Exodus 5.13 where 'work' and 'task' are the appropriate translations. Similarly in Ezra 10.3–4 and Proverbs 31.15. God's word has power to survive when other things fail (Isaiah 40.8; Jeremiah 23.29), promising the fulfilment of God's purposes in the life of the world. So the term *word* comes to mean more than the message; it is the driving force which causes something to happen (Joshua 5.4; 1 Kings 11.27: *reason* in both verses). In other places the word has the ability to act as God's messenger, personally achieving his purposes (Isaiah 9.8; Psalms 107.20; 147.15, 18). Books produced between the Old and New Testaments include

The Wisdom of Solomon which carried this idea further, speaking of
the Word as a warrior attacking Israel's enemies in order to give
them freedom (Wisdom 18.14–16):

> For while gentle silence enveloped all things,
> and night in its swift course was now half gone,
> thy all-powerful word leaped from heaven, from the
>   royal throne,
> into the midst of the land that was doomed,
> a stern warrior carrying the sharp sword of thy
>   authentic command,
> and stood and filled all things with death,
> and touched heaven while standing on the earth.

So the evidence points towards the time when writers could call Jesus
the Word of God, and some Jews would understand their meaning,
because of these earlier revelations.

The Spirit of the LORD

The Old Testament uses the word *spirit* very often. The translators
who produced the RSV used a capital S to distinguish references to
the Spirit of the LORD from those relating to other lesser spirits,
and to the spirit of a human. Yet the same Hebrew word appears in
almost all places where the translators used the English word
spirit, whichever meaning is intended. They also translated the
same Hebrew word in many places as *wind* or *breath*. Because the
same Hebrew word can mean so many things, we are often unable
to be certain which sense the writer intended in any particular
verse. There is an example of this difficulty in Genesis 1.2. Many
translations of the Bible take the Hebrew word here to mean
'Spirit', as another way of naming God. But the New English Bible
translates the verse 'a mighty wind swept over'. The New Revised
Standard Version attempts to employ both meanings by saying 'a
wind from God swept over'. However, the translators have done
their best in each case to discover the meaning the writer
intended, by examining the whole sentence and also the paragraph in which it stands, and thus to provide an accurate translation. Our interest here is in the Spirit of the LORD; we shall discuss
other meanings in Chapters 4 and 5.

In many passages the writers used the word *Spirit* merely as
another way of naming the LORD. But from very early times they
used the word *Spirit* to describe an impersonal power that was
under the control of the LORD, and which he used to equip people
for his service. This power enabled Moses to be leader among the
Israelites, and God gave it to others so that they could share his
responsibilities (Numbers 11.17, 25). In a similar way, God gave

Elisha power to follow as leader after Elijah was taken up to heaven in a chariot (2 Kings 2.9–10). The same power came on other people to equip them for their work. For example, Gideon (Judges 6.34), Samson (Judges 14.6), Saul (1 Samuel 10.6, 10). In all these instances the Spirit produced dramatic effects in the lives of the people concerned, but they lack any suggestion of a personal relationship between the Spirit and the person receiving it.

At a later stage in the history of Israel, people thought the Spirit enabled prophets to speak in the name of the LORD. The earliest prophets were unwilling to accept this as an explanation of their authority, because they wanted to avoid being compared with the ecstatic spokesmen of the Baalim and other false gods, who claimed to be working as a result of inspiration received from the spirits of their gods. But Micah did use the idea (Micah 3.8). Prophets in the Exile and after it used this explanation of their authority (Ezekiel 8.3; 11.1; Isaiah 61.1; Zechariah 7.12). Joel 2.28 contains a promise of the widespread gift of the Spirit in a later time.

Towards the end of the Old Testament period, the writers increasingly used language which suggests that the Spirit of the LORD is a person, alive and active. It says that the Spirit does many things which other passages describe as the work of the LORD. He abides with his people (Haggai 2.5); he leads (Psalm 143.10); he instructs (Nehemiah 9.20); he enables his people to live good lives (Psalm 51.10–12); he grieves over the sins of those who rebel against the LORD (Isaiah 63.10). The Spirit is everywhere present, so that nobody can escape from him (Psalm 139.7).

The Jews never supposed that the Spirit was anything other than part of the essential nature of the LORD, just as the spirit of a person is an essential part of that person's human nature. But at the very beginning of the Early Church, Peter was able to quote Joel 2.28–32 in order to describe the work of the Holy Spirit (Acts 2.16–21). Again, the way had been prepared for new truths to be expressed in terms which were already familiar. The Jewish crowds were able to appreciate what Peter was saying on the first Pentecost, even though the Christian theology of the Trinity had yet to be fully developed. The Apostles were dealing with the same experiences of God which people in Old Testament times had known, and were learning to express them with the fuller understanding that was available through Christ. Later writers, including Paul, expressed the revelation of the Holy Spirit even more fully.

📖 Check Your Understanding 10

1 We often express the Christian teaching about the Trinity by saying that we believe in *Three Persons; One God*. Which two of the following terms are nearest in meaning to the word *Persons* in that statement?

DISTINCT BEINGS   INDEPENDENT REALITIES

RECOGNIZABLE INDIVIDUALS   SEPARATE EXISTENCES

SUPREME CREATURES

2 It is possible to use the word *unity* in different ways. Which one of the following most fully expresses the meaning of the word in the phrase *Unity of God*?
    (a) Every part working in harmony.
    (b) Sharing a common purpose, and working together to achieve it.
    (c) All one without distinction.

📖 Study Suggestions

FOR GROUP DISCUSSION

1 God is Almighty
    (a) Is there anything that he refuses to do? If so, what?
    (b) Is there anything he is unable to do? If so, what?
2 Some people say, 'The world is a better place today than it was a century ago.' Do you agree? Explain as fully as you can the reasons for your own thinking on this subject.
3 What other forms of religion apart from Christianity do some people within your own country share? Do these religions involve guidance for living good lives? Should people judge a religion by the quality of life that it encourages?
4 A Christian can be several different things: for example, parent, teacher of school children, and lay preacher. Some people think that God is three persons in a similar sense, simply by doing different things at different times.
    (a) Can you suggest reasons why the Church in general dismisses that view as an error?
    (b) What evidence is there in the Bible of the relationship between the three persons?

FOR ESSAY WRITING

5   (a) How would you describe the work of scientists?

    (b) In what chief ways do the Old Testament writers think differently about nature from the way in which scientists describe it?

6 (a) What prompted the Israelites to write a connected account of the development of their history?

    (b) Were they interested in the history of other nations? If so, in what way did the writers of the Old Testament express that interest?

7 Some people contrast the Ten Commandments with the commandments of Christ, saying the former are all negative 'You shall not . . .', while the latter are positive 'Love the LORD . . . Love your neighbour'. Is it right that the Old Testament is restrictive in its rules, while the New Testament is positive in its rules? Give biblical references to support your answer.

8 How would you explain the meaning of the following verse to somebody puzzled by it?

'As yet the Spirit had not been given, because Jesus was not yet glorified' (John 7.39).

WORK WITH THE BIBLE AND A CONCORDANCE

9 (a) Use a concordance to examine the use of the words 'work' and 'works' in the Psalms, and make a list of things that are described as the LORD's work.

    (b) Are the things you have listed mainly activities in nature, or are they mainly activities in the hearts of people? Give three examples of each.

10 (a) The Old Testament writers often express the initiative of the LORD by the use of the phrase 'Raised up'. Use a concordance to examine the use of this phrase in the various parts of the Old Testament.

    (b) Make a list of the people which these verses say have been raised up by God. What status did they have: priests, prophets or anything else?

11 Study Psalm 119 and list all the different words it uses to mean rules which describe God's will for his people. Use an English dictionary to discover the precise meaning of each of these words.

12 'The Spirit does many things which other passages describe as the work of the LORD' (page 54). Use a concordance to discover a verse in the Old Testament for each of the following phrases which describe the activities of the Spirit: 'abiding', 'leading', 'instructing', 'enabling people to live good lives', 'grieving over the sins of those who rebel', 'being everywhere'.

Other Spiritual Beings 4

> Praise the LORD!
> Praise the LORD from the heavens,
> Praise him in the heights!
> Praise him, all his angels,
> Praise him, all his hosts.
>
> (Psalm 148.1–2)

A Warning about the Worship of Spirits

In many parts of the world people have believed in a Supreme God, but have given their worship and service to lesser spirits. The Supreme God has seemed so remote and inaccessible that people have felt that they could have very little hope of approaching him. Often these people have believed that many lesser spirits have greater power to affect their lives directly. For this reason they have made sacrifices and given offerings to these beings, hoping to gain their protection from trouble or sickness. In general these people have approached two sorts of spirits in worship:

- Some people have believed in spirits of nature as having power over the natural world and particularly over fertility
- Some people have believed in the spirits of the dead as having continuing influence over the life of the local community and of its individuals.

We need to study the attitude of the writers of the Bible to the worship of spirits, because this will help us to form our own understanding of these matters, and enable us to respond in the right way to the revelation of God that the Bible presents. The Old Testament provides most of the help we need on this subject.

The first thing we discover as we examine the books of the Old Testament is that the Israelites seldom thought of the LORD as remote or inaccessible. The writers normally describe him as present among his people, actively making himself known and desiring personal fellowship with them. All the Old Testament writers and editors were people who believed that they had had an experience of God themselves or were passing on to others the testimonies of people whose words they believed to be trustworthy. Again and again the prophets and poets urged people to respond to the LORD in worship and service, and to discover for themselves his blessings. Nothing is clearer in the books of the Old Testament than the reality of the presence and activity of the LORD.

For this reason, belief in other spiritual beings should have had much less importance in the lives of the Israelites than was often the case. The writers of the Old Testament never encouraged the worship of such lesser beings, and many of them openly condemned it as foolish and unworthy of those who know the LORD.

Types of Spirits

Nature spirits

The nearest thing to worship of nature spirits described in the Old Testament is worship of the Baalim. In the time of the divided kingdoms (931–721 BC) some of the Israelites supposed that they should worship the Baalim as well as the LORD. They thought that the Baalim could ensure good crops, increasing herds and large families. Elijah opposed this cult, because he saw that the Israelites might turn away altogether from the service of the LORD (1 Kings 18.21). King Josiah's reform of religion included the destruction of things used in worship of the Baalim (2 Kings 23.4). Hosea and Jeremiah both condemned this worship (Hosea 9.10–17; Jeremiah 11.13). The prophets needed to remind people that the LORD created the universe and everything in it. These prophets knew that many forces exist in nature which can affect humans. But they believed that these were under God's control. Wind (Exodus 10.13; Psalm 104.3–4; Isaiah 59.19) and water (Genesis 6.17; Psalm 29.3; Isaiah 40.12), fire (Exodus 13.21–22; 1 Kings 18.24; Jeremiah 21.14) and frost (Psalm 78.47; Zechariah 14.5–6) can all harm us, but we can also use them for our good. But these powers are impersonal, they fail to qualify as *spirits*. They lack any authority to be worshipped instead of, or alongside, God. They are unable to think or feel, or to answer people's prayers.

Ancestral spirits

Like many other peoples, some Israelites believed in ancestral spirits, and their power to affect the lives of individuals and their societies. King Saul looked for guidance from the spirit of the dead Samuel (1 Samuel 28.3–25). But Saul was going against his own better judgement, because we read that he had forbidden his people to seek help from the dead (verses 3 and 9). Men or women who people thought could contact the dead are called mediums. But the woman who was the medium in this story thought she was in contact with 'a god' (verse 13). This points to part of the danger involved in trying to make contact with the dead: the danger of giving them worship that really belongs to the LORD. The prophet Isaiah condemned such activities in Israel: 'should not a people consult their God?' (Isaiah 8.19–22). The Law Code of Deuteronomy includes the activities of mediums among the things which are an abomination to the LORD (Deuteronomy 18.9–12). The Holiness Code warns that mediums defile those who turn to them (Leviticus 19.31; 20.6), and it says that they must be punished (Leviticus 20.27). We shall study the Old Testament ideas about the dead in a later chapter, but what is important here is that the spirits of the dead are still human. We should refuse to worship them, even if others are doing so. The Israelites honoured the memories of their ancestors, but their scriptures taught that they must avoid looking to them for help when things go wrong. We might want to add that our deceased parents still have a concern for us, but that the most they can do is to look to God for our help, and we can approach the LORD directly ourselves. All help comes from the LORD (Psalm 121.1–2).

In general, then, the Old Testament writers rejected the worship of spirits, and stressed that people should serve the LORD alone (Exodus 20.5a). But they do recognize that there are other spiritual beings who live to serve the LORD. This is the main subject of this chapter. But first we must examine a strange situation concerning the use of the term *the angel of the LORD*.

The Angel of the LORD

Some of the earliest writings of the Old Testament refer in a special way to *the angel of the LORD* or *the angel of God*. These phrases are more than a reference to one of God's many messengers. As we read the passages concerned we find that the angel *is* the LORD himself. For example, in the story of Hagar (Genesis 16.7–13) we read, 'The angel of the LORD said . . .' (vv. 9 and 11). Then follows the statement that Hagar 'called the name of the LORD who spoke to her, "Thou art a God of seeing" ' (v. 13). In the story of the proposed sacrifice of Isaac (Genesis 22.9–14) the angel of the LORD said, 'you have not withheld your son, your only son, from me' (v. 12). We would be wrong to think that the writer meant that Abraham was worshipping an angel! The writer was using the phrase *the angel of the LORD* as another way of referring to God. Abraham's response throughout this story showed that he feared God and wanted to obey him.

In the story of Jacob's life while living with the family of Laban we read 'Then the angel of God said . . . "I am the God of Bethel" ' (Genesis 31.11–13). When Jacob blessed Joseph he first used the word *God*, and then at the climax he used the term *the angel* to describe the source of power for the fulfilment of his blessing (Genesis 48.15–16). Gideon laments that he has seen *the angel of the* LORD, and he believes that the result must be his death. But the LORD reassures him (Judges 6.22–23).

We very seldom find this special use of the idea of the *angel of the* LORD as a way of speaking of God himself in the prophetic books, but it still exists in Zechariah, written after the return of some of the Jews from exile in Babylon. We need to notice that only the title *the angel of the* LORD carries this special meaning; we can find other references to *an* angel of the LORD which refer to one of the many angels who serve God.

Probably the writers who used the distinctive phrase *the angel of the* LORD wanted to preserve the wonder and glory of the LORD. They recognized that God in his power and glory is separate from and greater than anything in the whole universe, and as such remains beyond our wisdom and understanding. To use a technical term we noted earlier (see p. 28): God is *transcendent*. They wanted to express the grandeur and detachment of God. To see God would tempt us to think that we understand him, and even that in some ways we can control him. Yet according to all these stories God really was aware of, and concerned about, his people. He was present in a mysterious way with people like Hagar, Abraham and Jacob. The writers used the term *the angel of the* LORD to talk about this. They were also trying to find words to express the *immanence* of God, which exists alongside his transcendence. The mystery remains: how does God Almighty dwell among his people?

People have told me that the word *immanent* creates difficulties for Indian students because in their country the word is used to express the Hindu idea of pantheism. This is the belief that God is in all things, so that everything in our world is an aspect of God himself. In fact the English word is used in two distinct ways. I am using *immanent* to mean that God is close by us, readily accessible to us. We could use the biblical term *Immanuel* to save confusion in areas where Hindu people live. It simply means *God is with us* (Isaiah 7.14; 8.8; see also Matthew 1.23). This word is sometimes written as *Emmanuel*. Both spellings are attempts to express the Hebrew word in English lettering.

The Hosts of the LORD

Throughout the Old Testament we can find references to God either as LORD of Host, or as LORD of Hosts. The various writers use each of the two forms of this title to refer to three distinct servants of the LORD: Israel as God's people; the heavenly lights, sun, moon and stars; and those who share the life of heaven with God. Nobody has yet discovered the significance of the contrast of these two versions of the name. Perhaps it is simply that when they refer to the LORD of Hosts, they intend to draw our attention to the unity of each of these groups, and use Hosts to refer to the wide variety of those who serve God. Now let us look at each group.

1 *The People of God, Israel* Exodus describes the people that God brought out of Egypt under the guidance of Moses as his hosts (Exodus 7.4; 12.41, 51). The armies of Israel who fought their enemies were known as the hosts of the LORD (1 Samuel 17.20, 45; 2 Samuel 5.10; 2 Kings 3.14; 1 Chronicles 17.24; Psalm 24.10). This was probably the original use of the phrase *LORD* of hosts. The Hebrew noun comes from a verb meaning *to wage war*. We find this use of the verb form in Numbers 31.7, 42; Isaiah 29.7–8).

The Scriptures say that the battles fought by the Armies of Israel were carried out under the orders of the LORD of hosts (1 Samuel 15.2; 17.45–46; Psalms 46.6–7; 59.5). The Ark of the Covenant was at times carried into battle, signifying the LORD's presence and support for Israel. 1 Samuel 4.4; 6.2 described it as belonging to the LORD of Hosts.

2 *The Hosts of Heaven* These are '*the sun and moon and the stars, all the host of heaven*' (Deuteronomy 4.19a). These are part of God's creation (Genesis 1.16; Psalms 8.3; 33.6; Nehemiah 9.6; Isaiah 40.25–26; 45.12b; Jeremiah 31.35). They seem to be given some personal status because writers describe them as giving praise to God (Psalm 148.3), helping to defeat Joshua's enemies (Joshua 10.12–13), and fighting against Sisera (Judges 5.20). Manasseh, king of southern Israel, encouraged worship of these objects (2 Kings 21.1–3). The next king Josiah had to dismiss the priests who had encouraged God's people to worship them (2 Kings 23.5). Close to that time Jeremiah condemned the worship of the host of heaven (Jeremiah 19.13). Isaiah describes the destruction of the stars as part of the judgement that the LORD sets over the nations of the world, because they have abused Israel (Isaiah 34.1–4). Deutero-Isaiah jeers at Babylonians who study the stars (Isaiah 47.13). This verse points to the development of astrology in Babylon. This is the belief that the stars can reveal the future for individuals and so enable them to face what is to come. Newspapers in Britain often run a regular column describing the effects of being born at different times of the year, when particular stars become prominent. Most people treat this as amusing, but some take it very seriously. Astrology is distinct from astronomy, which is a scientific study of the stars and the movements which we can see or detect from earth. No predictions about our personal prospects follow!

3 *Heavenly beings* These are the angels and other spiritual beings who share heaven with God. Since this is a major topic in itself we will study it in the second part of this chapter.

📖 **Check Your Understanding 11**

1 Write the following words on separate lines of your page. Then place the correct sentence from the list given below against each of these words. One of them can provide two answers!

IMMANENT   IMMANUEL   TRANSCENDENT

. . . means for Christians that God is mysterious and wonderful beyond our human understanding.

. . . means for Christians that God is near to us, and responds to our prayers.

. . . means for Hindus that we are each of us an aspect of God, as is all the created world.

. . . can be used to teach Hindus about God's immanence.

2 From what you have studied in this part of the chapter, what do you think should be the Christian response to astrology? Should we take notice of its predictions, or reject them as nonsense?

The Angels

Let the heavens praise thy wonders, O LORD,
thy faithfulness in the assembly of the holy ones!
For who in the skies can be compared to the LORD?
Who among the heavenly beings is like the LORD?
a God feared in the council of the holy ones,
great and terrible above all that are round about him?

(Psalm 89.5–7)

These verses set the angels in their right context. They share with God in being holy, which we learnt means that they are *apart* and *sacred, different from human beings*. But they are very different from God, because he far excels them in his holiness and glory. These verses describe them as members of God's assembly, and others elsewhere describe them as forming God's court. We shall return to these ideas later in this chapter, but first we need to look at some difficulties in translating the Hebrew words which the writers sometimes use to describe angels.

What do the Hebrew Words Mean?

First let us look at the meaning of the Hebrew word *malak*, which people often translate as *angel*. This word comes from a root word meaning *messenger*. Old Testament writers sometimes use the word to mean human messengers, and sometimes to speak of angels carrying God's messages. We can see the human use, for example, in Genesis 32.3, 6; 1 Kings 19.2; Ezekiel 23.16, and reference to heavenly messengers in such verses as Genesis 28.12; 2 Samuel 24.15–16; Daniel 3.25, 28. But sometimes translators find difficulty in deciding which meaning is appropriate in any particular verse. So, for example, in the story of Elijah's escape from the wrath of Jezebel, the person who provided food for him could have been a human. What he certainly did was to carry God's message and act on his behalf, but humans do sometimes serve God by what they do! Traditionally translators have taken this messenger to be an angel.

Now let us look at the meaning of the Hebrew word *Elohim*, which people often translated as *God*. Old Testament writers use this word in a number of ways quite different from its common use in naming the LORD. They also use it for the gods of other nations (Genesis 35.2; Judges 8.33; Psalm 16.4). The RSV translates Psalms 29.1 and 89.6 as 'heavenly beings', where the Hebrew says 'sons of *God'*. These verses speak clearly of those who are with God in heaven, and so indicates angels. The same phrase appears in Job 38.4–7, describing those who rejoiced with God at the creation of the world.

These possibilities raise problems for modern translators in working on Psalm 8.5. Some take the word *Elohim* to stand for *God*, and say that humans are 'made . . . little less than God'. Others take it to stand for angels, and say that people are '*made . . . little less than angels*'. Usually the translators give one of these two translations in their main text and a footnote offering the other meaning as an alternative. The RSV only offers *God*, possibly because everywhere else in the Old Testament *Elohim* never stands alone for *angels*, without the words *sons of God*.

Another use for the Hebrew word *Elohim* is to describe somebody who is powerful. The RSV translates it as *mighty* in Genesis 23.6, where the Hittites describe Abraham. This raises another problem for translators: scholars disagree about the use of *gods* in Psalm 82.1. Some believe that this is a reference to foreign gods, as being under God's rule. But this is doubtful, because it gives room for polytheism in a faith which is essentially monotheistic. Others take it to be a reference to powerful humans, and possibly those appointed to settle disputes among the people. But in verses 6–7 the writer compares gods to ordinary humans *like men*. So we are left with angels as the appropriate interpretation. We have here the idea that the angels share with the LORD in his rule over creation.

The Divine Council

Psalm 82, which we quoted above, describes the angels as 'the divine council', sharing in God's rule over creation. They possess greater knowledge and wisdom than humans (2 Samuel 14.20). They know the difference between good and evil (2 Samuel 14.17). They do what is right (1 Samuel 29.9; 2 Samuel 19.27). Part of their responsibility is to sing the praises of the LORD (Psalms 29.1–2; 103.20; 148.2). They also serve the LORD by carrying out his purposes (Psalm 103.21). They provide help for humans: as guides in life (Genesis 24.7; Exodus 23.20); as those who help in times of distress (Numbers 20.16); as those who protect humans from harm (Genesis 19.15; Psalm 91.11–12); as those who bring wrong-doers to judgement (2 Samuel 24.16); as those who punish wrong-doing (Exodus 23.20–21; 2 Kings 19.35; Psalm 78.49) and above all as messengers from the LORD. Other passages describe individual angels as sharing in God's activities (Exodus 23.20; Numbers 22.22–35; Zechariah 1.9–10). In Daniel 7.10 we can find a description of the court of heaven, corporately carrying out justice. We will look at other examples of this court when we study fallen angels.

Special Types of Angels

Archangels

The Old Testament never mentions these, although traditionally people have considered Gabriel and Michael to have this special rank among angels. The apocalyptic book of Daniel mentions both of these beings. It describes Gabriel as a *man*, that is, a male, bringing wisdom and understanding to Daniel (Daniel 9.20–22). As we have seen, angels possess special wisdom and knowledge. It describes Michael as Daniel's 'prince' (Daniel 10.21; 12.1). Perhaps this is in line with Deuteronomy 32.8, which pictures God dividing people into nations which each have an angel ruling over them. We find mentions of both Gabriel and Michael in the New Testament (Luke 1.19, 26; Jude 1.9; Revelation 12.7), but it calls only Michael an archangel.

Cherubim and Seraphim

The Old Testament mentions these two other special types of heavenly beings. The first mention of the Cherubim is in Genesis 3.24, where they guard the entrance to the Garden of Eden against the return of Adam and Eve after their eviction. The Priestly Code of Laws prescribed two golden images of Cherubim with outspread wings to adorn the Ark of the Covenant, protecting the mercy seat which lay between them (Exodus 25.18, 22). People thought that God ruled the world from this throne (2 Kings 19.15; Psalm 99.1) and revealed his compassion and care there (Psalm 80.1). The Israelites were to embroider the curtains of the tabernacle with Cherubim (Exodus 26.1, 31). In the time of the first Temple the Ark of the Covenant stood in the Holy of Holies, the sacred inner sanctuary. But the Ark was lost, probably looted at the fall of southern Israel to the Babylonians in 587 BC.

Ezekiel's visions of God's heavenly chariot refer many times to the 'living creatures', and in Ezekiel 10, he calls them Cherubim. They depart heavenward from the disgraced and punished city of Jerusalem (Ezekiel 11.22–23), and the last mention of them is in connection with Ezekiel's vision of a restored city and a new temple (Ezekiel 41.17b–20).

The book of Isaiah contains the only mention of the Seraphim. It pictures them as worshipping God, and active to cleanse Isaiah (Isaiah 6.2, 6).

Fallen Angels

We have seen that the Old Testament rejects the idea of a spiritual being who is eternally responsible for the creation of evil, in contrast to the LORD who is responsible for all that is good. So where did evil come from? In many parts of the Old Testament 'evil' describes the punishment which comes from God because of our wrong-doings (Judges 2.11–15; 1 Kings 14.9–10; Isaiah 13.9–11). The writers picture the LORD as repenting of evil when people turn to him in repentance (Exodus 32.11–14; Jeremiah 26.3–6; Amos 7.3, 6). When people suffer, they need God's help to search their hearts to see what they have done to displease the LORD (Psalm 139.23). Sin does cause suffering to others and to ourselves, but the book of Job describes the suffering that came to a righteous man, and robbed him of his many blessings. So we must reject any thought that God is responsible for all human suffering as punishment for evil-doing.

So, can we blame the angels for the evil in the world? Certainly Scripture describes them as fallible, capable of disobedience (Isaiah 24.21; Job 4.17–18; 15.14–16). The writer of 1 Samuel suggests that Saul suffered from an evil spirit from the LORD; and this being is seen as the cause of his wrong-doing (1 Samuel 16.14–16; 18.10). But other writers steer clear of using this idea.

There is an odd story in 1 Kings 22.19–23, in which God is involved in an act of deceit, inviting one of the heavenly court to volunteer to carry it out. Ahab wants to know whether he should go into battle, and a spirit from God tells him all will be well, knowing that in fact he will be killed! (See also Ezekiel 14.9 for a similar idea.)

Have a look at the story at the beginning of the book of Job (Job 1.6–7). It gives a picture of the sons of God coming to report to the LORD about their activities in his service. Among them comes The

Satan, a title describing his responsibilities in challenging the motives of people in their service of God (see RSV footnote translating Satan as 'the adversary'). He reports that he has been travelling to and fro, up and down the world. The LORD asks him whether he has noticed the honesty and goodness of Job. The Satan immediately suggests that Job has a motive of personal gain in acting in this way. He says that God has blessed Job abundantly, and so Job serves the LORD gladly. But if God takes the blessings away Job will curse the LORD openly. So the LORD challenges the Satan to prove it. Great suffering occurs, and is redoubled after the Satan has again reported to the LORD. But Job never does curse God! Notice that the story-teller avoids suggesting the LORD had himself planned to punish Job. In fact God is confident about Job's integrity (Job 1.8; 2.3; 42.7, 8). But the LORD accepts the Satan's right to challenge Job, and allows him to put Job to severe tests. He is allowing Satan the free will that is essential for all creatures that are given spiritual natures.

We can see how Old Testament thought developed if we compare the two accounts of a story about David. In 2 Samuel 24.1 the writer pictures the LORD as tempting David to take a census of the people of all Israel, and then punishing him for doing this (see verses 10–14). In 1 Chronicles 21.1 the writer puts *Satan* in place of the LORD as source of the temptation. Clearly he felt unhappy with the earlier story! Perhaps he felt the injustice of the record in 1 Samuel. But we must notice the difference in use of the word *Satan* in the Hebrew. In this passage *Satan* has become a personal name, since it lacks the word *the* essential to a title. This led eventually, through later writings not included in our Bible, to the New Testament concept of Satan as an independent spiritual being.

In Zechariah 3.1–3, which was probably written later than 1 Chronicles, the Satan stands ready to accuse the high priest Joshua. The LORD rebukes him, and commands that the people should honour Joshua. The reversion to use of 'the Satan' in the Hebrew as a title rather than a personal name seems to underline the fact that this being can only act with permission of the LORD and God can rebuke him for his rebelliousness in wanting to do what is clearly against the LORD's will.

What Should We Believe About Angels?

Other spiritual beings exist beyond ourselves

First let me say that if we dismiss the idea of angels as simply a part of the biblical traditions that Christians today should ignore, we are probably claiming that human beings are unique in God's plans for creation. Naturally the whole Bible is concerned with God's purposes for humankind, and the Old Testament shows the gradual development of spiritual understanding which was the outcome in those

Figure 5. The prologue to the book of Job provides the fullest description of Satan in the Old Testament. But Satan is never described in physical terms. Many Christians have heard that Satan has horns, cloven feet and a tail; but these ideas are not found in the Bible. They seem to come from pagan ideas of demons or gods of evil, such as the demon Pazuzu, shown here in a small statue from Mesopotamia.

days of God's activity as the Good Teacher. But why should we suppose that God was only concerned for this world, and our species? Psalm 8.5 probably does mean that we are a little lower than the angels. The LORD has a care and concern for angels as well as for ourselves. Indeed he watches with love over the lives of all who have personal nature and are capable of fellowship with him. There may well be other personal beings besides those we know in this world and think about in heaven.

Astronomers often say that the universe is so vast that there is every likelihood that there are other personal beings somewhere else in creation. But we should reject any thought that this is a major challenge to our faith. God is far more wonderful than we can ever know or think while we live in this world in this time. So we have ample room for belief in other personal beings who have a relationship with the LORD. Zoologists keep discovering more about the personal life of animals, and sometimes point to similarities with humans. So we cannot be sure that such creatures as dolphins, whales and gorillas are not at least developing towards becoming fully personal, able to think for themselves, able to come to conclusions leading to action and able to relate to other personal beings including humans, and even including God himself. C. S. Lewis, a writer with a vision of a reality within and beyond this world, has suggested that this is so. If he is right, we have even more to praise God for, and a greater need to treat animals with respect.

God does use messengers

Some people find difficulty in the very idea that God needs messengers to convey his purposes to us. We believe that God's purpose for all of us is that we should know him for ourselves (Jeremiah 31.34). He is very close to us, even though he is very different in important ways from us. But we could compare the question, 'Why does God need angels?' with the question, 'Why does God need people to pray to him?' There is a real sense in which God is complete in himself and fully able to respond to people's needs, and to help us to follow his way. But because he is the God of love, his delight is in building up the fellowship of his people, whether this means humans or angels. We need to learn to care for each other in our prayer life, and to care about those who suffer or are in need of what we think of as human necessities. We need, by word and action, to be available for God's service in caring for the world.

The existence of Satan

The importance of our study of the development of ideas about Satan is that none of the Old Testament writers made the mistake of suggesting that evil is caused by some eternally independent being, acting at all times in opposition to the Lord. They have firmly grasped the fact that *all* things come from God, and then struggle with the problem of evil in a world which God created in freedom and well-being. Jewish literature outside the contents of the Old Testament (for example in *The Secrets of Enoch*) eventually resolved the difficulty by the writer supposing that one of the angels whom the LORD created has turned against him, and is using his freedom to upset God's purposes. The Old Testament writers point to the idea without fully expressing it. Once it is expressed it gives hope, because Satan is a creature of the LORD and is unable finally to disrupt his purposes. Jesus used this understanding of Satan in his own teachings, for example Luke 10.18, and in the account of his own temptations before the start of his earthly ministry.

 **Check Your Understanding 12**

1 What does the Hebrew word *Elohim* mean? Give the four distinct types of beings, whether real or fictional, who are sometimes given this name in the Old Testament.
2 Which of the following words are associated with the idea of immanence, and which with the idea of transcendence?

ALMIGHTY   AVAILABLE   CREATOR   ETERNAL   HELPFUL
LOVING   NEAR   PERFECT   PERSONAL   SEPARATE

Study Suggestions

FOR GROUP DISCUSSION

1 What did the people of your tribe or caste believe about the origin of evil in the past? If more than one ethnic group is represented within your society, compare the different ways of answering this question. Are these ideas still widely held today among your people?
2 Some Christians say that belief in Satan is part of the Jewish religion which Christians should reject. They say that people are glad to have somebody to blame for their failures and sins. What do you think about this? Give full reasons for your own opinion.
3 Does the Old Testament give us physical descriptions of all the angels, of only some of them, or of none of them at all? In what ways are angels described? How does this help us understand their role in God's plans?

FOR ESSAY WRITING

4 Describe as carefully as you can, by giving textual evidence, the difference between the angel of the LORD in Genesis, and the angels in the Psalms.

5 We have studied the Old Testament belief that the LORD is transcendent. Is Satan also transcendent? Does he possess the four qualities of transcendence described on pages 30–33?. Give evidence, with the appropriate Old Testament references, which shows what the writers believed about the spiritual nature of Satan (page 70).

6 What would be your own reaction if scientists were able to provide clear evidence that there are other spiritual beings besides humans in this world, and in the universes beyond our reach today?

WORK WITH THE BIBLE AND A CONCORDANCE

7 Use a concordance to discover what the Old Testament writers say about evil spirits.

8 'Does evil befall a city, unless the LORD has done it?' (Amos 6.3). Does this mean that God is wicked or sinful? Find six other examples which say that the Lord planned or carried out evil. What is the real meaning of *evil* in these verses?

9 Use a concordance to study what Jesus had to say about Satan. Then summarize your findings in a short essay. Why do you think Jesus called Peter 'Satan' in Mark 8.33? Do we ever deserve that name?

Humanity 5

Human Creation and Destiny

When I look at thy heavens, the work of thy fingers,
the moon and the stars which thou hast established;
what is man that thou art mindful of him,
and the son of man that thou dost care for him?
(Psalm 8.3–4)

The Psalmist wonders at the sky which is beyond his reach, and is
aware of his own limitations. Today we can do the same with
much more knowledge of all that God has created. People have
travelled to the moon and spaceships have been sent to some of
the planets. Yet we know that the sun is in fact one of the stars.
There are many more out there in space beyond our reach, all part
of God's creation. So we should ask ourselves, 'What is man that
thou art mindful of him? And the son of man that thou visitest
him?', as the Authorized Version puts it. The Psalmist goes on to
say that we are 'little less than God' (RSV), and that God has given
humans dominion over the works of his hands. He says that God
has placed under our authority both domestic and wild animals,
and birds and fish as well. This psalm says we are less than God,
but greater than other living creatures on earth. We have already
studied God's own relationship with his creation (pages 35–9). We
are to be his agents within creation. We are to use our authority for
the benefit of the whole world. For the sake of readers who insist
that *man* can only refer to the males of our species, I should add
that the Hebrew word often translated 'man' can stand for
humans of both sexes (see especially Genesis 1.27). This is the
word used in Psalm 8.4 in the phrase 'son of man'.

The two stories in Genesis support the belief that God has made
us to be his agents in the world. According to Genesis 2.4–25, God
made man first of the animal world, and then gave him responsibility for the welfare of the garden of creation. Nothing else in creation
was suitable as a helper for man, until God created woman. The fact
that the Psalmists describe God himself as 'helper' of people (for
example, Psalms 10.14; 30.10; 54.4; 72.12) shows us that we would
be prejudiced to suggest that God intended women to be

subordinate to men. Further evidence that such an idea is false is provided in Genesis 1.1—2.4. God created male and female together on the sixth day at the climax of creation. God made both male and female in his own image, and gave them dominion over all living things (Genesis 1.28).

The two stories give different accounts of how the world was made and in what order creation took place. Yet the editor who included both stories in preparing the book of Genesis clearly refused to believe there was any important conflict between the two stories. He treated as unimportant the precise details of the order of creation, and the processes by which the world was made. He believed that both stories taught the same basic truths: that the LORD created the world, and that he gave humankind a central place in our world.

The two stories of creation involve important beliefs about the nature and destiny of humankind. We must study these more closely now.

Humans Are Part of Creation

Both stories recognize that humans are part of creation, and that they are closely related to the physical world and to animals.

Genesis 2.7 and 19 tell us that both animals and humans are living creatures; in some ways they are the same sort of being. These verses also tell us that humans were made of 'dust from the ground', and animals were formed 'out of the ground'. This also implies a close physical relationship between animals and humans. Both animals and humans have in them 'the breath of life', which in the Bible means a vitality that comes from God (Genesis 2.7; 7.22).

Genesis 1 includes a special Hebrew word to describe God's work as creator. It uses the same word to describe how he made the heavens and the earth (Genesis 1.1), living creatures of the seas, birds (Genesis 1.21), and humans (Genesis 1.27). We would be wrong to think that there is a distinct word to describe the origin of humankind. Humans are part of creation, like all other things.

Humans Have Authority Over Other Creatures

Both traditions in Genesis recognize that humans are different in some substantial way from other created beings.

In Genesis 2 humans are at the centre of the whole story of creation. God prepared the garden of Eden as the home for humans (Genesis 2.8). God made animals and gave a human authority to name them. In Hebrew thought, anyone who knows the name of a living creature has power over that creature. So the significance of Genesis 2.19 is that humans have power over animals and other living creatures. Eve shares Adam's authority, because she shares his own essential nature, and is not a lesser creature under his control (Genesis 2.22).

In Genesis 1 God gave humankind, both male and female, dominion over other living creatures (Genesis 1.26). Dominion means the right to rule, and so in God's purposes humans were made to rule over the other created beings. God also instructed the humans to take responsibility for the physical world in which they lived: 'fill the earth and subdue it' (Genesis 1.28).

This latter verse has often led to serious misunderstanding of God's purposes. Those who are selfish and proud of their humanity have taken the verse to mean that we have total freedom to tyrannize other creatures, using them solely for our own benefit and enjoyment. Such people ignore the fact that what they do often causes pain and suffering to animals, and can even help to destroy the earth's material resources. All humans are capable of misunderstanding what God-given freedom involves. We need to see the whole of creation and especially animals as deserving our understanding and care. The writer of Genesis I tells us that everything God made was very good. Everything has a right to its own existence, and as humans we have a responsibility to take care of our part of creation, and to ensure the well-being of every part of it.

The words 'fill the earth' (Genesis 1.28) have sometimes led people to believe that they should have as many children as possible, regardless of thought about how they are to provide for them. Taking the creation story in its most literal sense, Adam and Eve had the work of filling the world with peoples. But our responsibilities are different. Many people today face hardship and suffering because the countries in which they live are unable to provide a good life for everybody. Disputes over ownership of land are commonplace in many parts of Africa. They spring from the fact that fertile land is in short supply and fails to meet everybody's needs. Careful family planning is important and should be based on the need for parents to provide adequately for their children. But all of us need to care about these disputes, and to work together to bring peace and joy to our communities.

Humans Have a Special Relationship with God

Both stories of creation recognize that humans have a special relationship with God.

In Genesis 2 the LORD God 'breathed' into the man's nostrils the breath of life (Genesis 2.7). This suggests a close relationship in creation, as a contrast to the statement that the LORD God 'formed' every beast, etc. (Genesis 2.19). The LORD God talked with humans, and shared a knowledge of his purposes with them (Genesis 2.17).

In Genesis 1, God told humans how to serve him (Genesis 1.28–30). But the statement that 'God created man in his own image, in the image of God he created him' (Genesis 1.27) clearly expresses the special relationship involved.

However, scholars differ greatly in their interpretation of the phrase 'image of God'. Some believe that the writer intended an actual physical likeness between God and humans. They draw attention to the fact that God is often described in the Old Testament as though he were a man. Some texts say that God has hands (1 Samuel 5.11), feet (Genesis 3.8), and a face (Genesis 32.30). Others say he has ears and eyes to know things (2 Kings 19.16), and an arm to achieve his purposes (Isaiah 52.10). There are also texts which describe him as doing human things: laughing (Psalms 2.4; 37.13), smelling things (Genesis 8.21) and whistling (Isaiah 7.18). These scholars suppose that the people of Old Testament times thought that by having a physical resemblance to God, humans could best represent God within the world he had created.

Obviously some of the Israelites did take these ideas literally. But that fails to provide a satisfactory explanation of the meaning of the phrase *image of God*. The term comes from a later tradition which developed in the time of the Exile or perhaps afterwards. Long before that time, the Israelites knew that they must avoid using any physical likeness to represent God (Exodus 20.4). Those who make idols have control over them, which humans have never possessed over God. The evidence of the Old Testament, and of archaeology, is that physical images of God were never used in Israel; even human images were totally rejected.

All the verses mentioned above which describe God in human ways were intended to express mental and spiritual realities about his life, knowledge and activities. The Israelites were unable to find any better words to express the truth about God beyond those they used to describe human life, and the knowledge and activities of human beings. They used such words because they wanted to share with others knowledge of the ways of God, and this was the only language they could use.

God himself had used this way of expressing the truth about his personal reality and activity. He appeared to people in dreams and visions as a human being (for example, Isaiah 6.1; Daniel 7.9) in order that they should understand the things he wanted to reveal to them. But these physical appearances were only a way of making people aware of his presence and power. They were never used to imply that God is actually human-shaped. He is something more wonderful and beautiful than the best of humans.

So the use of the phrase 'image of God' means something different from a belief that humans and God share the same physical appearance.

Figure 6. 'Scholars differ greatly in their interpretation of the phrase "the image of God". Some believe that the writer intended an actual physical likeness between God and humans' (p. 75). The Egyptians believed that there was a close relationship between the Pharaohs and their gods. In this inscription inside the pyramid of Unis at Sakkara the dead Pharaoh is spoken to in these words: 'Thy arm is Atum, thy shoulders are Atum, thy belly is Atum, thy back is Atum, thy rear is Atum, thy legs are Atum, thy face is Anubis.' Clearly the Egyptians supposed there was an actual physical likeness between the Pharaoh Unis and the gods Atum and Anubis.

But scholars who look for another meaning do not all agree on the way it should be interpreted:

- Some believe that this is another way of speaking of the authority which God has given to humans. Just as God has dominion, so humankind has dominion.
- Some believe that the phrase means that people are God's representatives in the created universe, and that human dominion springs from the fact that we have been given this responsibility.
- Some believe that people have been made in the image of God in the sense that we share God's moral nature: being able to distinguish between right and wrong, and able to choose to do what is good.

Probably all these ideas are included in this phrase, but one way of expressing its meaning covers them all: humans are spiritual, as God is spiritual. So far as we know, our world lacks any other creature that combines in its being the two qualities of physical and spiritual nature in the way that we do. Because of our spiritual nature we can rightly use human terms, rather than those of other animal or vegetable life, to describe God. Eventually human spiritual nature made it possible for God to become incarnate, to be born as a man in Christ Jesus. The potential of human nature reached its highest fulfilment when the Son of God came to live among us as a man.

God's Concern for Human Beings

Both creation stories recognize God's concern for the well-being of humans. There is a positive purpose and value in God's creation of human beings. Both creation stories express this belief in the commands that God gives to humans (Genesis 2.16; 1.28). Chapter 2, which was was based on traditions much older than those used in chapter 1, goes on to describe how humankind acted against the purposes of God, and brought trouble into the world (Genesis 3.1–19). We shall study the nature and results of sin in a later chapter. It is sufficient here to notice that God intended people to have life, and life that involved a personal relationship with God himself. The commandments in the creation stories imply this relationship. We shall study the Israelites' understanding of death later, but we must notice here that what they hoped for was resurrection to life here on earth, with the continuing possibility of relationship with God.

The Place of Science

Many people have been troubled by talk of evolution ever since Charles Darwin wrote his books in the second half of the nineteenth century. The contrast between what he wrote and what the editors of Genesis presented in Genesis 1—2 has disturbed many people and still does. But in fact this is all based on a misunderstanding of what is involved. So let me try to clarify the issue. In the first place we have to accept that Genesis presents two different accounts of creation. We should not dispute this since Genesis 1 tells us that God created humans as the final act of creation, while Genesis 2 says God created Adam before animals, and only created Eve at the end of his work. We have seen that this means that the actual details about the events which led up to the world in which humankind lives did not matter to the editors who included the conflicting accounts when they produced the book of Genesis.

Let us try to imagine what happened. The people who created these stories felt inspired to teach the important facts about human creation which we have studied in this section of the chapter. They tried to find words to express this truth, and looked at the world as they knew it, and each saw it in a different way. The story-teller who produced Genesis 2 saw the world as a desert at the beginning of time (Genesis 2.5), and described the planting of a garden and the subsequent developments of God's act of creation. The writer of Genesis 1 saw the world as a vast ocean which God used in the processes of creation (Genesis 1.2). Each was using such knowledge as he had, and provided for his people something they could understand because they shared the same ideas of the world around them. Today scientists are the people who are eager to discover the true nature of the universe in which we live, and they base their description of the beginning of creation as a big bang on such knowledge as they possess. No honest scientist would say that they have everything right in their accounts. They work by trying to interpret what they already know and then to go on to carry out research to see whether they are right. From time to time scientists publish fresh results of research which sometimes support, and at other times contradict, the theories with which they have been working. In another 100 years the scientists of that time will have a different story to tell. This is how knowledge develops. There are many scientists who find no difficulty at all in believing in God, and learning to serve him. Even Fred Hoyle, who in the 1950s published a popular account of the universe denying the need for God, came later to say that the creation is so marvellous it must have a conscious designer. Since his time many scientists have recognized that the order of the universe depends on a creative and sustaining God.

Check Your Understanding 13

1 A person may see their own image by looking at any of the following things. Which of them shows an image of a similar type to the image of God in humans?

THE PERSON'S CHILD   THE PERSON'S MIRROR

THE PERSON'S PHOTOGRAPH

THE PERSON'S PORTRAIT   THE PERSON'S SCULPTURE

2 'The two stories of creation involve important beliefs about the nature and destiny of humankind' (page 73).
Which of the following definitions best describes the meaning of 'destiny' as we have used it in this chapter?
  (a) A goal to be reached, a final event to be worked for.
  (b) A way of life that is the real reason for living.
  (c) Something that cannot be avoided, which is certain to happen.

Human Nature

You shall love the LORD your God
with all your heart, and with all your soul,
and with all your might.

(Deuteronomy 6.5)

All the writers of the Old Testament were concerned with human life. They described the thoughts, feelings and actions of people in many different ways. Scholars have found evidence in the Old Testament to support several different views of each person's essential nature. Some speak of people as having three parts: body, soul and spirit. Some prefer to describe the two parts of a human as the physical and the spiritual. But by far the most important belief was that, whatever parts of human nature they distinguished from each other, Israelite thinkers believed that human life is a unity, and that the various parts are neither in conflict, nor capable of being independent of each other.

The difficulty in describing the exact nature of the Old Testament ideas about humans comes from the fact that in Hebrew, as in other languages, many words have more than one meaning. Often their meanings overlap, so we are unable to say that a particular Hebrew word means one thing, and that another Hebrew word means something quite different. At times both of these Hebrew words may bear similar meanings, and at other times they may express quite different ideas.

The work of discovering by research a recognizable pattern of Israelite thought about humans is impossible for most people, because the English and indeed other translations of the Bible fail to show what Hebrew words lie behind the interpretations given. Let me explain more fully.

1 Scholars may in fact translate Hebrew words in different ways in the various English translations. For example, the words the RSV translates as 'Serve the LORD with gladness', the Good News Bible translates as 'Worship the LORD with joy'. Those who prepare a new translation often use the same Hebrew word in different ways according to the needs of the sentence they are translating. For example, in the RSV they translate the ordinary Hebrew word for heart in many places as *heart* (Genesis 6.5, etc.), but they also translate it as *accord* (Psalm 83.5), *sense* (Proverb 6.32), and *understanding* (Job 36.5).

2 Scholars sometimes translate different Hebrew words by the same English word. For example, in the RSV they sometimes use the English word *mind* as a translation of the Hebrew word for *heart* (Deuteronomy 29.4); or as a translation of the Hebrew word for *soul* (Nehemiah 4.6); or even of the Hebrew word for *spirit* (Ezekiel 20.32).

If you can find an analytical concordance in a library, this can help you to discover the Hebrew words which lie behind the English words. The most useful book of this kind for people who use the RSV is *The Eerdmans Analytical Concordance to the Revised Standard Version of the Bible*, compiled by R. E. Whitaker. But to benefit from it you need at least to be able to recognize the letters of the Hebrew alphabet, which are quite different from English lettering.

We must make some attempt to bring order out of what may seem like confusion. So let us discover what we can about Israelite thought by using the three-part division of human nature: body, soul and spirit. We shall see that the word *flesh* usually refers to the body, that *soul* expresses personality, and that *spirit* refers to that part of our nature which makes it possible to share fellowship with God. The Israelites themselves were strongly convinced of the unity of human nature, and we shall find that they gave these three aspects of human nature close connections with each other. We shall discover that the Old Testament writers believed that the physical universe is the only place of existence for humans. They abhorred the idea of human spirits existing in separation from their bodies, either denying that life continued beyond death, or that it was a dreary kind of existence, without the ability to be or do anything significant. See pages 90–91 under the heading *Sheol*. Towards the end of the Old Testament we can find a fleeting glimpse of hope for the dead in the briefly-mentioned idea of resurrection to this world at the end of time (Daniel 12.2). So we use this subdivision into the physical, personal and spiritual nature of humankind for analysis purposes rather than to express anything the Jews believed and held to be an important division.

A Person's Physical Nature

The Old Testament seldom uses the ordinary word for *body*. Where it does, it can, like the English word 'body', mean a living person (Genesis 47.18; Nehemiah 9.37), or a corpse (1 Samuel 31.10, 12; Psalm 110.6). It can describe the carcase of a dead animal (Judges 14.8). It can also describe the physical appearances of a spiritual being seen in a vision (Daniel 10.6; Ezekiel 1.11, 23).

Much more often the Old Testament uses the Hebrew word for *flesh*. This can describe the material which makes up animal bodies (Leviticus 4.11) and human bodies (Leviticus 13.10). The word also describes the closeness of human relationships (Genesis 2.23; 37.27, etc.). Some texts use it to express the weakness of created beings, including humans, in comparison with the almighty power of God (Genesis 6.3; Job 34.14–15). But the Old Testament writers never used the term to suggest that flesh is corrupt (contrast Romans 7.18).

The Israelites failed to discover much about the workings of the human body. The Old Testament never mentions the brain, even though we know it controls the activities of the body. Muscles and sinews merely join the parts of the body together (Ezekiel 37.8). Nobody suggested that movement depends on their use in response to our nervous system. But the Israelites did know about some of the internal organs of the body, and supposed that these were the source of human mental and emotional life.

Chief among these organs is the *heart*. The Hebrew word can mean a person's physical heart (Psalm 22.14). But it can also describe the source of appetite (Psalm 104.15) and the centre of emotions (Exodus 4.14; Psalm 55.4). The Israelites believed that thought takes place in the heart: and that it is the place of understanding (Isaiah 6.10) and of memory (see Deuteronomy 30.1, where *mind* translates the Hebrew word for heart). They believed that a human's will is formed in the heart (Proverbs 6.18), and that character comes from it (Psalm 24.4; 1 Kings 9.4), even bad character (Deuteronomy 8.14; 15.7). In English we use some of these ideas in our everyday use of the word 'heart'. This probably comes from the influence that Bible reading has had over the centuries in Britain.

Old Testament writers also used other words which mean various internal organs of the human body. But their ideas are only partly formed and fail to give a precise meaning to each word. The translators of the RSV have tried to discover the appropriate English words, based on the traditional ideas we relate to each part of our bodies. So we discover that the Hebrew word for *bowel* can be translated in some verses as *belly*, or *body*, or *breast*, or *heart*, or *soul*, or *stomach*, or *womb*. This hides from us the ideas expressed by the Hebrew writers, whose understanding was more limited than ours. But we can notice some specific links between Hebrew words and English equivalents. So we must take brief notice of these here.

The Old Testament writers thought of the belly as the source of a person's willpower (Job 15.35), and the kidneys as the source of conscience (Psalms 16.7; 73.16; Proverbs 23.16). Grief came from the liver (Lamentations 2.11), and compassion from the bowels (Isaiah 16.11; Jeremiah 31.20) or the womb (Isaiah 63.15; Psalm 77.9). Most scholars agree that these ideas came from the writers' physical experiences. The Israelites recognized the physical feelings which go with strong emotions like joy, grief, shame and desire, and they supposed that these feelings showed the sources of the emotions, mostly in the abdomen.

These ideas illustrate the Israelites' belief that there is a close relation between the physical, emotional and spiritual natures of human beings. We should notice that modern doctors and psychiatrists are more and more stressing the interrelation between body and mind. Physical ill-health can affect the mind, and mental distress can affect the body. Healing must involve the whole person. These modern ideas are very similar to those of the biblical writers, and partly arise from similar human experiences.

A Person's Social Nature: The Soul

The Hebrew word we usually translate into English as *soul* is used about 700 times in the Old Testament, but the RSV translators use more than 40 different ways of presenting it. Many of these translations only occur very occasionally, and we can safely ignore them here. Apart from *soul* itself, which occurs 188 times, the translations which appear by far the most often in the RSV are *life* (185 times); *anyone* (120 times) and *person* (64 times). The Hebrew word also reinforces the reflexive mood of Hebrew verbs, thus emphasizing *myself, yourself*, etc. Let us look at a few examples of each of these translations of the Hebrew word we are thinking about:

> *Soul* (Genesis 35.18; Job 30.25; Psalm 23.3; Isaiah 10.18)
> *Life* (Genesis 19.17; 1 Kings 19.2; Psalm 6.4; Jeremiah 8.3)
> *Person* (Genesis 12.5; Deuteronomy 10.22; Proverbs 19.15;
>   Jeremiah 43.6)
> the reflexive *yourself, themselves*, etc. (Job 9.21; Psalm 25.13)
> for emphasis *me, you*, etc. (Numbers 23.10; Psalm 124.7).

These examples show that in Israelite thought *soul* is the name given to a person's essential self: the human quality of being active and creative, which a corpse has lost. The soul is the personal identity which makes social life possible. Every human possesses a unique quality of life which others can recognize and appreciate. Sometimes people say that animals such as the dolphin and the gorilla show human levels of understanding and ability to respond to humans. This means that they possess what the Israelites call a soul. Perhaps dogs are the most obvious example, since few of us have regular contact with dolphins and gorillas. It is certainly true that dogs have their own identity and nature. But as yet there is no evidence at all that they possess a spiritual nature, able to respond to God.

A Person's Spiritual Nature: The Spirit

The Hebrew word we usually translate as *spirit* occurs about 400 times in the Old Testament, but the writers use it about God, and about other spiritual beings, as well as about human beings. Scholars have to decide the sense which the writers intended in each verse that they translate. Then, where the reference is to God, their custom is to place a capital letter at the start: *Spirit*. If they are confident that the word is used about a human they write it without the capital: *spirit*. In some passages in the Old Testament, however, scholars are uncertain whether the Spirit of God or the spirit of a human is intended. The fact that human encounters with God are the main substance of the Old Testament sometimes makes it especially difficult to distinguish the two uses.

Apart from *spirit*, the commonest translations of this word in the Old Testament are *wind* (109 times) (Genesis 8.1; Psalm 1.4; Isaiah 7.2); and *breath* (27 times) (Genesis 2.7; 2 Samuel 22.16; Job 7.7). These translations suggest that spirit is the driving force of life, providing energy for action, and enabling body and soul together to have life (Job 27.3). The human spirit is a gift from God (Isaiah 42.5), and if God withdrew the gift, a person would cease to exist (Job 34.14–15). Living things die when God takes away their breath (Psalm 104.29).

God's Spirit enables people to achieve many things which they would be unable to achieve without it. The coming of God's Spirit to human beings enriches their life, and enables the human spirit to reach its fullest powers. The Spirit of God enabled Bezalel to be a skilled craftsman (Exodus 31.3), and Samson to exercise his great strength (Judges 14.6). By the same power the judges defeated the enemies of Israel (Judges 3.10), David ruled in Israel (1 Samuel 16.13), and the prophets spoke in God's name (Isaiah 61.1). We have already noticed that the Old Testament emphasis on the Unity of God prevented the Israelites from recognizing the fully personal nature of the Holy Spirit. But they could recognize the difference made to the lives of some of their leaders when the Spirit of God 'came upon' (Judges 14.6; 1 Samuel 16.13), 'took possession of' (Judges 6.34), 'filled' (Exodus 31.30), or 'poured upon' (Isaiah 44.3) them.

The spirits of humans are often impure. The Old Testament writers describe people as erring in spirit (Isaiah 29.24), or having a spirit of confusion (Isaiah 19.14), harlotry (Hosea 4.12) or unfaithfulness (Psalm 78.8). But the LORD can revive their spirits (Isaiah 57.15); and put a new and right spirit within them (Psalm 51.10; Ezekiel 36.27). The presence of God's own Spirit makes this possible (Isaiah 11.2), and in its fullest power it produces in his people a spirit of wisdom, understanding, counsel, might, knowledge, and fear of the LORD.

So we can say that the spiritual nature of humans is that aspect of our whole being which enables us to have fellowship with God, and to receive inspiration and guidance (Jeremiah 31.34). Ultimately this is the most significant part of human nature since our personal experience of God assures us of eternal life, a thing the Old Testament writers failed to recognize.

📖 **Check Your Understanding 14**

1 'the three-part division of human nature: body, soul and spirit' (see page 80). Which two of the following words would best describe the meaning of 'part' in this sentence?

COMPONENT DETACHABLE DISTINCT

INTEGRAL SCATTERED SEPARATE

2 Name the seven distinct ways in which the Israelites believed the heart provided different aspects of human nature.

Birth, Life and Death

> I cry to thee, O LORD
> I say, Thou art my refuge,
> my portion in the land of the living.
>
> (Psalm 142.5)

The writers of the Old Testament had quite a lot to say about the origin of individual human beings, the part they are able to play in the life of the nation, and their experiences after death. So now we must look at this sequence of ideas in order to complete our study of human nature.

Christians who have only studied the Old Testament at a shallow level often suppose that its ideas are the same as those found in the New Testament. But some of the ideas of the Old Testament's writers

and editors are quite different, especially in the subject we are looking at in this new section of Chapter 5. A useful example is in the last
verse of the popular Psalm 23. Many people misunderstand the
words 'I will dwell in the house of the LORD for ever' as a promise of
eternal life in heaven. The Good News Bible gets this matter right
when it translates the verse as: 'Your house will be my home as long
as I live'. The Hebrew words that some versions of the Bible translate
as *for ever*, really mean *for the present period of time*. The writer was
thinking of this present life, as the only time which he would be
sharing with God.

So you must be careful to look at the biblical quotations given
here, to see that they really do confirm the ideas you meet here.

Birth

Old Testament writers believed that the secrets of birth are under
God's control, but especially so in the procreation of our human spiritual natures and our endowment with gifts and abilities. Scientists
may be able to define many of the physical processes involved, but
they still have many unanswered questions about these. There is
some kind of relationship between the origins of personality and of
aptitudes, and our physical development, but they are a far greater
mystery than scientists can explain by suggesting that everything
stems from our physical bodies. The Old Testament writers lacked
scientific knowledge and the tools for research, but they did recognize the mystery of what makes humans more than animals, and saw
God's hand at work creating each one of us. They expressed this idea
most fully in the story of Jacob and his two wives. Leah bore many
children, but Rachel seemed to be barren. She complained to Jacob,
but he replied, 'Am I in the place of God, who has withheld from you
the fruit of the womb?' (Genesis 30.2; compare 29.31). The same idea
underlies stories of barren women who pray for children and, as a
result, receive them. For example, the mother of Esau and Jacob
(Genesis 25.21), and the mother of Samuel (1 Samuel 1.19–20). But a
normal conception is often described as a gift from God (Genesis 4.1;
Ruth 4.13).

Because the Israelites knew none of the physiological reasons for
the development of the foetus in the womb, they believed it to be a
mystery directly controlled by the LORD (Job 31.15; Psalm 119.73).
They described the way the LORD works to make each human being,
though in very general terms which suggest that the physical as well
as the spiritual side of human nature develops under his control
(Psalm 139.13–15; Job 10.8–11). But there are verses which suggest
that it is especially the spiritual part of human nature which comes
from God in the birth of each child. According to Ecclesiastes 11.5
the great mystery is, 'how the spirit comes to the bones'. To this we

can add, 'The L ORD . . . made our souls' (Jeremiah 38.16) and 'formed the spirit of man within him' (Zechariah 12.1). The prophet Jeremiah believed that he had been chosen to serve God before he was born, and even that God had made him for that very purpose (Jeremiah 1.5).

Role in Life

We have already noticed that the Israelites believed that the L ORD was active within the events of history (see pages 40–3). We saw that the L ORD often brought his purposes to fulfilment through the obedience of those who responded to his call: Abraham, Moses and David, among others. Such people believed that they had a special part to play in the history of God's people.

But they knew that they were chosen to enable the whole nation to fulfil its role within God's purposes. At the centre of these purposes was the L ORD's intention that the Israelites should know him (Hosea 6.6). Some of the prophets expressed God's anger and distress that his people failed to honour him (Hosea 4.1; 5.4; Isaiah 1.3; Jeremiah 4.22). The Law was intended to show the Israelites what God wanted from his people, and so to reveal his heart and mind. But, 'those who handle the law did not know me' (Jeremiah 2.8). These same prophets looked forward to the time when God's people would know their L ORD (Hosea 2.20).

> I will be their God, and they shall be my people. And no longer shall each man teach his neighbour and each his brother, saying, 'Know the L ORD', for they shall all know me, from the least of them to the greatest, says the L ORD. (Jeremiah 31.33–34)

Here we find expressed God's purpose for every human life in Israel, and for his chosen nation within the world. The prophets believed that eventually all peoples would recognize this as God's purpose for all humankind (Isaiah 2.3).

In order to reach this goal the L ORD chose people to serve him and to do important things for him. He chose Abraham to establish a new family and lead them towards their new home. In this way God began to prepare for the salvation of humankind. According to Genesis 17.4–5 Abraham would be called 'father of a multitude of nations'. As we have seen already, Jews, Christians and Muslims all look back to Abraham as the first man to have shared in God's work of redemption. God chose Moses to rescue the Israelites from Egypt, and to bring them to a meeting with him at Sinai. In this way God created Israel as a nation under his rule. God chose Joshua to lead the people into Palestine, and to help them settle in their new home. In this way God brought Israel to a strategic place which linked Africa, Asia and Europe. There the people had a part to play in the life of many nations. So one by one the leaders came, gave their service, and departed. Each carried out a special role, a significant part of God's plans for his people.

Each of these people needed special qualities and abilities to fulfil the role that God gave them. How were they equipped for their work? Did God search out from among the people somebody who possessed the necessary qualities? Did God endow his leaders with special qualities, which they would have lacked as part of their natural and personal characteristics apart from God's special gift at the time of their call? Or is there some other explanation of their ability to do his will, and so fulfil the role he gave them?

We can find the answer to these questions by looking at stories which tell of God's choice of new leaders and especially those in which the person he chose doubted his ability to do the work that God gave him. The story of the call of Moses is given in Exodus 3.1—4.23. Moses felt inadequate for his work: 'Who am I that I should go to Pharaoh?' God's answer was, 'I will be with you' (Exodus 3.11–12). The presence of the LORD would make all the difference. With God's help he would be able to do his duty. Later in the story Moses again raises doubts, 'Oh, my LORD, I am not eloquent . . . I am slow of speech and tongue' (Exodus 4.10). He assessed his own natural ability and felt that he lacked the qualities needed for this work: 'either heretofore or since thou hast spoken to thy servant'. God's presence had failed to alter that. The LORD's reply was, 'Who has made man's mouth . . . Is it not I?' (Exodus 4.11). Moses had forgotten that God was his creator and knew what abilities he possessed better than Moses knew them himself. The LORD would enable him to use his hidden resources of speech in a way that Moses himself had never used them before. His lack of confidence hindered him from discovering the truth, and so the LORD provided Aaron as a spokesman for him (Exodus 4.14). When Moses and Aaron confronted Pharaoh it was usually Moses who spoke, and Aaron who worked the miracles!

There are similar ideas in other parts of the Old Testament. When David was chosen to be king, the LORD said to Samuel, 'the LORD sees not as man sees; man looks on the outward appearance, but the LORD looks on the heart' (1 Samuel 16.7). God is able to see what a person is capable of doing; his assessment goes beyond what that individual is already doing. Seven of Jesse's sons lacked the qualities needed for such responsibilities, but David was capable of being a good king, even though he was the youngest among them. The LORD knew where to send Samuel to find the one he wanted. God had provided himself a king among Jesse's sons (1 Samuel 16.1).

Jeremiah's call began with the idea that God had been involved in his creation as an individual in his mother's womb. God had equipped him for the work of a prophet from his conception (Jeremiah 1.5). Jeremiah doubted his own ability, as he felt too young and inexperienced to be a prophet (Jeremiah 1.6). But the LORD promised to be with him to enable him to do his work (Jeremiah 1.8). The inborn qualities of Jeremiah would come to maturity through service in fellowship with the LORD.

These examples of the way in which God equips people for service will help us to understand the other calls to service which we find in the Old Testament. They cover a wide range of activities, involving all the leaders who, people thought, were serving the LORD in some special role: patriarchs (for example, Abraham: Genesis 12.1–3), judges (for example, Gideon: Judges 6.14), priests (Numbers 18.6), prophets (for example, Amos: Amos 7.15), craftsmen (2 Chronicles 2.13–14), musicians (1 Chronicles 15.22). In fact the writer of the books of Chronicles recognized God's call as underlying the work of 'every willing man who has skill for any kind of service' (1 Chronicles 28.21).

Death

The Israelites accepted death as part of normal human experience. They referred to the 'common death of all men' (Numbers 16.29). A psalmist asked, 'What man can live and never see death?' expecting the answer 'nobody' (Psalm 89.48). The death of an important person served to mark the date when something else happened. Notice the mention of death in the first verse of Joshua, Judges, 2 Samuel and 2 Kings. They knew that death could result from natural causes, such as drinking dirty water (2 Kings 2.19–22) or eating the wrong things (2 Kings 4.38–41). They believed that certain crimes should be punished by death (see especially the Book of the Covenant, Exodus 20.22—23.33). They thought that God sent disease and famine to punish evil-doing, and that those who died unnaturally were the evil-doers (Exodus 12.29; 2 Samuel 24.15). The book of Deuteronomy describes the way of life that is pleasing to God, and explains that disobedience leads to death (Deuteronomy 30.15–20). The Israelites also believed that God is able to deliver people from death (Psalms 68.20; 107.17–20), and that this provides them with a further opportunity to serve him (Psalms 9.13–14; 56.13).

Yet even righteous people die eventually. Throughout most of the Old Testament the only privileges allowed to the righteous are long life, many children and their memory preserved in Israel. The extraordinary ages to which the the Old Testament says the patriarchs lived were probably well beyond their true ages, but simply a way of honouring the great people of the past. The writers seem to say 'They were so righteous that God allowed them to have a very long life' (see Genesis 25.7; 35.8; 47.28).

In other parts of the Old Testament the writers use the phrase 'a good old age' (Judges 8.32; 1 Chronicles 29.28), and, 'full of days' (Job 42.17; 2 Chronicles 24.15) to express the same idea; that long life is a gift of God to the righteous. Prayers were offered that God would prolong the life of the king (Psalms 61.6; 72.5, 15). The unrighteous are 'cut off' (see Leviticus 20.3; 1 Kings 14.10; Ezekiel 14.8). The Israelites also regarded children as a reward for obedience (Deuteronomy 7.12–13; Psalms 37.37; 127.3), a blessing the unrighteous never received (Job 18.5, 19). The memory of the righteous would remain for a long time among the living (Psalm 112.6; Proverbs 10.7), while the people would soon forget the unrighteous (Deuteronomy 32.26; Psalm 34.16; Job 18.17).

These ideas are simply blessings which hide the cruelty of death. Most of the Old Testament lacks any suggestion that the righteous would have a continuing personal life after death. Some Psalmists say quite bluntly that death is the end of personal existence (Psalms 39.13; 146.4; compare Job 7.21). Some biblical writers describe death as the reverse of creation. God made the first human 'of dust from the ground' and breathed into him 'the breath of life' (Genesis 2.7). If God withdraws the breath of life from people, they die (Psalm 104.29; Job 12.10), and they return to the dust (Genesis 3.19; Job 34.14–15; Ecclesiastes 12.7). According to Ecclesiastes 12.7, 'the spirit returns to God who gave it'. The writer never intended readers to think of the spirit as having independent life and sharing a personal relationship with God in heaven. He meant that the power of life had been withdrawn. The departure of the spirit was part of the break up and disappearance of the human individual, as suggested by Job 34.14–15.

Two stories in the early tradition of Israel do however suggest that certain people escaped the destruction involved in death. One was Enoch, who 'walked with God; and he was not, for God took him' (Genesis 5.24; compare Hebrews 11.5–6). The other was Elijah, who 'went up by a whirlwind into heaven' (2 Kings 2.11). These stories express a growing desire among the Israelites to discover some future for the truly righteous. At this stage in the development of their ideas they were unable to accept that life was possible without the survival of the complete person: both body and soul. So they supposed that Enoch and Elijah had taken their physical bodies with them. Perhaps a similar idea lies beneath the tradition of the death of Moses, buried by God (Deuteronomy 34.6). But even if so, later story-tellers were very doubtful whether it was possible for a human to escape in this way, and they simply recorded that 'no man knows the place of his burial'.

These rare expressions of hope for life beyond death all refer to people who had served God and been faithful to him in all circumstances. This is a step forward in thoughts about this subject beyond that which existed in Egypt, where it was only the Pharaohs who were thought to have a right to life after death.

Sheol

The first evidence for belief in some form of survival after death is found in the use of the Hebrew word *Sheol*. Some English versions regularly translate it as *grave*, but a careful study of Old Testament use of the word shows that it meant something different from the place where a body is buried. The translators of the RSV treat it as a special technical word which totally lacks any exact English equivalent. They use the same word *Sheol*, transliterating from the Hebrew alphabet into the lettering we use.

The belief about Sheol was approximately as follows: Sheol is situated in the depths of the earth (Psalms 63.9; 88.6). All the dead are gathered there (Isaiah 14.9–10) from every nation (Ezekiel 32.18–32). The wicked go there after an early death (Psalms 9.17; 31.17) but the righteous men of Israel are there too (Genesis 37.35; 49.33). Sheol is a place of gloom and darkness (Job 10.21–22). Those who are there survive in weakness (Isaiah 14.10). 'There is no work or thought or knowledge or wisdom in Sheol' (Ecclesiastes 9.10) because without a body, activity is impossible. In his worst moments of suffering Job looked forward to Sheol as an escape from the sorrows and troubles of life. He believed he would have rest there (Job 3.13, 17). But in fact it is a place of hopelessness (Job 17.13–16; Isaiah 38.18). Those who live in Sheol are cut off from God (Psalm 88.10–12). They completely forget God (Psalm 6.5), and exist without praising him (Psalms 30.9; 115.17). Yet they are still under his rule, without escape (Psalm 139.8; Amos 9.2; Isaiah 7.11). 'Sheol is naked before God' (Job 26.6). The worst thing about Sheol is that the dead are unable to escape, and exist without any hope of return to the world of the living (2 Samuel 12.23; Job 14.12).

This picture of Sheol as the place of the dead is exactly what we should expect from the Israelites, when we remember that for them real life involved the whole person: body, soul and spirit. When people die, their bodies are left in the grave, and only their bones survive (Genesis 50.25; Exodus 13.19). The personality of each human must therefore either disappear altogether or else linger on without the body as a means of life, and without the spirit as a power for life.

Yet the Israelites' belief in Sheol expressed a growing hope that people could expect something better beyond this life than mere decomposition. The shadowy existence was preferable to total extinction. Some of the Psalmists expressed their desire for the possibility of an escape from Sheol. Scholars disagree about the sort of escape: some think that the Psalmists are only speaking of a prolonged earthly life, but others think that they hoped for a real life after they left this world. Whichever view we take, it is clear that they based their hope on their knowledge of God's love for them, and his care and protection. They believed that God's love would continue, and that his care and protection would save them from ending up in Sheol. The psalms which express this confidence in God are 16.10–11; 17.15; 37.27–28; 49.165; 73.4–6. There is a similar idea in Job 19.23–27, though in other parts of the same book we find the more traditional views of death and Sheol (but see footnote x in the RSV).

Resurrection

There is one final idea about the dead which writings that probably come from the latest period of Old Testament thought mention briefly. This is the idea of resurrection; the idea of restoration to full human life after a period of death. This idea may have sprung from the three stories in the books of Kings about people who were raised to the life of this world again (1 Kings 17.17–24; 2 Kings 4.17–37; 13.21). But writers seldom used the idea of resurrection, possibly because they recognized that human life in this world is for a limited time, and even for a person to be restored to full life would still involve a later death. They chiefly used the idea figuratively to speak about the Exile and the Return. Some of the prophets spoke of this as the death and resurrection of Israel (Hosea 6.1–3; Ezekiel 37: the valley of dry bones).

There are only two passages in the Old Testament which seem to accept the resurrection of dead people as part of God's plan for humankind. Both these passages come from apocalyptic writings which emphasize God's power to achieve things that are impossible to humans. Isaiah 26.19 describes a joyful resurrection for the righteous, although some scholars believe that even this verse refers to the return from the 'death' of exile (compare Hosea 6.1–3). Daniel 12.2 refers to resurrection for many, 'some to everlasting life, and some to shame'. The writer found it necessary to speak about a return to this world in order to explain that people could be restored to true life: body, soul and spirit. The writers of the Old Testament never tackled the problem that the human body is subject to decay and is unable to keep its physical nature to all eternity. When we come to the New Testament, the changed body of the risen Christ gives some clue to the truth. St Paul expressed the answer by speaking of a spiritual body, suitable for the new form of life in heaven (1 Corinthians 15.42–44). He adds, 'we shall all be changed, in a moment, in the twinkling of an eye, at the last trumpet' (1 Corinthians 15.51–52).

📖 Check Your Understanding 15

1 Which two of the following words come nearest in meaning to the word 'role' as we have used it in the phrase 'Role in Life', which is the heading of part of this section?

CAREER   CAST   CHARACTER   FUNCTION

LIVING   PART   POLICY

2 How were the people God called able to possess the skills needed to do the things God required them to do?
Which one of the following is correct?
  (a) God searched for people who possessed the natural talents that would enable them to do his will.
  (b) God implanted special skills within them at the time of their call to enable them to do his will.
  (c) God endowed people with gifts at the time of their conception, and inspired them to make full use of these gifts when he called them.

📖 Study Suggestions

FOR GROUP DISCUSSION

1 Make as full a list as you can of the characteristics which humans share with animals. Are people always more capable in all these things than animals? Do some animals possess greater powers than humankind in some aspects of life? Give examples to support your answers.

2 How far would it be true to describe Old Testament ideas about a person's *soul* and a person's *spirit* as two ways of referring to the same aspect of human nature? In what ways do these two terms differ in meaning from each other?

3 The name given to attempts to make contact with the spirits of the dead is 'spiritualism'.
  (a) What are the traditional attitudes of most people in your country to spiritualism?
  (b) In what way, if any, does this conflict with biblical teaching?
  (c) In what ways, if any, does the custom of some Churches of praying to the Virgin Mary, and to saints, differ from spiritualism?

FOR ESSAY WRITING

4 Any religion or philosophy which attempts to explain the meaning and significance of human life must also attempt to describe the nature of humans.

(a) Describe as fully as you can what any religious teachings known to you, other than Christian teaching, believe about the nature of humans.
(b) In what respects is this belief different from the ideas held by the Israelites? How far do you think such differences make it difficult for people of other religions to understand the teaching contained in the Bible?

5 Deuteronomy 6.5 gives one of the two commandments which Jesus said were the greatest in all the Old Testament (Mark 12.30). What is the significance of the three elements of human nature included in the Deuteronomic version of this law?

6 'Throughout most of the Old Testament the only privileges allowed to the righteous are long life, many children and their memory preserved in Israel' (page 88). How did the following people fare so far as these privileges are concerned: Abraham, Jacob and David? Give Bible references in evidence of your answers.

WORK WITH THE BIBLE AND A CONCORDANCE

7 Look up the word 'face' in a concordance and pick out the verses which refer to the face of God. Look closely at each reference and discover how the Israelites thought about God's face. None of us have seen the face of God, so what does this word mean when applied to God?

8 Look up the word 'mind' in a concordance. Study the verses in the book of Proverbs which it lists as containing this word. Try to create a definition of the word 'mind' as they use it. All these verses are using 'mind' to translate the Hebrew word which often stands for 'heart'. Do the verses in Proverbs illustrate what is said in this chapter about 'heart'?

9 Look up the verses in Ecclesiastes which say 'This also is a vanity'. Make a list of the things that the writer believed are worthless, and then try to discover why he was so pessimistic.

Human Failure

6

The fool says in his heart,
'There is no God.'
They are corrupt, they do abominable deeds,
there is none that does good.

(Psalm 14.1)

Obedience and Temptation

We have seen from our studies so far that the Old Testament provides
us with a basic understanding of the fact that God created the world.
He had a primary purpose of creating human sons and daughters
who would live in fellowship with him and with each other, and
have responsibility for the physical universe, its vegetation and animals. Genesis 3 provides us with a picture of the first humans disobeying God, and turning to evil ways. Some people believe that
Adam and Eve created trouble for everybody who descended from
them. They speak of Original Sin, meaning that they think we
inherit a tendency to disobey. According to this interpretation,
Adam and Eve were responsible for the failure of every human to fulfil God's purposes for us. But there is nothing in the writings of the
Old Testament to support this interpretation. Jesus never mentions
the idea. But Paul does present this view briefly in his letters
(Romans 5.12–14; 1 Corinthians 15.22). He was a Pharisee who had
given much attention to study of the Jewish scriptures and other
Jewish literature, so probably drew this idea from contemporary Jewish sources. We must look more closely at this subject, but for now let
us notice that Paul's main emphasis is on the difference between
Adam's influence on humanity, and that of Jesus Christ.

Good and Evil

In the writings of the Old Testament 'good' and 'evil' are related to
God's purposes. Whatever leads to the fulfilment of God's will is
good. This is the meaning of the word in Genesis 1.31. The whole of

creation is so planned that it makes possible the fulfilment of the LORD's purposes for humankind. The Old Testament writers describe many things as 'good'. For example, a good land (Exodus 3.8), good people (Proverbs 12.2), good words (Isaiah 39.8). Each of these things is good because it helps to achieve God's will for his people.

Anything which goes against the will of God and hinders his purposes is *evil*. Many of the writers of the Old Testament describe the evil things which people do (for example, Genesis 6.5; Isaiah 13.11). These things are evil because they are contrary to the will of God. But the word 'evil' is also frequently used in the Old Testament to describe something which God has done (2 Kings 21.12; Nehemiah 13.18a; Jeremiah 4.6). God never seeks to do humans any harm, because that would be against his purposes. The writers of such verses refer to the suffering that is involved in our punishment for disobedience. Its purpose is to correct sinful people. If we respond to his punishment by repenting, then the LORD 'repents' of this evil, and returns to his usual activity of blessing us (Exodus 32.14; Jeremiah 26.19). We must avoid thinking that God has acted unjustly or with cruelty. He never needs to repent of anything that is selfish or unkind (1 Samuel 15.29), of anything contrary to his own purposes for us. When writers say that God 'repents', they mean that he changes the way in which he is dealing with people, because a different approach will now enable him to achieve his purposes.

Freedom to Choose

God has given humans freedom to choose between good and evil. Each of us can either respond to God by obedience and service, or turn away from him and do things contrary to his will. Three Hebrew words express a response which can be obedient, but may be the reverse.

1 One of these words simply means *to choose* (Deuteronomy 30.19; Psalm 119.30; Isaiah 7.15).
2 Another word means *to consent*, and always describes response to a command or suggestion. The Old Testament almost always uses this word in the negative, to describe an act of rebellion against God's purposes (Deuteronomy 1.26; Psalm 81.11; Isaiah 30.15).
3 The third word means to do something *willingly* (Exodus 25.2; Judges 5.2; Psalm 110.3). This implies that the people concerned are glad to do something. Whatever the something is, they are happy with it and readily agree to do it.

We can see from these words that the Israelites believed that people have a choice in what they do. Humans are free to behave as they wish without any forces or powers outside themselves compelling them to choose what they should do. God refuses to compel us to be obedient, even though his commandments are wise and good, and bring blessing. The reason for God giving us such freedom is that he wants us to be responsible people, and he rejects any idea that we should be machines designed to always obey his commands.

The Israelites became aware of their freedom to choose because they recognized the existence of evil. Even their great national heroes, such as David (2 Samuel 12.7–9; Psalm 51), were sinners. At times they disobeyed God, and they were rebuked and punished for it. Lesser people were undoubtedly sinners too. The editor of 1 Kings describes Solomon as praying about a time in the future when God's people might be taken into Exile, and explains 'there is no man who does not sin' (1 Kings 8.46). Psalmists ask God to abandon the judgement of people, for 'who could stand?' (Psalms 130.3; 143.2). They thought nobody could avoid condemnation. The wisdom writers said much the same sort of thing (Proverbs 20.9; Ecclesiastes 7.20). These writers all believed that sin is universal, and that all humans have failed to live a life of perfect obedience to the LORD.

Notice the problem here: if God created human beings, how can we explain why they have all turned against him? We can more easily believe that since people are given a free choice to obey or rebel, some have chosen to rebel. But we find difficult in understanding why all humans share together in sin. What drives us on to choose evil instead of serving the LORD? Is there some fault in human nature that makes us all behave in this way? Does Genesis 3 really teach that the first man, Adam, fell into sin, and passed on his fallen nature to all his children? We can be sure that the story deeply influenced the thinking of the Israelites. It comes from the earliest of the written records in Israel, and was probably amongst the earliest traditions. Yet even so, the later writers of the Old Testament never used the story to explain the universality of sin. Scholars are unable to be sure whether any of them intended even to mention Adam's name, except in 1 Chronicles 1.1. This is because his name is one of the ordinary Hebrew words for 'a man' (see Job 31.33 and the RSV footnote). Why were they so silent about this matter?

Another difficulty exists in this interpretation of the story of Adam and Eve. The story describes the experience of temptation, but it fails to describe the tempter, except as 'the serpent'. Most Christians take this to be a name for Satan, but the Old Testament writers totally ignore the idea that the serpent was Satan. This idea was first introduced in one of the books of the Apocrypha: 'through the devil's envy death entered the world, and those who belong to his party experience it' (Wisdom 2.24). In fact the Genesis story describes the serpent in the Garden of Eden as directly opposed to God, and wanting to encourage evil. Yet the rest of the Old Testament describes Satan as an angel whose work was simply to test the sincerity of those who served God. The two ideas remained unlinked until people had begun to think of Satan as having completely rejected the rule of God, and this idea only arose after the completion of all the Old Testament books.

The Problem of Evil

But even if we suppose that the purpose of Genesis 3 was to describe the work of Satan, despite the fact that the writers of the Old Testament failed to relate the two ideas, there are still problems. If Satan is a fallen angel, as the New Testament suggests, we shall want to know what caused him to fall. We may perhaps place the blame for the origin of evil on this spiritual being instead of on Adam. But we still lack an answer to the question: why did a creature made by God rebel? The Bible writers never explain Satan's choice of evil. Perhaps Satan delighted in the sense of power that his work gave him, and that he used it more and more for his own benefit (Job 1.12; 2.6). Sadly we know that those who are given power experience temptation to do that (Deuteronomy 8.17–18; Ezekiel 22.6–12; Micah 2.1).

Yet we are all aware of temptation in our daily lives, once we have accepted Jesus as our Saviour and Lord. Before that happens, we prefer to exercise our free will, choosing for ourselves our way of life. We are only troubled by a sense of shame when things go wrong and we cause trouble for ourselves and for others. But when we accept Christ, we commit ourselves to his service knowing he is wise and caring. Then comes temptation to return to our earlier independence. We find promptings within ourselves to do something which we feel we should hide from God. According to the story, Adam and Eve experienced the same. Their story sets down many ways in which we find we meet the temptation to choose for ourselves what we should do. The story of Adam and Eve points a warning finger at many of the ways in which we experience temptation:

1 The suggestion that we do not know exactly what God wants us to do: 'Did God say . . .?' (Genesis 3.1).
2 The suggestion that God's commandments are unfair and misleading: 'You will not die. For God knows that when you eat of it your eyes will be opened' (Genesis 3.4–5a).
3 The suggestion that we can gain something by disobeying God: 'you will be like God, knowing good and evil' (Genesis 3.5b). They knew good already, so the only new knowledge they could gain was how it felt to be guilty.
4 The encouragement to sin which comes simply from thinking about a disobedient act: 'when the woman saw that the tree was good for food, and that it was a delight to the eyes, and that the tree was to be desired to make one wise . . .' (Genesis 3.6a).
5 The encouragement to sin which comes because somebody else is willing to share our disobedience: 'she also gave some to her husband, and he ate' (Genesis 3.6b).

In a later part of the story God challenged first Adam and then Eve to explain their disobedience. Each in turn looked for somebody else to blame. They felt somebody else had persuaded them to do evil. God recognized the power of persuasion, but he also recognized that each of them was free to refuse temptation. Each could have been obedient, and each deserved punishment for choosing to disobey.

The one new thing that came into the lives of both Adam and Eve because of their sin was their separation from God. God drove them out of the garden, and away from their intimate fellowship with him that the earlier part of the story describes. What they lost was *knowledge of God*, and the grace to do his will that comes from fellowship with him. If there is some inherited form of corruption which encourages people to disobey, it must lie in this separation from God, which makes obedience impossible. The whole Bible is the story of God's work to bring people back into fellowship with himself, and so to establish a community of righteousness.

📖 Check Your Understanding 16

1 Which three of the following words *always* describe situations in which we face the temptation to do something wrong?

APPEAL   COAXING   ENTICEMENT

INVITATION   LURES   SEDUCTION

2 'The LORD repents of evil' (page 95). Which of the following alternatives best expresses the meaning of 'repents' in that sentence?
  - (a) admits wrong-doing
  - (b) asks pardon
  - (c) turns to a different way
  - (d) regrets previous action

Sin and Its Results

When we come to study this subject we face the same problem about translation as we thought about at the beginning of our study of Human Nature (pages 79–80). Only with a knowledge of Hebrew can we be sure that we are distinguishing accurately between different terms that we face as we study. But if we have at least a knowledge of the Hebrew and Greek alphabets, we can use an analytical concordance to help solve this problem, because it indicates under each English word the different Hebrew and Greek words that are in the original text. The translators of the RSV have tried to be consistent in the way they translate a particular word, provided that they believe those who used it meant the same thing. Sometimes the word has more than one distinct meaning and the translators then use different English words to make the necessary distinctions clear in their translations. In this book I have tried as far as possible to select verses which actually contain the specific words we are studying. If you are using a different translation, you may find that the people who prepared that translation chose a different word, and you will need to guess which word in the verse illustrates the Hebrew word we are trying to study. Let me give you an example to make this clear. Suppose we are studying a word which occurs in Micah 6.8, and in other places. The RSV translates the word as *love kindness*, but in the the New International Version of the Bible you would find *love mercy*, and in the Good News Bible you would find *show constant love*. The Hebrew word used has a special meaning which is without an exact equivalent in English, but we can properly translate it in any of these ways. The word refers to God's continuing love and concern for people even when they have been disobedient and deserve severe punishment. The word assures readers that the LORD never gives up trying to draw us back into a loving relationship. The prophet Hosea uses this Hebrew word in Hosea 2.19, where the RSV translates it as *steadfast love*, and he adds that the LORD requires the same attitude from humans, and between them (Hosea 6.6).

Sin

The RSV uses two English words to describe things done against the will of God.

1 The first of these is *sin*, which stands for a Hebrew word which has a very general meaning. The word can mean things done intentionally (Isaiah 3.9; 30.1), as well as things done without any intention to disobey (Leviticus 4.13; Genesis 20.3–7). It may refer to something done against another human (1 Samuel 20.1), and it may also refer to something done against God himself (Exodus 32.33). The original meaning of the word *to sin* was *to miss the mark*, or *to miss the road*. For example, the word was used about an archer who failed to hit a target, or a traveller who lost the way. So now, when the word is used theologically, *sin* carries the meaning of *failure*: something we have neglected that we should have done, or something that humans have done that they should have avoided. A sinner is a person who has failed to do God's will, and has failed to live on good terms with his or her neighbour.

2 The second word is *transgression*. The RSV uses this word many times to translate a Hebrew word which always means an intentional act against the will of God. A *transgressor* is a person who chooses to disobey God, and who goes his or her own way without accepting the authority of God. Sometimes the word scholars normally translate as *transgression* is translated as *rebellion* (for

example, 1 Kings 12.19). This was probably the original meaning of the Hebrew word. This translation is used in Job 34.37, where Elihu describes Job by saying 'he adds rebellion to his sin'. He was suggesting that Job had failed to live as God wanted him to, and had done it deliberately.

We now need to look at two words relating to human sinfulness:

1 *Iniquity* describes the attitude of mind which leads a human towards acts of sin or rebellion (Job 3 1.24–28; Psalm 36.1–4). This fact helps us to understand Exodus 20.5 and similar verses: 'For I the LORD your God am a jealous God, visiting the iniquity of the fathers upon the children to the third and fourth generation of those who hate me.' The attitude of every person influences other members of their family, and can possibly affect people of the third or fourth generations because they can all be alive during the life of the original person, influenced by him and continuing to influence each other. The father's iniquity is likely to be shared by his family, to his great grandchildren, and all of them may be guilty before God.

2 *The wicked* is a frequent description of people who are rebellious against God, and who refuse to do the LORD's will (Job 8.22; Psalm 10.3; Isaiah 3.11). Old Testament writers often set such people in contrast with *the righteous*, who do the will of the LORD (Genesis 18.23; Proverbs 4.18; Ezekiel 18.5). Job complains that both come to the same end in death (Job 9.22; compare Ecclesiastes 9.2). The prophet Ezekiel recognized that a human might change from being wicked and begin to live righteously (Ezekiel 33.14–16), and that the righteous also could change, turning aside from God, and become wicked (Ezekiel 33.13).

Guilt

A wicked person lives in a state of *guilt*, and is liable to be punished for the evil he or she does. The prophets were deeply aware of the guilt of God's people, and continually warned them of punishment to come (Isaiah 14.20b–21; Jeremiah 30.14–15; Hosea 12.7–8). They believed that the leaders of the nations were particularly guilty (Jeremiah 23.1–4). Among these were the kings (Hosea 5.1), prophets (Jeremiah 28.15–16), priests (Isaiah 28.7), and the richer and more powerful people generally (Amos 6.1). But the prophets believed that the ordinary people had failed to escape being guilty themselves (Hosea 4.12). Some of the Israelites supposed that they had escaped punishment, but the prophets warned them to avoid speaking too soon (Jeremiah 5.12–15; compare Psalm 94.7). Hosea especially noticed their attitude, and warned the people that God was storing up judgement against them (Hosea 7.2; 13.12).

The writers of the Old Testament never used a Hebrew word that could be translated *conscience*, but they were well aware of the feeling of guilt that that English word expresses. In the story of Adam and Eve we read that they hid themselves when God approached. Adam explained, 'I heard the sound of thee in the garden, and I was afraid, because I was naked; and I hid myself' (Genesis 3.10). When David had done wrong he felt guilty (1 Samuel 24.5; 2 Samuel 24.10). Isaiah felt distressed because he was 'a man of unclean lips' (Isaiah 6.5). The compilers of Deuteronomy described the uneasy conscience that follows disobedience (Deuteronomy 28.66–67). A Psalmist describes his own feelings of guilt before he repented (Psalm 32.3–4). All of these are accurate descriptions of an uneasy conscience. Sinners know they are guilty in the presence of God.

God's Wrath

God's response to all evil is *wrath*. Genesis 6.5–7 well describes God's wrath towards humans: 'The LORD saw the wickedness of man . . . And the LORD was sorry that he had made man on the earth, and it grieved him to his heart.'

The prophets spoke often of the wrath of God (for example, Hosea 5.10; 13.11; Isaiah 9.19; 10.6; Jeremiah 7.29; 10.10; Ezekiel 21.31; 22.31; Zephaniah 1.18). Some of the Psalmists rejoiced that God's wrath would fall on evil-doers (Psalms 2.5; 21.9; 59.13). Others recognized that God's people deserved his wrath (Psalm 106.40–41). Some pleaded with God that he should turn away from showing wrath towards them (Psalms 88.13–18; 89.46–48).

Many passages in the Old Testament describe how God restrains his wrath and holds back the punishment that sinners deserve. The earliest traditions in the Torah, the J-traditions, include two promises which God made. The first, included in the story of the flood, was that the LORD would never again destroy in the same way (Genesis 8.21–22). The second, given to Abraham, was that if there were ten righteous people in Sodom the LORD would refrain from destroying the city (Genesis 18.32). Moses pleaded with God not to destroy the Israelites after they had made the golden calf and worshipped it at Mount Sinai, and the LORD restrained his wrath (Exodus 32.11–14). Amos was a prophet of judgement, yet we read that he also pleaded with God for Israel, and that God turned aside from carrying out his wrath (Amos 7.1–6). Ezekiel's words explain the significance of God's restraint: 'As I live, says the LORD God, I have no pleasure in the death of the wicked, but that the wicked turn from his way and live' (Ezekiel 33.11) Notice also Lamentations 3.33, where we read 'he does not willingly afflict or grieve the sons of men'.

Judgement

We should never imagine that God's wrath is a blind fury, or an uncontrolled anger. He is roused to wrath by sin (Deuteronomy 7.4; Isaiah 5.24–25). His wrath leads to judgement and punishment as a reasonable consequence of sin. From the earliest times people recognized God as 'the Judge of all the earth' (Genesis 18.25), but in the Torah judgement was a responsibility God gave to humans (Deuteronomy 1.9–18). Those responsible had rules about fair treatment of the accused. They were never to be unjust, or partial in their judgements (Leviticus 19.15). They were to follow God's ordinances (Numbers 35.24).

The prophets recognized that the judges of their time were failing to give fair judgements, and were helping the rich and neglecting the poor (Amos 5.7, 12). The prophets believed that they themselves were sent to declare God's righteous judgements (Hosea 6.5–6; Micah 3.8), but it is the Lord who truly judges his people (Isaiah 3.14–15; Jeremiah 1.16; Ezekiel 5.5–8).

Judgement and the Day of the LORD

The Old Testament often refers to God's judgement as a future event, which would take place on the *Day of the LORD*. But often that Day was quite distinct from any idea about the final end of all history. Many writers suggested that the Day was a moment due to happen in the course of their own history, at a time that for us is long ago. For example, scholars suggest that the Day which Amos predicted (Amos 5.18–20) actually came when the Assyrians conquered the Northern Kingdom of Israel. Certainly at that time the Northern Kingdom was destroyed for ever, leaving only the kingdom of Judah as God's people Israel. The Day for Isaiah was the time when Judah would be punished for all her sins (Isaiah 2.12–19). That Day was postponed by God's purpose when the Assyrians failed to capture Jerusalem, but came when the Babylonians took her people into exile.

But these Days failed to bring a time of justice and peace on earth, because people continued to live as transgressors, disobedient to God. So other writers taught the Israelites to believe in another, greater Day that was yet to come, when all evil-doers would be punished and righteousness would triumph. This idea is expressed most fully in the apocalyptic writings of the Old Testament (see Isaiah 24—27, and Daniel).

Punishment

An important part of the teaching of the Old Testament about punishment is that, in a world ruled by God, sin brings its own results, which are trouble and conflict. Solomon prayed at the dedication of the Temple that God would condemn 'the guilty by bringing his conduct upon his own head' (1 Kings 8.32). The same idea occurs in the Psalms (Psalms 9.13–18; 10.2; 141.10), and among the proverbs (Proverbs 5.22). The writers believed that God had made the world in such a way that creation itself would help to fulfil his purposes. Evil often derives from wrong-doing, without any action from the Creator. Evil deeds can only cause trouble in such a world, and especially trouble for the people responsible and those around them.

Several writers asked why the wicked prospered (Psalm 73.3; Jeremiah 12.1). The answer they gave was that the wicked only seemed to be secure (Job 12.5–10). They would be 'requited', paid back, for what they had done (Judges 1.7; Proverbs 11.31; Psalm 28.3–5; Jeremiah 51.24), 'what his hands have done shall be done to him' (Isaiah 3.11). This is an example of what the Romans called *lex talionis*, that is, the belief that fair judgement involves a punishment equal to the crime. The earliest law code after the Ten Commandments includes the most famous statement of this rule: 'life for life; eye for eye, tooth for tooth . . .' (Exodus 21.23–25). The prophets believed that God's own judgements were based on this rule (Hosea 4.6; Isaiah 33.1; Jeremiah 30.16). Some people find intolerable the idea that the punishment should fit the crime in its measure of violence. But probably the *lex talionis* was first used in a time when court procedures were unable to exercise firm control in providing proper ways for dealing with evil. The rule limited the degree of revenge that could be tolerated and removed the danger of a continuing feud, with each side taking increasing retaliation against the most recent trouble caused by the other side. So the rule set down limits which would settle a dispute permanently.

Because the people of Old Testament times lacked any clear idea of life after death, they believed that punishment of the wicked must take place in this life. In one place the writer suggests that death is an escape for the wicked from the punishment due to them in this life (Job 11.20). The writers of Job picture his friends as thinking that the disasters that fell on him were an example of the sort of thing that happened to the wicked: their possessions carried away (Job 20.28–29), their children destroyed (Job 27.13–14), their health ruined (Job 15.20). But the writer described such popular beliefs in order to deny them. These same things happened to Job, even though 'there is none like him on earth, a blameless and upright man, who fears God and turns away from evil' (Job 1.8).

Many writers in the Old Testament describe the punishment of the wicked as the direct opposite of the blessings of the righteous, which were thought to be long life, many children, and their memory preserved in Israel. 'The LORD does not keep the wicked alive' (Job 36.6; Proverbs 10.27), they go down to Sheol (Psalms 9.17;

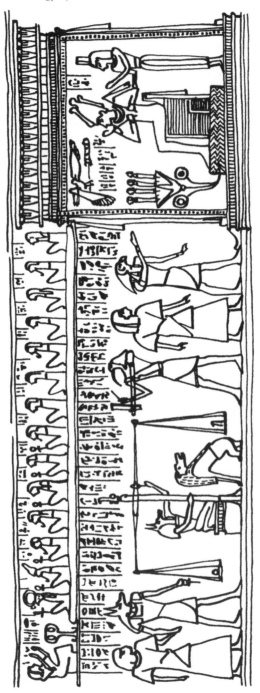

Figure 7. 'Because the people of Old Testament times had no clear idea of life after death, they believed that punishment of the wicked must take place in this life' (p. 104). The Egyptians, however, believed that the Pharaohs, and perhaps other royal leaders, could enter a new life after death. This papyrus shows the god Anubis weighing the soul of Hu-nefer to discover if he is worthy of life, and then introducing him to the god Osiris. To enter the underworld, it was believed, the king had to be innocent of evil and reverent towards the gods.

31.17), they will fail to have any children (Job 18.19, compare Psalm 37.28, 38), their memory will perish, so that nobody will know their name (Job 18.17; Psalm 9.5; Proverbs 10.7).

The writers seem to have felt strongly that God is unable to tolerate the wicked. Such people have failed to reach the quality of life God planned for them and are a hindrance to his purposes, so they must be removed (Psalm 37.10, 36; Proverbs 10.25). They vanish (Psalm 37.20), destroyed by God (Genesis 18.23; Psalm 9.5). They are cut off (1 Samuel 2.9; Psalm 37.28, 38) and are no more (Proverbs 10.24–25, Psalm 37.10, 36). One way or another they perish (Psalm 68.2). But we need to remember that all these words could describe physical death, since the Israelites believed that death brought the break-up of human nature. Only in Daniel 12.2 is any mention made in the Old Testament of judgement and punishment after death, and even then only at a time when the dead would again live in the physical world.

📖 **Check Your Understanding 17**

1 (a) Use a dictionary to discover the various meanings of the two words 'present' and 'attend'. Then write one sentence for each of these words so that by comparing them you can see that they mean exactly the same thing. Follow this by writing one sentence for each in which the other word does not fit, thus showing that they do differ in some of their meanings.

(b) Give examples of a similar kind to show that in your own language two words can sometimes have the same meaning, and at other times they have quite different meanings.

2 Which two of the following words describe forms of 'iniquity'? (See page 100 for a definition of iniquity)

BRIBERY   MURDER   REBELLIOUSNESS
THEFT   UNKINDNESS   VIOLENCE

📖 **Study Suggestions**

FOR GROUP DISCUSSION

1 How would you answer a person who says, 'We are taught as Christians to be patient and forgiving, yet we often read in the Bible about the wrath of God. Why is it right for God and wrong for us to be filled with wrath?'

2 In what ways does belief in Satan help us to understand the nature of temptation, and in what ways does it hinder our understanding of temptation and of the reasons why we fall into sin?

3 Think about the following statement: 'The writers of the Old Testament preach judgement, but the writers of the New Testament preach salvation.' Is this a fair assessment of the two parts of the Bible? Explain your reasons for thinking as you do.

FOR ESSAY WRITING

4 (a) Why does God give people the freedom to choose how they will respond to him?
   (b) What difference would it make if people could only do good?
5 What explanation, if any, does Genesis 3 provide for the universality of sin? If you reject the idea that Adam led us all into sin, what do you think is the purpose of the story?
6 (a) What difference is there between 'a sin' and 'a transgression', as the RSV uses these words to translate Hebrew words?
   (b) Express the thought of Isaiah 59.12 in your own words, so as to show the difference between the three words that this verse uses about human evil.

WORK WITH THE BIBLE AND A CONCORDANCE

7 (a) Discover what the apocalyptical passages of Isaiah (chapters 24—27) say about 'the Day of the LORD' and make notes about your findings.
   (b) How do these ideas differ from what other parts of the Old Testament say about that Day?
8 The Old Testament often uses the word 'hell' to translate the Greek word 'Gehenna' (see RSV footnotes). This name comes from the Hebrew for 'Valley of Hinnom'.
   (a) Find out and make notes on what the Old Testament says about the Valley of Hinnom.
   (b) Why do we never find the idea of Hell in English translations of the Old Testament? (for example, in the RSV).
   (c) What connection, if any, is there between the Valley of Hinnom and the New Testament ideas about Hell?
9 The word 'requite' appears more than 40 times in the Old Testament. Use a dictionary to find out the meaning of the word, and then study the use of the word in the Old Testament. In the light of your studies, how would you explain the meaning of Proverbs 11.31: 'If the righteous is requited on earth, how much more the wicked and the sinner'?

Salvation

7

Say to them, As I live, says the LORD God,
I have no pleasure in the death of the wicked,
but that the wicked turn from his way and live;
turn back, turn back from your evil ways;
for why will you die, O house of Israel?

(Ezekiel 33.11)

God's Attitude to Sinners

The Need for a Fresh Start

Let us begin by looking at Genesis 6.5–6, which is the introduction to the story of Noah's flood. The editor who included this dismal statement was passing on a story that had probably existed among the Israelites for a long time before he used it in helping to prepare Genesis. He wanted his readers to know that from an early time the people of Israel had begun to puzzle over the existence of evil in the thoughts and actions of humankind. God had created the world and filled it with good things, and had given people the opportunity of enjoying the world God had created by serving him. Yet they had chosen evil instead of good. They had acted against God's purposes and had spoilt the world that he had made. What would God do about their disobedience? Why should he allow his creatures freedom to interfere with the fulfilment of his purposes?

The story of the flood suggests one answer that God might give to the problem. Genesis 6.7 describes God as saying, 'I will blot out man whom I have created from the face of the ground . . . I am sorry that I have made them'. The story goes on to tell how God destroyed all the wicked by drowning, and only Noah and his family survived. A later editor of the story explained that 'Noah was a righteous man, blameless in his generation' (Genesis 6.9).

The story-tellers suggest that God intended to make a fresh start this way, with only the righteous to share his world. But before they came to the end of the account of the flood, they made it quite clear that God would never use this method of dealing with the problem. We can read that God said, 'I will never again curse the ground because of man, for the imagination of man's heart is evil from his youth' (Genesis 8.21). The account of the flood goes on to give details of the indecent behaviour of Noah and Ham, showing that even then those who were supposed to be righteous failed to live as God intended them to do (Genesis 9.21–22).

All humans had richly deserved punishment and even death, because they had shared in spoiling the world God created and in rejecting the way of life he had offered them. Yet God chose to save them from the consequences of their sinfulness. Nothing in their character or behaviour could prompt him to turn aside from punishing them: 'man's heart is evil from his youth' (Genesis 8.21). He could justly destroy them, but he knew that in doing so his own plans and purposes would be thwarted. God's saving attitude to sinners exists without being prompted by any rights or privileges of humans; it derives from his own character and intentions, which are always merciful and rich with blessing.

The Israelites failed at first to understand the ways of God, and to know why he acted as he did. They only gradually came to understand more as they experienced his activities among them. When editors commented on the story of the flood, they failed to understand why God acted as he did. They simply knew that God had never in their time attempted to destroy the whole of humankind. They saw clearly that God continued to care for sinful people, and to work for their good, and only gradually did the full truth dawn on their minds.

God's Love for His People

Instead of destroying humankind, God chose one man through whom he would make himself and his purposes known. This man was Abraham. The relationship of Abraham and his descendants with God would show all peoples what God is like. This was the blessing they would find (Genesis 12.3).

Later writers discussed God's motives in choosing the Israelites. God's people were few in number, compared with the Egyptians and the Assyrians (Deuteronomy 7.7). The Israelites failed to live righteously, which might have made them different from other nations. Yet God punished other nations for their wickedness (Deuteronomy 9.4–5). The real reason why God chose Israel was because he had loved their ancestors, and had chosen them and their descendants (Deuteronomy 4.37). He loved his people still, and they had a responsibility to love him and to keep his commandments (Deuteronomy 7.8–9).

But what sort of love did God have for the people of Israel? The Hebrew word used for 'love' in these verses was *aheb*. This was an ordinary word used for the feelings of one person for another: a friend for a friend, a man for his wife, parents for their children. Such love is often attracted by the qualities and activities of the person loved, but God's motives are far removed from personal gain. Hosea discovered that his love for his wife was more than a response to her beauty, purity, or faithfulness. His love remained firm even when she did everything she could that would make her repulsive to him. Through Hosea's own experience of love he was able to understand and describe something of God's feelings for Israel. God's love for Israel remained firm despite their disobedience, and corruption. The motive of God's loving activity in Israel is sometimes said to be for his 'own sake' (Isaiah 48.11), or for the sake of 'his name' (Ezekiel 20.9). In English a person's reputation is often called their name: 'He has a name for honesty.' These verses seem to imply that God was anxious to defend himself against the contempt of other nations for choosing a worthless people. But really God's intention was to show that even with a despised people he could work effectively, bringing them to a time of peace and righteousness (Psalm 106.7–12). Other nations could learn from their knowledge of Israel that God's love is part of his essential nature, and that he is true to his character in continuing to show his love for people even when they sin.

God's love for humankind always involves a desire to enter into a creative relationship with people. The various covenants which we shall study in the next section of this chapter all resulted from God's desire to establish fellowship with humans. Often people failed to fulfil the hopes expressed in the covenants, and continued in disobedience and sin. But God himself never broke the covenants. He never withdrew from the relationships involved, so that whenever the people who had shared in the covenant returned to seek God's blessing, they always found him ready and waiting to renew his relationship with them.

God's Faithfulness

There is a special Hebrew word that describes the faithfulness of God to his purposes of love towards people. A difficulty exists in trying to put down the appropriate English letters in the place of the Hebrew letters in which they were originally written. The nearest we can get is to write *hesed*, but you need to know that the 'h' written here stands for a single sound like each breath of somebody panting. This sound is technically known as a voiced breath. Translators have always had difficulty in finding a suitable English equivalent to express the meaning of this word. The RSV translators have chosen *steadfast love*, and this does seem to express the motive of God which led to the creation of the various covenants, and made their continuance possible even after people had failed to fulfil their part.

Hebrew poetry often expresses the same ideas twice over, using different words. Take, for example, 'Thou wilt show faithfulness to Jacob and steadfast love to Abraham' (Micah 7.20). This use of parallelism helps us to understand the meaning of Hebrew words which might otherwise be difficult to translate. In this example *steadfast love* is similar in meaning to *faithfulness*. There are other examples of these two words being used in parallel, for example, Psalm 88.11. But the Old Testament writers use other words similar in meaning to *steadfast love*. Notice especially *righteousness* in Hosea 10.12. This means that if God's people are rightous, they will help to build a healthy society, and God's purposes of steadfast love for them will be fulfilled. Notice also that *compassion* is part of God's steadfast love according to Lamentations 3.32.

Some Old Testament writers group steadfast love with other words which describe the character of God and show us what we can expect from him. He is 'gracious and merciful, slow to anger and abounding in steadfast love' (Joel 2.13; compare Exodus 34.6). He is merciful (Isaiah 63.7) and willing to forgive (Numbers 14.19). His love is everlasting (Isaiah 54.8; Psalm 100.5). All these words taken together provide us with a very accurate idea of the nature of God's *steadfast love*.

God rejects the idea that he should restrict his steadfast love to his people Israel. As early as the time of Amos, prophets recognized that God had shown his care to other nations (Amos 9.7). The Psalmists were confident that all peoples could depend on his goodness (Psalms 36.7; 145.9). The writers of the books of Jonah and Ruth deliberately set out to describe God's care for people of other races and nations (Jonah 4.10–11; Ruth 4.11–14).

All this evidence shows that God was revealing his steadfast love for humankind throughout Israel's history. He revealed himself because of his love, and it was his love that he revealed.

📖 Check Your Understanding 18

1 'And the LORD was sorry that he had made man on the earth, and it grieved him to his heart' (Genesis 6.6). Which two of the following words best describe the feelings implied by the story in this statement?

> ANGER   ANXIETY   DISAPPOINTMENT
> FRUSTRATION   IRRITATION   RESENTMENT   PAIN

2 (a) Which three of the following words could you use instead of love in the expression 'steadfast love'?

> AFFECTION   ADMIRATION   APPETITE
> DEVOTION   NEED   SYMPATHY

> (b) The three words you have chosen have slightly different meanings. Explain how each expresses something about God's attitude to humans.
>
> (c) Explain why each of the remaining words would be inappropriate.

God's Way of Helping Sinners

We have seen that the motive of all God's activities among humankind is love. In the beginning he created people to share a loving relationship with one another and with him. At the centre of all evil is lovelessness. Pride, greed, selfishness, and all forms of iniquity are denials of the way of love, and therefore are contrary to the will and purpose of God. Evil has spoilt people's lives, so that they have ceased to give or receive love from one another. We have failed to be compassionate and caring as God intended us to be as a basis for our human relationships. People are out of harmony with God and at cross-purposes with each other.

But God continues to regard human beings with love. This love has the special qualities belonging to steadfastness. His love reaches humans without being motivated by any attractiveness in people, and simply springs from God's essential nature. God's purpose is to enable humans to reform their lives and to live the life of love which was his intention in creation. But he safeguards the free will of people, never compelling us to change. God's purpose is to work with humans to create loving human societies, in which everybody gladly seeks understanding and co-operation and produces harmony with one another in the presence of God. This re-creation is what we call 'salvation'. Many people think of salvation as solely a matter for individuals, but in fact its outworking should affect the whole of society.

The Covenants

But how is this to be done? God chose to work for salvation by making covenants with people and with Israel. A covenant is an agreement by which personal relationships are established. In human society marriage is a good example of a covenant. The relationship is based on love, but we express our love through the marriage vows, and fulfil it in married life. Love is the basis of God's covenants. The Bible expresses them in the terms of an agreement, and says they are fulfilled in a creative relationship between God and humans, and between people. We can see the importance of these covenants by the fact that the two parts of the Bible are known as the Old Testament and the New Testament. 'Testament' is simply another word for covenant. The Bible is all about God's covenants with humankind.

When we study the Old Testament, we discover that God made a whole series of covenants, instead of one. He made covenants with Noah, Abraham, the Israelites at Sinai and with David. And the people themselves completed covenants with each other in the presence of God at Shechem, and after the Exile in the time of Nehemiah. Jeremiah looked forward to a new covenant, which Christ established at the Lord's Supper.

Why did God make so many covenants? We would be wrong to think this was directly the result of people refusing the relationship which God was offering them, with the earlier covenants cancelled because of their rejection of God's loving purposes. God can and does continue to offer that relationship as long as his love endures, that is, for ever. We should also avoid thinking that God was experimenting with different sorts of covenant, hoping to find one which people would welcome. That idea would suggest that God failed to fully understand from the beginning what was necessary for the salvation of humankind.

The real reason for so many covenants was that at each stage in the life of Israel God offered a relationship which people were capable of understanding, and accepting *at that time*. Each covenant expressed something more of God's purposes. Each one challenged the people to a deeper response and a fuller relationship with him and with each other.

Sometimes those who introduced God's covenants to Israel could see further ahead, and could understand God's ways at a deeper level than others were able to do. Moses, for example, seems to have expected that the people would respond more readily to the experiences at Sinai than they actually did. Moses seems to have hoped that the Israelites would share his own experience of a direct relationship with God; but they refused and insisted that Moses should act as an intermediary between them and God (Exodus 19.19). They preferred that he should pass on God's Law to them, rather than that they should experience God's leadership in personal ways. God accepted the limitation placed on his relationship with his people, and provided the Ten Commandments. The priestly editors who produced the existing version in Exodus 19 had their own reasons for preferring Law to a loving relationship.

Let us now look at each of the covenants in turn and the revelation of God that each contained:

The covenant of Noah (Genesis 9.8–17)

Scholars have provided some evidence that the story of the flood was worked over and developed over a long period of time, and that these particular verses were probably produced by editors during or after the Exile. But the ideas the story contains are in harmony with the promises of God given in other parts of the whole story, especially in Genesis 8.20–22, which many think had its origin quite early in the development of the Torah. The covenant of Noah is between the Creator and his creatures. Life itself is dependent on God maintaining the world that he created. By this covenant God promised that he would never again loose the floods to destroy all living creatures. The rainbow was to be the sign of God's protective care. This covenant lacks any instructions about the way God's creatures should behave. But the idea contained in Genesis 8.20–22 seems to indicate that Noah believed that he should please God by making burnt offerings to him.

The covenant of Abraham (Genesis 15.7–21 and 17.1–27)
This covenant was to establish the special role for which God chose the Israelites from among the nations. The covenant of Noah still remained valid, but this new covenant prepared the way for even greater blessing for all humankind. It provided the basis for God's relationship with the family of Abraham, and promised blessings for all peoples in time to come. God would give the Israelites a land for their own use. He did expect obedience, but it was on a personal basis, without any law code. It was to involve each individual's response to God's will as he would make this known to Abraham and his descendants, through their relationship with him. Circumcision was to be a sign to show who were the heirs of this covenant. Perhaps this custom was meant to be a sign of the parents' submission and obedience to God.

This covenant was inherited by the descendants of Abraham, who were often reminded that they were included within the covenant God made with Abraham. God revealed his presence and purposes to Isaac (Genesis 26.3–5, 24). Similarly, he appeared to Jacob when he fled from home, having deceived his father and robbed his older brother of his inheritance (Genesis 28.13–14; 31.42; 35.10–12). By the time of Moses, God made himself known as the one who had made a covenant with Abraham, Isaac and Jacob (Exodus 3.6, 15–16; 6.6–8; 33.1). Both the Old and the New Testaments use this threefold mention of Abraham, Isaac and Jacob to indicate God's choice of Israel to be his people and to learn to serve him.

The covenant with Israel at Sinai (Exodus 19.2–8 and 24.3–8)
If you compare these two passages, you will see that there are two accounts of God making a covenant with the people of Israel. The first is concerned with a time before the Law was given, and the second after the giving of the Ten Commandments and the Book of the Covenant. Scholars give various reasons for the repetition of the story of God's people committing themselves to God's service. I believe that we should take careful note of the difference between the two accounts. The two passages give quite different views of the

significance of the Law in this covenant. They are probably dependent on two distinct sets of tradition passed down through the years in Israel. Exodus 19.2–8 records that the people promised obedience based on obeying God's voice before any Law was given, and the Law was added to help the Israelites understand what God required of them. Exodus 24.3–8 suggests that the Israelites were first given the Law, and that their chief commitment was to obey it.

Exodus 19.2–8 is in keeping with the earlier covenants. It shows that the foundation of the relationship with God was his love and goodwill. His people's obedience would follow as an outcome of the relationship. Walking with God, they would know and do his will gladly, knowing the LORD to be wise and loving as the Patriarchs had done. The second account implies that the foundation of the whole relationship with God was obedience and that it was totally dependent on the fulfilment of the Law. We can find these two contrasting attitudes among the Israelites all through the subsequent period of the Old Testament, and also at various times among Christians.

Why in fact did the Ten Commandments probably enter the experience of Israel at this particular time? According to Genesis, God had been making himself known to individuals, and had been giving covenants based on personal relationships. But at Sinai God made himself known to a larger group of people, who were gradually to be formed into a nation. Always some people among the Israelites would be able to enjoy the same sort of personal relationship with God that the Patriarchs had enjoyed. Moses himself was one of these. But many of them were unprepared for this sort of relationship with God, and were incapable of living obediently simply as a response to his love. So God gave the Law to bridge the gap, and to make known something about his will without forcing a personal relationship on those unready to receive it. This is the significance of Exodus 20.18–20. God was willing to provide a covenant relationship in a form that people could readily respond to, even though it fell short of the personal relationship that God wanted with his people.

According to the priestly traditions, the Sabbath was to be a sign of God's covenant at Sinai (Exodus 31.16). The custom of observing the Sabbath, a regular ceremony in which all could take part, was appropriate for those involved in a covenant for all God's people.

The covenant at Shechem (Joshua 24.14–28)

After the Israelites had settled in Palestine, they understood that God had given them the land. Joshua believed that in their gratitude for this they should make a vow of obedience to the LORD. Joshua warned them that they should avoid any attempt to make an agreement with God that could compel him to favour them (verse 19). God had freely given love to his people, and he was equally free to punish evil-doing. The foundation of this covenant, too, was God's goodwill. It provided for a continuing relationship among the people themselves, and between the people and God. The tribes of Israel were only loosely linked at that time and the covenant helped to draw them closer together, and so to prepare them for full national life.

The Shechem covenant was important because the people themselves as a group took the initiative in response to God's goodness. The only sign God required from them in return was that they should show their sincerity in promising to serve him alone, by ceasing to worship foreign gods.

The covenant of David (2 Samuel 7.8–17; 23.1–5; 1 Kings 8.22–26)

The appointment of kings in Israel came about because the people believed they would benefit from such an appointment, since Eli's sons were corrupt and failed to copy their father's concern for justice in the land (1 Samuel 8.4–5). Samuel was convinced by the LORD that the appointment of a king would prove disastrous for the people (1 Kings 8.10–18); but the people insisted. The LORD showed the extent of his patience and love by instructing Samuel to carry out their wishes, and the LORD himself took action leading to the appointment of Saul (1 Samuel 9.27—10.1). But he was disobedient and failed to obey God. So David was chosen to take his place after Saul's death (1 Samuel 13.14).

By the time that David had established his rule as king and had conquered Israel's enemies, the people were prepared to accept his reign as a gift from God. They believed that it was a fulfilment of God's purposes. Nathan expressed this belief by sharing in God's establishment of a new covenant with David. He assured David that his family would continue to reign after him. Solomon accepted that his own reign was part of the fulfilment of this promise (1 Kings 3.6). The people of the Northern Kingdom rejected Rehoboam's claim to inherit these promises, but the people of the kingdom of Judah accepted the rule of the descendants of David throughout the years that led up to the Exile.

After the Exile the Jews looked eagerly for the Messiah who would inherit David's covenant and so have authority to rule in the name of the LORD. First they thought that Zerubbabel might be God's choice (Haggai 2.23; Zechariah 4.10), and later Joshua (Zechariah 6.11); but neither filled the role. In New Testament times the Jews found difficulty in believing that Jesus was the Messiah because he never ruled as king over their people. But Paul taught that Jesus had always had the right to rule, even in his lifetime, and that after his death, resurrection and ascension he came to rule eternally over all God's creation (Philippians 2.6–11).

Covenant Renewals (2 Kings 23.1–3; Nehemiah 9.32—10.29)

The people of Israel often failed to fulfil God's purposes as the various codes of law in the Torah describe them. Then their leaders would call them to turn back to the LORD and to serve him faithfully. These leaders recognized God's goodness in all his dealings with Israel. They believed that the people's disobedience had caused times of national and personal distress, and only penitence could bring new hope. So they logically urged obedience, and asked the people to commit themselves to the service of the LORD. Josiah did so after the discovery of the law book in the Temple. Nehemiah did so when he shared in the re-establishment of Israel in Judah after the Exile. Ezra is missing from the list of people who entered into this covenant, despite Nehemiah 9.37. This is part of the evidence for believing that Ezra came later than Nehemiah (see Volume 2, first edition pages 136–9, and second edition pages 91–3). But disobedience was a constant problem in Israel. Earlier, Jeremiah had come to believe that God's people were incapable of changing their ways and serving the LORD (Jeremiah 2.22; 13.23). Complaints by prophets against the people who had returned to Jerusalem after the Exile confirmed his belief (Haggai 1.2–6; Zechariah 1.1–6). But Jeremiah and Ezekiel believed that God would provide a new covenant, one that the people would be able to fulfil.

The New Covenant (Jeremiah 31.31–34; compare Jeremiah 32.37–41 and Ezekiel 36.24–28)

Jeremiah was the prophet who recognized that humans are unable to change their ways and become righteous simply by deciding to do so. But he also recognized that God was preparing to do something new to enable people to serve him. 'I will put my law within them and I will write it upon their hearts' (Jeremiah 31.33). Even though humans failed to obey God because of their sinfulness, God himself would restore the relationship and make obedience possible.

What was the difference between Abraham, Moses, and others who had faithfully served the LORD, and the people of Israel who had failed again and again? The difference was in their relationship with God. The great leaders had entered into a living, active relationship with God, and this had given them the inward resources to be obedient. But most of the Israelites had only heard of the LORD at secondhand. They had been taught *about* him, but lacked any personal knowledge of him. So Jeremiah believed that there would come a time when it would be true to say: 'no longer shall each man teach his neighbour and each his brother, saying "Know the LORD," for they shall all know me, from the least of them to the greatest, says the LORD' (Jeremiah 31.34).

The personal relationship between God and humans, expressed in the early covenants, was equally important in God's covenant with the nation and through them with all peoples. However, the work of God's self-revelation needed to be carried much further before ordinary people would be ready for the blessings he had planned for them from the beginning. The coming of Christ was the completion of all that God had been doing in Old Testament times to make himself known to humankind, and to offer to them that personal relationship which was at the centre of all his purposes. Ezekiel wrote, 'A new heart I will give you, and a new spirit I will put within you' (Ezekiel 63.26), and this promise was made available to all peoples through the work of Christ. The work of revelation leading to salvation was complete in him. The New Covenant is totally adequate to meet the needs of all humans. The presence of God in our hearts today is known through the working of the Holy Spirit. Jesus promised 'you shall receive power when the Holy Spirit has come upon you' (Acts 1.8). And Peter was right when at Pentecost he quoted Joel 2.28–32 and claimed that the gift of the Holy Spirit was available to all believers (Acts 2.16, 38–39).

 Check Your Understanding 19

1 Which two of the following words best express the same ideas as the word 'covenant' as we have used it in this chapter?

AGREEMENT   BARGAIN   CONTRACT
GUARANTEE   PACT   PROMISE   ULTIMATUM

2 Which one of the following ideas best expresses the meaning of 'relationship' as we have used it in this chapter?
   (a) ancestry and kinship between people
   (b) association and behaviour between people
   (c) comparison and contrast between people

Sacrifice

We need now to look at the place of sacrifice in the life of Israel. Our concern will be to recognize as far as we can the theological significance of the ritual, the underlying importance of these customs which God's people believed came from God. The Old Testament mentions many different forms of sacrifice, from the earliest records right through to the latest writings. In *History of Israel*, Volume 1 of this *Old Testament Introduction*, you will find a study of this subject in the third section of each chapter, where we think about ritual and social developments in each period of Israel's history. You will find the relevant passages in the first edition on pages 36, 62, 76, 144, 163. In the revised edition you should look at pages 41, 69, 85, 155, 176. Here I will try to provide an account of the way that ideas concerning sacrifices developed in Israel, and their significance.

The Development of Communal Sacrifices

In the time of the Patriarchs
The Patriarchs were the first among God's chosen people to use altars to mark places where God had made himself known to them. So the initiative was with God, rather than with his people. We can take as examples Abraham building an altar at Shechem (Genesis 12.6–7), Isaac at Gerar (Genesis 26.23–25), and Jacob at Bethel (Genesis 28.10–22). These were spontaneous responses to meeting with God. Until the time of Moses, laws never existed to guide humans in their approach to God. But one important issue was dealt with from the start: Abraham believed that God wanted him to sacrifice his son Isaac, but the Angel of the LORD prevented him from doing so (Genesis 22.10–13). In consequence, human sacrifice never became a customary part of the worship of the LORD. When the Patriarchs worshipped, the senior members of the families led the sacrifices and priests were unnecessary. Genesis mentions only priests who belonged to foreign people, starting with Melchizedek, king of Salem (Genesis 14.18–19).

In the time of Moses
The first development of detailed guidance for sacrifice related to the Passover, which celebrated the escape of God's people from the fatal plague which affected the Egyptians. Chapters 12 and 13 of Exodus provide us with details about the celebration of the Passover. But the book of Exodus only incorporated these records during or after the Exile. In consequence they included information from more than one source. Because the people who prepared the Torah were priests, there is a strong probability that they were responsible for adding more detailed instructions than existed at the time of Israel's escape from Egypt, by presenting rules that were familiar to the writers and had developed over the subsequent years of Israelite History.

Events at Sinai included the giving of the Ten Commandments, which laid down the foundations for worship for God's people: these included worshipping the LORD exclusively, rejecting all use of visual images of God; and the setting aside of the Sabbath for worship. Sacrificial instructions are totally missing from the Ten Commandments. Instead we find requirements for corporate and personal relationship with God. Notice that Jeremiah, centuries later, could say that all God required at the time of the Exodus was obedience to his voice (Jeremiah 7.22–23). In New Testament times Paul told the

Figures 8 and 9. 'Genesis mentions only priests who belonged to foreign people' (page 118). The function of priests has always been to bring the offerings of their people to the gods that they worship. Such customs are known to us in part through the use of seals. These were made by small cylinders with engraved pictures, which when rolled on clay or wax left imprints. The mark of an Assyrian seal illustrated above, from about 1000 BC, portrays sacrifice being made to a god. The one below, from Syria about 85 BC, shows the god Ashur as a winged being at the top, pouring out his blessing on a prince standing beside a sacred tree and attended by another god.

people of Galatia that the detailed laws of the Old Testament 'were ordained by angels through an intermediary', and that they were needed to quell the rebelliousness of God's people (Galatians 3.19).

Exodus depicts Aaron as the priest at Sinai, although he carried out this office in a disastrous way by making the golden calf. Even after that serious error Moses made Aaron responsible for the Tabernacle, which Exodus describes in a very elaborate fashion. Many scholars doubt whether these details were actually true of the place of worship during the years of wandering in the wilderness. The description fails to provide an easily moveable centre of worship. Scholars suggest that it better fits Solomon's temple, built in Jerusalem but destroyed by the Babylonians. As we have seen, the Jews finally compiled the Torah during or shortly after the return from Exile. At that time only the ruins of the temple existed, and the descriptions were based on tradition rather than personal knowledge.

In the time of the independent tribes

When God's people settled in Palestine, they took up agriculture and needed ceremonies to celebrate the seasons of the year. The Book of the Covenant, which we find in Exodus 20.22—23.33, gathered rules of behaviour which depended on guidance from God as disputes arose among his people. On the cultic side there are rules concerning altars and their use (Exodus 20.22–26), and about the three feasts which were to be shared: Unleavened Bread, Harvest and Ingathering. The Feast of Unleavened Bread was linked to the Passover, and probably represented the haste of preparation for departure from Egypt. The other two feasts involved making gifts of the people's first produce. Further guidance on these is given in Exodus 34.10–26, which some scholars call the Cultic Decalogue – ten rules concerning worship. Such scholars believe these were the Ten Commandments from Sinai, and that the ones we know developed later. They say that the Ten Commandments of Exodus 20 and Deuteronomy 5 contain rules for a settled life, rather than for people who were wandering in the wilderness of Sinai. But the ancestors of these people had lived settled lives in Egypt until they faced persecution, and they would understand the significance of the Ten Commandments, even though their own circumstances were different.

In the time of the kings

The book of Deuteronomy, which was found in the temple in the time of King Josiah, contains further guidance for the existing customs: Passover and the three feasts (Deuteronomy 16.1, 16–17). Each of these ceremonies was to recall the history of the Exodus from Egypt. The Passover sacrifice was again associated with the Feast of

Unleavened Bread. But Deuteronomy introduced a totally new idea: that everybody should gather in the one place chosen by the LORD to share in Israel's Passover sacrifices. Previously families had celebrated wherever they lived, as they did in Egypt. Seven weeks after the Passover, the people were to hold the Harvest feast, also known as Weeks and Pentecost, at the end of the corn harvest, and use it to celebrate the giving of the Law at Sinai. They were to hold the Feast of Booths at the completion of the grape harvests, and use it to celebrate the wandering of the Jews in the Wilderness.

During the Exile

We need to remember that, influenced by Deuteronomy, the Jews believed that the temple in Jerusalem was the only place where they should make their sacrifices. So after the destruction of the temple and the exile of the people, they lost their opportunity to make sacrifices, and the priests became redundant. Scholars believe that they set to work to preserve the traditions of Israel, so that the Jews would never forget their history or their former rituals. So the Torah began to take shape. They naturally included many details about sacrifice and the function of priests. They probably presented their highest ideals of what should be, rather than the facts of what had been done. The priests probably also led the people in worship and taught them from the records they were producing. In such a way they could prepare the people for a time when they could return to Jerusalem and re-establish their worship there. Certainly Ezekiel had a high vision of what the temple would be like when this happened. He was one of the priests (Ezekiel 1.3)!

After the Exile

Very few people returned from Exile to re-settle in Jerusalem, and they took a long time meeting their own need for homes to live in and gardens to grow their food. The prophet Haggai rebuked them about the fact that they had failed to build a temple for the LORD (Haggai 1.1–6). They needed to have a way to express their penitence. So a new ceremony developed: the Day of Atonement (Leviticus 23.26–32). This was an annual event of national mourning. The details of its ritual are given in Leviticus 16. The sacrifices involved one for the atonement of the priest and his family and another for the atonement of the temple and its contents. Then came the sacrifice for the sins of the nation.

Aaron was to choose two goats: one as a sin offering, the other to receive the iniquities, transgressions and sins of the people and to be driven off into the wilderness to *azazel*, whatever that means! We should remember that animals for sacrifice had to be perfect, and the Old Testament lacks any suggestion that such animals were bearing the sins of the people. Perhaps the offering of a perfect animal was a sacramental way for the donor to give his own life into the hands of God.

The noticeable thing about this account of development in Israel's sacrificial worship is that throughout the Old Testament people believed that God initiated changes and developments; it was far from being a matter of their own whims, or even the wisdom of the priests, who were expected to give guidance when fresh understanding of God's will became necessary with changing circumstances. You need to be sure that you recognize the sequence of events recorded in the Old Testament, which we have used in describing the development of Israelite worship. The first exercise in Check your Understanding 20 on page 127 will refresh your memory; you will find it helpful to answer it now.

Personal Sacrifices

So far I have described the development of sacrifices relating to times set aside for all God's people to share together in ceremonies that helped strengthen their sense of community and mutual responsibility. But we also need to remember that many sacrifices existed which provided for the needs of individuals and families. These sacrifices enabled people to express their relationship with God in three main ways:

- When Israelites wanted *to thank God* for his goodness to them they were able to share in sacrifices which expressed this thanksgiving, especially the thank-offerings (Leviticus 7.12), and the burnt offerings (Leviticus 1.10–13).
- When they wished *to share fellowship with God*, they could do so through sacrifices in which the worshippers ate part of the sacrificial animal, for example, the peace offering (Leviticus 3.1–5).
- When people were moved *to make atonement for their sins*, rituals existed which expressed their desire to heal broken relationships, and went alongside confession and restitution. For example, the sin offering (Leviticus 4) and the guilt offering (Leviticus 5).

Sacrifice and Obedience

We should remember that the people using the sin offering and the guilt offering belonged to God's chosen people. They believed they were already in a saving relationship with him through the covenants. They knew the proper response to the love which God had shown through his covenants: obedience. They believed that God had given them sacrifices as a means to maintain their relationship with him. But sacrifice alone could never be a substitute for obedience (1 Samuel 15.22; Psalm 51.17; Proverbs 21.3). Several of the prophets spoke fiercely against the Israelites for supposing that God would be pleased with them because of the many sacrifices that they made. The prophets made sure the Israelites understood that sacrifices were an inadequate response to God's love (Amos 4.4–5; 5.21–24; Isaiah 1.10–17; Jeremiah 7.21–26). Sacrifices should be an outward sign of the inward and personal response to God, which only fully showed itself in obedience to God's will and purposes.

Deliberate and Unintentional Sin

However, the people of Israel failed to respond fully to all that God was doing among them. As a people and individually they still acted against God's purposes, even after they had accepted the covenants. If they deliberately disobeyed God, then they lost their right to claim the privileges of the covenant relationship. People who refused to accept their responsibility to obey God were to be 'cut off' (Genesis 17.14; Exodus 12.15; Leviticus 18.29). They were excluded from membership of the covenant community. Jeremiah believed that the whole nation had rejected their relationship with God, and could only expect punishment (Jeremiah 7.28–29). Sacrifices were unable to help those who were deliberately disobedient (1 Samuel 3.14; 15.24–26). They had sinned with a 'high hand' (Numbers 15.30).

But actions contrary to God's will were sometimes unintentional. People at times failed to realize the significance of what was happening. They lacked awareness that their action was contrary to God's purposes, until they saw the result of what they did. Notice the distinction made between murder and manslaughter (Deuteronomy 4.42; Joshua 20.2). The first is deliberate, the second without intention. Both are treated seriously, but the person responsible for manslaughter was freed from the harshest penalties because their motive for action was innocent. The same is true of all wrong things done in innocence (Numbers 15.27–31). Knowledge of God and his purposes is essential to those who want to live righteously, because only so can they truly serve him. But only one source exists for such knowledge: the LORD himself. If we are to be faithful we must go on learning throughout our lives what God wants us to be and to do (Psalms 25.4–5, 9–10; 119.64–66). Even the righteous man Job (Job 1.1; 42.8b) was wrong in one thing, he forgot how ignorant he was as compared with God (Job 38.1–3; 40.1–5). But he was treated as innocent because he had done all he knew to serve God (Job 42.8b). Notice again what we learnt about the meaning of the word 'transgression' in contrast to the term 'sin'.

Confession and Restitution

The rituals of the sin offering and the guilt offering were only accept-able to God when they were accompanied by confession and restitu-tion (Numbers 5.7). The opposite attitude is shown in Jeremiah 2.35, where the outcome is judgement.

Confession was an essential part of the personal guilt offering (Leviticus 5.5–6), and also of the national ceremony of the Day of Atonement (Leviticus 16.21). Many of the Psalms express confes-sion, and were without doubt used in temple worship, serving as part of the preparation for sacrifices (Psalms 32.5; 38.18; 41.4). Some of the Psalms reminded the worshippers that sacrifice alone was insuffi-cient: what God really demanded was obedience (Psalms 40.6–8; 51.16–17). Nobody could approach God and find blessing if they refused to admit their need for forgiveness, or if they intended to go on in sin.

But restitution was also necessary in order to remove the barrier to fellowship with God and friendship with the person bearing the injury that sin had caused. The guilt offering was a gift to God on account of a breach of faith and unwitting sin (Leviticus 5.14–16). But if someone had injured a neighbour by their sin, then they must restore the relationship they had broken with their neigh-bour before coming to bring a guilt offering to the LORD (Leviticus 6.1–7).

Atonement

When an individual had shared in a sacrifice with real sorrow for their past sins, and with real intention to serve God, then the sacri-fice opened the way for the atonement for their sin. The sacrifice was a sign of repentance, of the removal of the hindrance to right rela-tionship with God that the sin had created. Scholars are uncertain of the origin of the Hebrew word for atonement, but by comparison with the ideas of other religions of Old Testament times they suggest that the word means either *to wipe away* (that is, to remove the stain of sin), or more probably *to cover* (that is, to ensure that the past sin is never seen or remembered again). Whichever is the more accurate interpretation, we should notice that *God* deals with the problem of sin. Sinners are unable to claim any merit for their confession, resti-tution or sacrifice. What people do by these actions is to become receptive to God's loving concern for them, instead of being rebel-lious and resentful towards him. In the following verses, and others besides, the RSV translators chose to interpret the Hebrew word for atonement by using the English word 'forgive': Deuteronomy 21.8; Psalms 65.3; 79.9; Isaiah 6.7.

Isaiah 52.13—53.12

As early as New Testament times, Christians made use of this passage in trying to understand the death of Christ. The Ethiopian Eunuch was puzzled by this passage, and Philip helped him to understand about Jesus, and led him to conversion (Acts 8.26–39). When Jewish Christians in New Testament times wanted to share their faith that Jesus was the Messiah with other Jews they knew they would be opposed unless they could show quite clearly that the Old Testament contained a prophecy about the death of the Messiah, because the Jewish scriptures were the foundation of their faith. So they probably made great use of this passage. The Apostle Peter certainly used these verses to advise servants how they should behave if they were mistreated, placing his emphasis on the fact that they knew Christ's suffering had brought them salvation (1 Peter 2.22–25). Christian writers in the early second century used this same passage to convince people of the truth of their message. As we would expect, Jewish writers of the time rejected this interpretation, preferring to see the verses of Isaiah as laying down the general principle that the sufferings of the righteous could benefit sinners.

Down through the ages many discussions have taken place among scholars about the significance of Isaiah 52.13—53.12. Some preachers have chosen these verses to suggest that God's wrath could not be turned aside until the due punishment had been carried out, and that his concern for righteousness demanded such suffering. So they have taught that his Son died in our place, bearing our punishment and setting us free from our burden of guilt. They have believed that only this way could God welcome us back as his children. This does seem to explain some words in this passage: 'wounded for our transgression . . . bruised for our iniquities . . . the chastisement that made us whole . . . the LORD has laid on him the iniquity of us all'. This interpretation is said to be salvation by substitution.

But this way of interpreting the death of Christ has substantial problems for many people.

1 First, the death of Christ seems to be totally unjust. What human court would rule that somebody else must suffer execution or life imprisonment in place of a convicted murderer, setting him free?
2 Second, and more importantly, this explanation sets a divide between the Father and the Son in the Godhead. The Father is said to be concerned that justice must be done, and the Son has compassion for sinners and so offers himself to be punished in their place. But the whole of the Old Testament contains records of God's activity in order to rescue humans from the state of sinfulness and his efforts to build creative relations with his people through his covenants. And the New Testament tells us that Jesus

never needed to reconcile an angry Father to the people he had created. He was fully committed to human salvation (2 Corinthians 5.17–19).

As we might expect, Jewish teachers today continue to reject the idea that Jesus was the Messiah and that through his death he provided the possibility of salvation for all and the promise of eternal life for those who believe. They often take the view that the Jewish people as a whole bear the sins of the world, seeing in this the cause of the persecution and suffering they have endured through the centuries. We should recognize with great sorrow that Christian nations and peoples have often in the past persecuted Jews because those who have done so have seen the Jews as directly responsible for the crucifixion of Jesus. These Christians have failed to recognize that the sins of the Jews were very similar to those they themselves and their people have committed, and that if Jesus had been born among us we would probably have acted in a similar way in bringing him to trial and punishment.

So how else can we understand Isaiah 52.13—53.12? Many twentieth-century scholars have begun from the fact that sin causes divisions between individuals, communities and nations. This happens because those who have suffered at the hands of others have been unwilling to forgive them and so been unable to seek reconciliation. But throughout the history of God's people there have been saints who have put aside their anger and forgiven their hurts, and have been able to bring peace and reconciliation as a result. These can be considered the suffering servants for their own times and communities. Scholars have chosen a wide range of people of Old Testament times as being among those who have endured suffering and forgiven those who have treated them badly. They have chosen such people as Moses, Hezekiah, Isaiah himself, Jeremiah, Jehoiachin, and Zerubbabel to illustrate this behaviour. Perhaps one of the outstanding ones is Jeremiah, who had the dreadful responsibility of telling the Jews that God had given up on keeping them safe from their enemies, and would send Babylon to conquer them and take them into exile. The people of Jeremiah's time were angry with him and treated him badly. Jeremiah would never have suffered as he did if they had never sinned as they did. But the writers of Lamentations showed that they had at last accepted, at least in part, the truth of his message. They saw him as one they had caused to suffer, when in reality he was offering them God's warning of what was to happen. This and other examples of the righteous suffering for the unrighteous seems to lie behind Isaiah 52.13—53.12: 'He was despised, and we esteemed him not . . . We esteemed him stricken, smitten by God, and afflicted . . . But he was wounded for our transgressions, he was bruised for our iniquities'. If we do approach the passage from Isaiah from this angle, we need to go on to recognize that Jesus Christ revealed on the cross that forgiveness is costly to God as well as to human beings. God came in Jesus Christ to reveal the extent of his love, even going to the extreme of dying a terrible death to teach us the truth. He waits to forgive us, and to welcome us as his children.

📖 Check Your Understanding 20

1 On a sheet of paper write down the numbers of the sentences below, filling their blank spaces with the correct periods of Israelite history listed here.

THE EXILE THE EXODUS INDEPENDENT TRIBES THE KINGS
THE PATRIARCHS AFTER THE RETURN FROM EXILE

(a) _____ was the time when the priests recorded traditions because they were unable to make sacrifices.
(b) _____ was the time when the Day of Atonement began to be used by God's People.
(c) _____ was the time when worship was largely a spontaneous response to God's revelations.
(d) _____ was the time when the major sacrifices were by law to be shared by everybody in one place.
(e) _____ was the time when rules for corporate and personal relationships with God were first set down.
(f) _____ was the time when three annual feasts became part of Israelite worship.

2 Which two of the following words best express the purpose of sacrifice in the Old Testament? Why?

COMPENSATION DEDICATION DESTRUCTION
LOSS OBEDIENCE PUNISHMENT

📖 Study Suggestions

FOR GROUP DISCUSSION

1 What is the meaning of the statement 'for the imagination of man's heart is evil from his youth' (Genesis 8.21)?
(a) In particular, what does the word 'man' mean here? (i) an individual, (ii) a male person, (iii) human beings in general, or (iv) the whole human race?
(b) Also, what does 'imagination' mean here? (i) his temptations, (ii) his idle thoughts, (iii) his intentions, (iv) his feelings?
(c) What conclusions does the story-teller provide about God's activities, based on this statement?

2 'It was the will of the Lord to bruise him; he has put him to grief' (Isaiah 53.10). Say how you think that this statement applies to:

   (a) the righteous in Israel at the time of the Exile;

   (b) the Jewish people today, and the nation of Israel;

   (c) our Lord Jesus Christ.

3 (a) Does the Lord's Supper have a similar significance for Christians as the sin offerings and the guilt offerings of Old Testament times had for the Israelites? Explain the similarities and the differences.

   (b) Do some Christians make similar mistakes about their use of the Lord's Supper, as the Israelites were accused of doing about their sacrifices by the prophets?

FOR ESSAY WRITING

4 Describe in your own words the two different traditions about the relationship between the Covenant and the Law at Sinai. Which of the two is nearest to the Christian attitude to the Law? Give reasons for your choice.

5 Read the account of the Day of Atonement in Leviticus 16, and answer the following questions:

   (a) For what individuals and groups is atonement made in this ceremony?

   (b) In what way do you think 'the holy place and the tent of meeting and the altar' (verse 20) need atoning for?

   (c) Which of the animals used in the ceremony does this passage consider to be sin offerings or guilt offerings? Which of the animals remained unsacrificed?

   (d) What was done with the blood of the bull and the goat which were sacrificed? What do you think was the meaning of this action?

   (e) What was done with the goat over which all iniquities, transgressions and sins of the people were confessed?

6 Give three examples from present day life, either from your own experience or from your knowledge of other people's behaviour, of sin which was unintentional but led to remorse.

WORK WITH THE BIBLE AND A CONCORDANCE

7 (a) Use a concordance to discover all the things that the Psalmists believed God would do for his own sake or for his name's sake.

   (b) What do these things suggest about the character of God as the Psalmists understand it?

   (c) What do you think is meant by the words 'for the sake of thy steadfast love'?

8 Not all covenants in the Old Testament are introduced and established by God, or the people with him.
   (a) What other covenants can you discover in the book of Genesis?
   (b) Are similar covenants known in the community in which you live? If so, in what ways are they helpful to the life of your society?
9 The original language of the book of the prophet Hosea uses the Hebrew word *hesed* several times. It occurs in Hosea 2.19; 2.20; 4.1; 6.4; 6.6; 10.12; 12.6. Which word or words does the RSV translation of these verses use to translate *hesed*?

The New Life

8

Two questions arise from all that we have studied so far. What do the Old Testament writers say about

- The present outcome of God's work of salvation?
- The final outcome?

These are the subjects of this chapter and the next. First we must think about the results of God's work among his people in the times described in the Old Testament. These results are relevant for us today because God continues his work of salvation among us.

The Remnant

> In that day the remnant of Israel and the survivors of
> the house of Jacob . . . will lean upon the LORD,
> the Holy One of Israel, in truth.
>
> (Isaiah 10.20)

Many of the prophets make reference to the remnant of God's people. The word 'remnant' normally means *what is left over, the residue, the stub*. This meaning is clearly seen in one of the earliest uses by Amos, who gives a startling picture of the nature of the remnant: 'As the shepherd rescues from the mouth of the lion two legs, or a piece of an ear, so shall the people of Israel who dwell in Samaria be rescued' (Amos 3.12). He is describing the outcome of God's punishment of faithless Israel. Because God still plans to provide for himself a people of faithfulness, he must first find a few righteous among the many corrupt. These will be the foundation on which God will build his kingdom. Amos preached judgement on the nations for their evil-doing, and led up in his sermon to judgement on Judah and Israel. 'For three transgressions of . . . and for four, I will not revoke the punishment' (Amos 2.4, 6). Yet later in the book we read of Amos pleading with God to release Jacob, meaning Israel, from judgement (Amos 7.1–6). Amos asks 'How can Jacob stand?' (Amos 7.2), which is a way of asking how God can destroy the people he has created to be his own and to bring blessing to others. The final vision in the chapter points to justice as God's motive in carrying out his judgement

(Amos 7.7–9). We know that the Northern Kingdom of Israel was conquered soon afterwards and taken into exile, never to be heard of again. But Judah remained to provide the remnant through whom God could fulfil his purposes. Yet even they were due for judgement and thorough punishment close to extinction, but with a puzzling promise, 'The holy seed is its stump' (Isaiah 6.13). Micah uses the idea of remnant to describe those who would share in God's rule in Jerusalem over the nations (Micah 4.6–7, which follows the prophecy which Micah and Isaiah share in Micah 3.1–3, Isaiah 2.2–4).

When the majority of God's people from Judah had gone in exile to Babylon, Jeremiah denied to the people remaining in Israel the right to consider themselves the remnant of God's people. He was certain that God would work through those who eventually would return from exile (Jeremiah 24.1–10). Zephaniah, who worked at about the same time, thought differently about the people who remained in Judah (Zephaniah 2.7; 3.12, 13). But the history of that period shows that Jeremiah was right, even though far fewer of the exiles returned than the prophets expected, and only a minority of those who did were committed to God's purposes. During the Exile, Ezekiel confirmed Jeremiah's idea (Ezekiel 11.13–21). After the Exile, Haggai referred to those who had returned from it as 'all the remnant of the people' (Haggai 1.12, 14); Zechariah does the same (Zechariah 8.6, 11–12); as also does Deutero-Isaiah (Isaiah 45.22–25).

All these prophets believed that God in his mercy would save a few from among the multitude of God's people who were disobedient and deserved judgement. They believed that those God saved to help fulfil his purposes would serve the LORD faithfully. They seem to have failed to understand that even among the remnant who God actually saved from destruction, there would be many who failed to respond to his steadfast love and refused to live as he intended them to do. Throughout the history of Israel there would be a conflict between the faithful and the unfaithful, between the righteous and the wicked. The faithful remnant were always a small minority among those who survived the national disasters. Though many of the writers of the Old Testament clearly believed that God's work of salvation might be completed in their own time, they came to realize that those who were faithful in serving the LORD would always be few compared with those who disobeyed him. The remnant had to live their lives of obedience among many who failed to serve the LORD.

Since God's purpose has always been to create a community of men and women who would serve him gladly and live in peace and harmony with each other, his work of salvation is directed to that purpose. Throughout history he has been drawing people into fellowship with himself and with each other. Such fellowship has been possible wherever people have been willing to respond to his steadfast love. We are called to share in God's work of salvation, by living as his faithful and obedient people. Let us now examine what the Old Testament writers had to say about these relationships.

Human Relationship with God

The earliest stories of human relationship with God are the accounts of the experience of God shared by Abraham, Isaac, Jacob and Joseph. But the oldest account of how all humans living in community should relate to God is contained in the Ten Commandments (Exodus 20.2–17; Deuteronomy 5.6–21). So we must now think about the significance of those commandments.

The Ten Commandments: 1–5

They begin with a statement of God's right to rule his chosen people. He reminds them that he has given them freedom from slavery in Egypt. Even Moses had doubted the LORD's power to do this, when Pharaoh refused to let the people go. But God had done what seemed impossible. Throughout their journeying, despite their own complaints and rebelliousness, God had led them safely to Mount Sinai where he gave them Ten Commandments. YHWH saved his people, and would go on guiding and supporting them if they listened to his commands, and lived according to his will.

After the introduction, the Ten Commandments contain four rules about how God's people should relate to him. We will study each in turn, and head each paragraph with a brief statement of the nature of the command.

You shall have no other gods besides me (Exodus 20.3; Deuteronomy 5.7)
We have already looked closely at this on pages 23–7 under the heading 'One'. We have seen that people in Old Testament times could interpret the first commandment in different ways, depending on the depth of their spiritual insight. We have seen that they never regarded Satan as an equal authority with God. The ultimate reality of the Trinity, Three-in-One, underlines the truth that God is One, and we now know that his nature is expressed through three persons: the Father, the Son and the Holy Spirit.

You shall not make idols to worship (Exodus 20.4–6; Deuteronomy 5.8–10)
The people were quite used to seeing pictures and models representing the gods of Egypt. So when Aaron proposed making a golden calf, none of the people objected and Moses was absent and unable to

prevent it happening (Exodus 32.1). How did the descendants of Abraham come to behave in this way? Probably because they saw the one calf as a suitable symbol for the one God. Certainly Jeroboam at a later time created similar images for the High Places in the Northern Kingdom of Israel after they had broken away from Judah (1 Kings 12.28–30). But nothing on earth could truly represent God. Idols would only provide the opportunity for people to mistakenly worship the object rather than the spiritual being their makers may have rightly expected the people to recognize that they represented.

The reference to God's jealousy seems odd and destructive if he poured it out on descendants to the third and fourth generation. This sounds like excessive revenge. 'Jealous' does express a strong emotion, but we could perhaps better translate it as 'zealous'. God is very keen to maintain truth and righteousness against competing false ideas. About the generations, we should remember that four generations may be alive at the same time, and three generations very often are. Family attitudes and behaviour strongly influence each member of the family when they live as a close community. So that whenever people choose to adopt bad habits their example can affect their children and their children's children. In consequence, God is unable to ignore the behaviour of each generation. Our example, good or bad, is very important!

Do not misuse the name of God (Exodus 20.7; Deuteronomy 5.11)

We should never support our promises by saying such things as 'The Lord knows . . .', when in fact we are being dishonest. Jesus extends this command by saying we should never use God's name for our own advantage even when what we say is true (Matthew 5.33–37). The fact is we should always speak the truth, then people will learn to trust us without needing such oaths. But we must recognize that there may be times when people confide in us, telling us their secrets perhaps to gain our advice, and we have a solemn duty to avoid passing on what they have said. We must refuse both to answer direct questions about the secret, and to avoid including any reference to the secret in our conversation. People will then feel confident to ask our advice or our prayers concerning their personal needs. Perhaps this commandment made the Jews reluctant to use YHWH, even when reading the Bible. How could they be sure that they were always using his name wisely?

Keep the Sabbath (Exodus 20.8–11; Deuteronomy 5.12–15)

The seventh day of the week, known now as Saturday, is the time for corporate worship among the Jews. Work was to be banned on that day because the day was dedicated to the LORD. Exodus and Deuteronomy both give a reason for this commandment. In Exodus the day was to commemorate the fact that God created the world in six days and rested on the seventh (Genesis 2.2). In Deuteronomy the Sabbath was to provide rest for everybody, in memory of the fact that God rescued the Jews from their heavy work as slaves in Egypt. Time for relaxation once every seven days is an important principle, because otherwise life becomes one long effort without time to recover from tiredness. Christians as a whole now observe Sunday, because that was the day Jesus rose from the dead. But the purpose is similar: to worship, to rest and to spend time with our families.

Honour your father and your mother (Exodus 20.12; Deuteronomy 5.16)

A fifth commandment follows these, which places our parents next to God in our lives. The reason the verses give is that we may have stability in national life. Ties such as those still found in African family life are important. Happy families are a good basis for peaceful and co-operative social life. In many places these ties are breaking down because of the need to travel far to find work, and so to rear families away from the homes of parents and other relatives. Education can cause rifts between parents and children because those with schooling are tempted to despise those who still live in traditional ways. This commandment is important because it reminds us that we owe our lives to those who brought us into being and guided us in our early years. We have a responsibility for them as they grow old, and especially if they lose their ability to live independently.

The Ten Commandments provide basic guidelines in our relationships with God. They spell out some of our responsibilities in our fellowship with God, and help us to plan our lives as we live as his people today. But we need to obey these rules, and our obedience depends on our whole attitude to God. If we have the right motives we shall be glad to live as God requires us to do. Old Testament writers were well aware of this fact. They use three terms to express a healthy attitude in our worship and obedience to God: fear, faith, and love. So we will look at these now.

The Fear of God

Christians often describe their religion by saying. 'I believe in the Lord Jesus Christ.' The Jews expressed their religious experience by saying, 'I fear God' (Genesis 42.18; Job 4.6; Jonah 1.9), or 'I fear the LORD' (2 Kings 4.1; Isaiah 11.3). This way of expressing their experience of God probably resulted from the Israelites' deep sense of God's holiness. We have already noticed that the Hebrew word for *holy* probably means *separate*. So God's holiness is all that makes him different from human beings, everything that makes him seem mysterious and strange. There is an English word, 'awe', which sums up the human response to the holiness of God. It includes both wonder and dread: a desire to know, and also a fear of finding out, what God is like (see Genesis 28.17; Exodus 15.11).

The whole evidence of Old Testament revelation is that this holy God intends human beings to know him. Hosea expressed this in the words of God: 'I am God and not man, the Holy One in your midst, and I will not come to destroy' (Hosea 11.9; compare Isaiah 55.6–9; Ezekiel 39.7). Isaiah of Jerusalem and Deutero-Isaiah shared this idea, and referred to God as 'the Holy One of Israel' (Isaiah 1.4; 41.14). This suggests that God is different from humans, but seeks fellowship with them. For humans, fear in the sense of awe remains a real part of their experience of God's presence, even though God's purpose in making himself known is for their good (Isaiah 54.4, 5).

Rightly understood, God's holiness leads to joy, as people share in his good purposes for them (Isaiah 41.16; compare 48.17). This fear and this joy can he combined, because fear of the LORD turns humans from evil, and they are able to share in good (Proverbs 3.7; 8.13). They see the Law as a guide, showing them how to reverence God (Deuteronomy 17.19b; 31.12–13). The fear of the LORD leads people to walk in his ways (Deuteronomy 10.12; Joshua 24.14; Psalm 86.11). This is the true basis of all wisdom (Proverbs 9.10).

Faith in God

We find frequent mentions of God's own *faithfulness* throughout the Old Testament (for example, Deuteronomy 32.4; Isaiah 49.7; Psalm 89.8). People can trust God because he is always the same. His attitude to humans is always one of *steadfast love*. Old Testament thought nearly always links the two ideas. In many of the psalms the writer sets faithfulness and steadfast love in parallel to each other (for example, Psalms 36.5; 88.11). In prose passages also the writers often set the two ideas side by side (Exodus 34.6; 2 Samuel 2.6; Hosea 2.19, 20).

In the Old Testament, the writers often also link God's faithfulness with his *righteousness* (Psalm 85.11; Zechariah 8.8). We have seen that righteousness meant 'everything that is in tune with God's purposes' (see page 29). So God's righteousness is shown by the fact that he acts according to his purposes. The fact that he always does so is a measure of his faithfulness.

Another related idea is that the LORD is a God of *truth* (Isaiah 65.16; Jeremiah 10.10). In Hebrew the words for truth and for faithfulness come from the same verbal root. But the connection in thought is even more important than the link of the word forms. Truth is something which brings understanding and provides meaning and purpose for life. For example, if I believe that God loves me, this is so wonderful that it must affect my whole life. Or again, if I know that I am a sinner, then I need to search out the way of salvation and find God's forgiveness. Truth is vitally important to me and to us all. According to the Old Testament writers, God is a reliable source of truth. That is part of the meaning of the word 'faithful' when used about God. He can be trusted to give us a proper understanding of life and of ourselves.

Some of the Psalmists looked to God for truth (Psalms 25.5; 43.3). Psalm 119, the great psalm in praise of the Law, teaches that the Law is true (verses 142, 151). The Law is a source of the knowledge and understanding which gives us a sure foundation for life. The purpose of some of the books in the third section of the Hebrew scriptures is to preserve and pass on truth (Proverbs 22.20, 21; Ecclesiastes 12.10; Daniel 11.2).

The human response to God's revelation of his faithfulness and his truth should be faith. There are many examples in the Old Testament. Notice for example:

1 Abraham 'believed the LORD; and he reckoned it to him as righteousness' (Genesis 15.6). By his faith Abraham entered into fellowship with God; he was responsive to God's purposes and so his relationship with him was rightly based.
2 Isaiah urged Ahaz to place his trust in God, by saying 'If you will not believe, surely you shall not be established' (Isaiah 7.9). Unless Ahaz responded to God he was unable to share in God's purposes, and his reign as king in Judah would be short and ineffective.
3 Habakkuk believed that God's purposes would be fulfilled and that those who opposed God would fail 'but the righteous shall live by his faith' (Habakkuk 2.4).

Faithfulness was clearly an essential part of serving the LORD. Ezra recalled Abraham's faithfulness with approval (Nehemiah 9.7, 8). A man of God delivered a message from God to Eli: 'I will raise up a faithful priest, who shall do according to what is in my heart and in my mind' (1 Samuel 2.27, 35). Ahimelech the priest describes David as more faithful than any other of Saul's household (1 Samuel 22.14). The descendant of David who would rule in God's name would wear righteousness as his belt (Isaiah 11.5; compare Isaiah 16.5). God's 'servants', that is, those in Israel who would serve him, would be faithful (Isaiah 42.1, 3).

In some of the verses we have studied, faithfulness seems to mean *trustworthiness*, rather than *trustfulness*. But we should remember that people become trustworthy through being trustful towards God. The security which we discover through our relationship with God enables us to be secure in our dealings with others (1 Kings 2.4; 3.6; and compare Psalm 26.3). Notice how the Psalmists use such words as 'fortress', 'rock', 'refuge', to describe the security they find in God, and the confidence he gives them for life (Psalms 18.2; 91.2; 144.2).

Love for God

The qualities of the right human response to God are the result of God's relationship with human beings. God is holy, we rightly respond by fearing him. Because God is faithful, we can rely on him and have faith in him. But we have already discovered that the most important thing about God's relationship with us is his love. We have seen that God's love is described by two different words in the Hebrew of the Old Testament (see pages 109–110). One is the ordinary word for love between human beings. The other includes the idea of faithfulness, as shown towards people. The RSV usually translates this word as *steadfast love* (see page 110).

How did the writers of the Old Testament describe people's response to God's love? Did they think that human beings could love God as he loves them? They rarely use the word we normally translate as *steadfast love* to describe the human response to God.

1 Hosea taught the people of his time that God desired steadfast love, and set this quality alongside *knowledge of God* (Hosea 6.6). He also complained that 'There is no faithfulness or kindness, and no knowledge of God in the land' (Hosea 4.1). In this latter verse Hosea was describing the outcome in human relationships because they had failed to enter a true relationship with God. He used the Hebrew word for *steadfast love*, even though in this verse the RSV translators have used the word *kindness* to express its meaning.
2 Jeremiah believed that in the early period of God's relations with Israel, people had shown steadfast love *to God*. The RSV translates Jeremiah 2.2 as 'I remember the devotion of your youth', but the word *devotion* translates the Hebrew word that this translation normally gives as *steadfast love*.
3 Similarly, in Jonah 2.8 the translators have used *true loyalty* to express the meaning of the same word. Here again the complaint is that this quality is lacking in the relationship of people with God.

The evidence of the whole history of Israel is that the Jews failed to respond to God with steadfast love, so we should expect that a description of the existing relationships between the Israelites and God would exclude mention of this quality in their contacts with him.

The ordinary Hebrew word for love occurs widely in the Torah. Jesus quoted Deuteronomy 6.5 as one of the two commandments on which all the Law and the Prophets depend (Matthew 22.39, 40):

'You shall love the LORD your God, with all your heart, and with all your soul, and with all your might'. The word the the RSV translates as 'love' here is the Hebrew word which is normally used for human relationships, for example, a man's love for his wife, a father's for his children. The same Hebrew word occurs in the Ten Commandments, in referring to the 'thousands of those who love me and keep my commandments' (Exodus 20.6; Deuteronomy 5.10), and appears throughout the book of Deuteronomy to describe our proper attitude to God.

So we can say that in the Old Testament both Hebrew words for love are used to describe how humans *ought* to feel towards God, rather than how they do in fact feel and believe. Both the complaints of the prophets and the instructions of the law-givers guide people towards the unfamiliar path of love towards God.

Yet there is also evidence in the Old Testament to show that some of the people did respond to God's love. We find this evidence in the frequent use of words expressing thanksgiving and joy.

The Hebrew word for thanksgiving appears again and again in the Psalms. One verse in particular is often repeated:

> O give thanks to the LORD, for he is good,
> for his steadfast love endures for ever.
> (Psalm 136.1, and many more places)

This verse expresses thanksgiving which is basically a response to God's steadfast love. Sometimes the Hebrew word for *thanksgiving* is translated as *praise*. But the RSV translators use the word *praise* more often in translating another Hebrew word, which we often use in an anglicized form, *Hallelujah*. The RSV translators express this word by using the words *Praise the LORD*. See especially what are known as the Hallelujah Psalms: 105–107, 111–118, 135–136, 146–150.

Several different Hebrew words express the idea of *joy*, or *rejoicing*. For example, they express the feelings of satisfaction which people have when a purpose is fulfilled or a task completed (Isaiah 9.3). The wicked *rejoice* in the evil they have done (Ezekiel 36.5; Proverbs 2.14). The righteous *rejoice* in what God has done. They rejoice in his salvation (Psalm 51.12; Isaiah 12.3), his judgements (Psalm 97.8), and his deliverance (Psalm 9.14). Some of these verses express joy in what God has done for individuals, others express joy in what he has done for the whole people. Joy is especially related to the well-being of Jerusalem. Joy disappears when the city is defeated, and reappears when its future seems good (Isaiah 51.11; Jeremiah 31.13). Joy is the people's proper response to God's steadfast love (Psalm 31.7). Because all God's purposes are good and his achievements are sure, it became natural for the Old Testament writers to speak of having joy, or rejoicing 'in the LORD' (Isaiah 29.19; 41.16).

📖 Check Your Understanding 21

1 Which two of the following words come nearest to expressing what Old Testament writers meant by the *fear* of the LORD?

> ANXIETY   APPREHENSION   HORROR   MISTRUST
> PANIC   RESPECT   REVERENCE   SUSPICION

2 Each of the following words refers to behaviour which depends on a particular quality in the person to whom it is shown. For example, *trusting* somebody depends on the person trusted being *trustworthy*.

What quality does a person need to deserve each of the following ways of behaving?

> BELIEVING   DEPENDING
> HAVING FAITH   LOVING   RELYING

Our Relationship with Each Other

> You shall not take vengeance or bear any grudge against the sons of your own people, but you shall love your neighbour as yourself: I am the LORD.
>
> (Leviticus 19.18)

Whenever God called someone to serve him, he did so in order that that person could have an influence within the community in which they lived. God called Abraham to establish a family that would serve him. He called Moses to draw the tribes of Israel together to become the people of Israel. He called David to establish the nation of Israel, freed from their enemies and able to serve the LORD.

But God intended that other people besides the great leaders should have an influence in Israel. Every person who was responsive to the steadfast love of God was able to set an example for the people of his or her time. God ruled their lives, and this should have an effect upon their relationships with their neighbours.

The Law, the Prophets and the Writings all contain guidance about the way people should behave as members of the Israelite community. There were many distinct codes of Law, which developed over the centuries: the Book of the Covenant, the Law Code of Deuteronomy; the Holiness Code and the Priestly Code. I describe their formation in *Books of the Old Testament*: volume two of my *Old Testament Introduction* (first edition pages 21–3; revised edition pages 45–8). All of these codes contain rules of conduct which had the purpose of helping to establish good human relationships in Israel. A great part of the message of the prophets was a warning about the sins which were dividing the people and hindering God's purposes for them. The writers of the Wisdom Literature, for example Proverbs, preserved teachings about life which they and their sources had drawn from practical experience, and which helped show the best way to live in God's world and among his people.

Some of today's Old Testament scholars believe that in studying Old Testament Theology we should include a study of all these teachings, but ethics is a separate subject from theology, whether we are studying the teachings of the Old or New Testaments or modern theory and practice. People write whole books on such subjects, and any attempt to condense such knowledge to a few pages would fail to do justice to the subject. But we do need to recognize the reasons behind the rules for moral behaviour in Israel.

Throughout the Old Testament, ethics, that is, the accepted customs, are much more than ways of behaviour which ease the problems which arise in human society and help people to avoid conflict. As we have seen, they attempt to express the righteousness which is in accord with the will and purpose of God. The purpose of all the lawgiving, preaching and teaching recorded in the Old Testament was to help people understand what God wanted them to do, and how best they might serve him. As people's understanding of God developed over the centuries, so their recognition of moral standards improved. This explains why we can find contradictions at times between what the various writers have to say about human behaviour and about God's will.

We shall understand the basic purpose of ethical teachings more fully if we turn now to study the ethical rules contained in the Ten Commandments. They show just what is involved in serving God in this world, and thus what sort of character people can develop through obedience to the Law. We shall go on to see that this can be summed up in the phrase 'the image of God' (Genesis 1.27).

The Ten Commandments: 6–10

We have already looked at the first five commandments which concern our relationship with God, and the special place of parents in our thinking and activities. Now we need to look more closely at the final five commandments, which provide basic guidelines for community life (Exodus 20.13–17; Deuteronomy 5.17–21).

You shall not kill (Exodus 20.13; Deuteronomy 5.17)

Respect for human life is central to Old Testament morality. This springs from the knowledge that human life is a gift from God, and should never be carelessly or violently destroyed. The later codes of law distinguish killing which is blameworthy from killing which is accidental (as in Exodus 21.12–14), or is a just punishment for evil

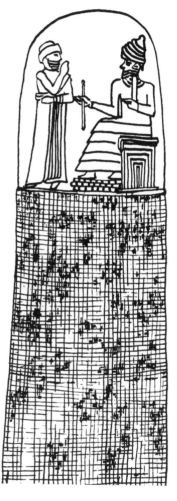

Figure 10. 'The purpose of all the law-giving, preaching and teaching recorded in the Old Testament was to help people understand what God wanted them to do, and how best they might serve him' (p. 140).

In the eighteenth century BC Hammurabi, king of Babylon, had this stele or pillar set up in his kingdom. The carving at the top shows the sun god, Shamash, giving Hammurabi a sceptre and ring, the symbols of authority. The inscription below gives laws for the guidance of community life (but it does not say that these were revealed by Shamash).

There are similarities between the code of Hammurabi and the law codes of the Old Testament, but also many differences. There is no evidence that Moses and the later law-givers borrowed ideas directly from Hammurabi's code, and it is doubtful whether all the peoples ruled by Hammurabi adopted his code as a guide for daily life. Here is a passage from Hammurabi's code:

'If a citizen has destroyed the eye of one of citizen status, they shall destroy his eye. If he has broken the bone of a citizen, his bone shall they break. If he has destroyed the eye, or has broken the bone, of a vassal, he shall pay one mina of silver.'

What similarities and what differences do you notice between this passage and the laws recorded in Exodus 21.2–35; Leviticus 24.17–20, and Deuteronomy 19.21?

(as in Exodus 21.15–17). God offers every human the opportunity of responding to him and sharing in his purposes. Since the Old Testament writers lacked belief in an afterlife, they believed that death prevented a human sharing in these blessings. Anyone who deliberately robbed another person of the opportunity to serve God, by killing them, themselves deserved death. Anybody who deliberately and openly defied God, or acted against his purposes, equally deserved death.

You shall not commit adultery (Exodus 20.14; Deuteronomy 5.18)

According to the stories of creation, sexuality is a gift from God, and normal relations between a man and his wife are something that God encouraged and approved. God had said 'Be fruitful and multiply' (Genesis 1.28, and compare Genesis 2.24). The later law codes condemn serious misuses of sex, for example, sexual relations outside marriage (Exodus 22.16), prostitution (Leviticus 19.29), homosexual relations (Leviticus 18.22), and, most especially, adultery. The codes made a distinction between a man committing adultery with a woman married to another man, and a woman sharing sex with a man married to another woman. The penalty for the first was death (Leviticus 20.10), but the penalty for the second was marriage (Deuteronomy 22.28–29)! These were logical rulings based on the fact that men were allowed to be polygamists. They also discouraged the break up of an existing marriage through a wife sharing sex outside her proper relationship with her husband. All these bans on sexual activities were necessary to avoid people creating relationships contrary to God's will, because the compilers of these laws believed such actions caused great misery and destroyed trust.

The law codes never condemned polygamy, and treated the possession of concubines as acceptable behaviour. Both could result in fairly permanent relationships, and children born from them would be well cared for. Yet towards the end of the Old Testament times the Israelites very rarely practised these two customs. Probably they came to consider them less than the best kinds of relationship, but even the latest of the law-givers failed to condemn them. This was probably because so many of the leading Israelites of earlier times had followed these customs, and the Jews were unable to accept any criticism of their forefathers.

Israelite law only permitted divorce when it considered the marriage relationship improper, for example, because the woman failed to maintain her virginity until the time of marriage (Deuteronomy 22.13–21) or because a man had married a foreigner (Deuteronomy 7.3; Ezra 10.10, 11).

Several of the prophets accused the Israelites of committing adultery by deserting the LORD in order to serve false gods (for example,

Hosea 2.7; Jeremiah 3.9; Ezekiel 16.30–34). They expressed great horror at what God's people had done, and thus showed how highly they valued the marriage relationship. They felt that they were right to compare the relationship between God and his people with that between a man and his wife.

You shall not steal (Exodus 20.15; Deuteronomy 5.19)

God's purpose is that all people should have sufficient of the good things of this world to enable them to live productive and healthy lives. When a person steals, they are usually trying to gain more than their fair share of these goods, by depriving somebody else of their share. This is made clear by the wide range of behaviour which the later law codes condemned as being forms of theft. These include dishonesty in trade (Leviticus 19.35, 36), in employment (Leviticus 19.13), in the exercise of a trust (Exodus 22.7–9), and in control of property (Deuteronomy 19.14; the word 'landmark' means a boundary stone, marking the edge of somebody's property).

The wrong done by misusing or destroying property belonging to somebody else, for example by trespass or arson, is another closely related idea (Exodus 22.5, 6). Anyone who breaks these laws fails to gain anything, but robs another of their possessions.

We may wonder what was meant by the ban on charging interest on a loan (Leviticus 25.35–38). We should avoid the mistake of thinking that this applies to ordinary commerce, where those who provide money for a business should share in the profits it makes. The law does apply to money-lenders who take advantage of people who are reduced to poverty and need financial or other help for a time until they can earn enough to pay for what they need and return the loan.

You shall not bear false witness against your neighbour (Exodus 20.16; Deuteronomy 5.20)

God's purpose is that every person should have a place in human society and good relations with their neighbours. Good relations are destroyed when one person tells lies about another, so the law condemns lies spread through conversation: this is slander (Leviticus 19.16). The law also condemns lies told by a witness in a law court: this is perjury (Exodus 23.1–3, 6–89). Nobody should lie for the sake of a bribe, but neither should they lie to protect somebody who is poor. Such lies will prevent justice being done, and others will suffer injustice because the truth is distorted.

Notice that the commandment to 'love your neighbour as yourself' comes in a passage which condemns false witness (Leviticus 19.15–18). People should treat one another fairly, because this is the only way that a healthy human community can be established. Desiring revenge or bearing a grudge are as bad as actually spreading lies. All these attitudes are the opposite of love and will help to destroy human relationships.

'You shall not covet . . . anything that is your neighbour's' (Exodus 20.17; Deuteronomy 5.21)

This commandment is close in meaning to the eighth commandment: *You shall not steal*. To *covet* means to have a strong desire to possess something belonging to another person (Deuteronomy 7.25). To *steal* means to secretly take for your own use something which belongs to someone else (Micah 2.2). Even when a person restrains their covetousness, so that they avoid actually stealing something, their desire to possess it can have a strong effect on their relationships with other people. Covetousness can destroy friendships because the wrongdoer is unhappy about the blessings received by their companions. This behaviour is wrong in the sight of God because it can destroys human relationships which are part of God's purpose in creation (Proverbs 21.26).

Sometimes people suggest that the tenth commandment is more important than the others we have studied here, because it is about feelings and intentions, while the other four are about outward actions. But all such actions result from feelings and intentions, and inward attitudes become important when they disturb human relationships. Sin is about both feelings and intentions, and the resulting actions are contrary to the purposes of God. Paul suggests that knowledge of God's purposes as revealed by the Law prompts people to further sin (Romans 7.7–12). Human beings have an unpleasant urge to be rebellious against authority, which drives us to act deliberately against the will of God, just as children are prompted to disobey their parents' instructions simply because they know they *are* orders.

The Image of God

According to Genesis 1.27, humans were created in the image of God. We have seen that this probably means something different from God and people sharing a physical likeness (pages 75, 77). Probably this phrase means that we share the fact that we are spiritual beings capable of fellowship. The finest qualities possible in human life are a reflection of the character of God himself. If, as we have seen, God is holy, faithful and shows steadfast love, then those who serve him are capable of showing the same characteristics in their relationships with other humans.

Human holiness

Holiness is probably the most difficult quality to achieve in human life. Yet God chose the people of Israel to be his *holy* nation (Exodus 19.6; Deuteronomy 7.6). They were urged 'to be holy, for I am holy'

(Leviticus 11.44, 45; 19.2). The prophets whose work is recorded in the book of Isaiah looked forward to a time when people would be holy (Isaiah 4.3; 62.12). Perhaps Leviticus 20.26 gives the best explanation of what the Old Testament means by human holiness: 'You shall be holy to me; for I the LORD am holy, and have separated you from the peoples, that you should be mine.'

We have already seen that the word 'holy' describes something separate, different, or even strange (see page 28). Those who have responded to God and are trying to live according to his purposes must be very different from those who have refused to accept his call. They will at times seem strange when judged by the standards of those who lack knowledge of the LORD. But just as God makes himself known to sinful people, so his holy people must be readily seen and known among those who lack faith, so that they may receive blessing by becoming aware of their true nature, that they are created to be children of God. This is what is meant by the statement that the faithful in Israel are to be priests representing God among the nations (Isaiah 61.6; Exodus 19.6). Others see and know that we care for all who are in trouble or need, and we must care so much that others come to know God's love through our service. We must, like God and under his guidance, work for the salvation of all humankind.

Human faithfulness

God's faithfulness is seen in the fact that he always acts according to his purposes. He is completely reliable in his purposes of steadfast love. Those who put their faith in the LORD will be equally reliable in their relationships with other people. They will always be concerned for the good of their neighbours, since they have agreed to follow the lead given by God in his relationships with all humans.

Human faithfulness shows itself in a concern for *justice* and *righteousness*. Both these words are often used to translate a single Hebrew word which covers both meanings. We can best distinguish between them by saying that *justice* is the quality of the actions done by good humans in their relationships with others, while *righteousness* is the quality of heart which makes such actions possible. See especially Amos 6.12, where 'justice' is placed in parallel with 'the fruit of righteousness'. The two ideas are set directly in parallel in Isaiah 28.17 and Amos 5.24.

The prophets repeatedly complained that justice was missing or corrupted in the life of the Israelite communities (Habakkuk 1.4). 'Justice is turned back' (Isaiah 59.14; compare Isaiah 10.2). The prophets urged people to avoid putting their trust in each other because nobody could be trusted (Micah 7.2–6; Jeremiah 9.4–6).

In contrast to this, righteous people serve God (Malachi 3.18), walk in his way (Hosea 14.9), and do what is lawful (Ezekiel 18.5–9).

The thoughts of such people are just (Proverbs 12.5), and others can trust their words (Psalm 37.30; Proverbs 10.11, 21). They know the rights of the poor (Proverbs 29.7), and are generous (Psalm 37.21; Proverbs 21.26). A community that is led by the righteous is a happy one (Proverbs 29.2).

Human steadfast love

The Hebrew word which translates as *steadfast love* when it describes a quality of God, also quite often in the Old Testament describes human relationships. But the scholars who prepared the RSV have almost always avoided using the same English translation in these cases. Probably they felt that steadfast love was so specially a quality of God that they had to avoid using the same phrase to describe human behaviour. Instead, they used the English words 'loyalty' and 'kindness'. In many passages in the RSV Old Testament these two words describe ordinary good human relationships. Abraham, Jonathan, Abner and David all speak about human *loyalty* (Genesis 21.23; 1 Samuel 20.15; 2 Samuel 3.8; 10.2). Abraham, Joseph and Rahab all asked for their neighbours to show them kindness (Genesis 20.13; 40.14; Joshua 2.12).

As the people of Old Testament times began to recognize God's steadfast love, they described it by using the best word that they had available. But their experience of God's steadfast love enriched the meaning of the Hebrew word. The scholars who prepared the RSV were right to want to make a distinction between the word as it applied to God and the word normally understood in human relationships.

But when the prophets came to appreciate the steadfast love of God, they began to teach that God required the same quality in relationships between human beings. So Micah told his hearers that God requires *kindness* from his people (Micah 6.8; compare Zechariah 7.9). The Wisdom writers took up the same idea. 'He who withholds kindness from a friend forsakes the fear of the Almighty' (Job 6.14). The word 'loyalty' in Proverbs came to have the same depth of meaning, and the the RSV translators could equally well have translated it as *steadfast love* (Proverbs 3.3; 16.6; 20.28).

📖 Check Your Understanding 22

1 This chapter has been about 'relationships'. Which one of the following words could you use instead of that word to express best the use which we have made of it here? Which one of the words would be totally unusable?

ALLIANCE   ANTAGONISM   ASSOCIATION

CONNECTION   FRIENDSHIP

2 (a) Explain the difference between each of the following ways of dying:

ABORTION   EUTHANASIA   EXECUTION

MANSLAUGHTER   MURDER

   (b) Which one of these ways of dying do people recognize as unintentional, and treat the person who performs the action with understanding?

   (c) Which, if any, of these do the laws of your country regard as legitimate behaviour? Should Christians accept these government rules as soundly based in reason and experience?

📖 Study Suggestions

FOR GROUP DISCUSSION

1 Some of the prophets believed that the people who would truly serve God would be small in number. In New Testament times the number of Christians in each place was very small.

   (a) Do you live in a country in which Christians are a tiny minority, or in one in which the great majority of people are Christians? Which situation do you think best encourages people to think deeply about their faith?

   (b) Do some groups of Christians in your country claim to be the only people who truly serve God? If so, why do you think they do so? Does your congregation believe they have this unique authority?

2 'You shall not make idols to worship'. Do pictures have an important place in the churches of your country? If they do, in what ways are they helpful in worship, and in what way can they be a hindrance? If the churches of your country ban them, why do they do this?

3 'You shall not take vengeance or bear any grudge against the sons of your own people, but you shall love your neighbour as yourself: I am the LORD'. Does this verse from Leviticus

19.18 mean that we should avoid quarrels with strangers, but truly love our own people? If so, is it in keeping with the teachings of Jesus, and the ways of righteousness? And how would you explain the existence of such a commandment in the Old Testament?

FOR ESSAY WRITING

4 'God's purpose has always been to create a community of men and women who would serve him gladly and live in peace and harmony with each other' (page 133). Give an example of this activity of God from each of the following sources: (a) The Old Testament, (b) the New Testament, (c) the Churches today.

5 'Whenever God called someone to serve him, he did so in order that that person could have an influence within the community in which they lived' (page 139). What sort of influence did God want each of the following people to exert in Israel? (a) Elijah; (b) Jeremiah; (c) Nehemiah.

6 In what ways can human holiness be similar to God's holiness, and in what ways is it impossible for us to be wholly Godlike?

WORK WITH THE BIBLE AND A CONCORDANCE

7 Job declared that he had lived righteously (see Job 29.12–17).
   (a) Does Job's idea of righteous behaviour agree with what the book of Deuteronomy says?
   (b) For each claim that Job made about having served others, suggest a verse or passage from Deuteronomy that confirms his understanding of what is righteous. (For the help he gave the poor, you could quote Deuteronomy 15.7.)

8 Study all the verses in the Torah which refer to the Sabbath. Make a list of all the different ways in which lawgivers believed its observance is helpful. Set against each of these ways all the biblical references in which the writer recognizes its importance.

   How far does the Christian observance of Sunday in your country involve the acceptance of these same purposes?

9 We have met the word 'fellowship' many times during these studies, and 'communion' as an alternative. Yet, in the RSV Bible, the word 'fellowship' only occurs once in the Old Testament (Psalm 55.14), and 'communion' fails to have a place at all. Yet there are ways of expressing the ideas that these words convey for us today. Examine the following words in

your concordance, with and without their suffixes, and see which ones occur most frequently. Do they truly express what we mean by the words we have used?

BROTHER(HOOD)   CLAN(SMANSHIP)

COMPANION(SHIP)

COMRADE(SHIP)   KIN(SHIP)   TOGETHER(NESS)

The Ultimate Goal

9

O let the evil of the wicked come to an end,
but establish thou the righteous,
Thou who triest the minds and hearts,
thou righteous God.

(Psalm 7.9)

The Hope of the Righteous

The Psalmists often remarked on the fact that the righteous live among the wicked. Some of the psalms are a cry for defence against the wicked (for example, Psalms 10.1, 2; 17.8, 9). Some call on God to judge and punish the wicked (for example, Psalms 10.15; 28.4). The Psalmists often expressed their confidence that God would deal with people according to their deeds: blessing the righteous, and punishing the wicked (for example, Psalms 32.10; 34.21, 22). Here then is plenty of evidence that the Jews believed that God's plans for his people had yet to reach fulfilment. Some people had turned to God. They had accepted him as LORD and were glad of their fellowship with him. These were the righteous. Often they suffered at the hands of the wicked, who refused to serve the LORD. The righteous eagerly looked forward to a future in which God's rule would be recognized and accepted in all the earth (Psalms 57.5; 59.13).

For the time being, however, the righteous must live in *hope*, waiting for the day when God will fulfil all his purposes. We must, however, notice that the Old Testament idea of hope is very different from the idea of hope in the New Testament and in Christian doctrine. The difference is that the Jews lacked any clear idea of a good life after death, and any expectation that God's purposes would be fulfilled in a different world from this earthly and physical creation. This was the reason for their great emphasis on personal salvation and the deliverance of the individual from the troubles of this life. The Hebrew word for *hope* is almost always used to express this type of hope (Psalm 71.5; Proverbs 10.28; Job 4.6). Our hope goes far beyond this to belief in an eternal future under God's rule caring for us all.

Some Old Testament writers do suggest that there will eventually be some final change when the wicked will be excluded and the righteous will prosper. These writers realized that their present life was unsatisfactory, and could never be fully satisfying while the wicked continue to harm the righteous (Psalm 9.18; Jeremiah 31.16–17). But they failed to explain how the righteous who suffered and perhaps died in their own time could share the joys of those future times. The book of Job emphasizes that the righteous individual who suffers hardship in this world has little hope for the future (Job 7.6; 14.7–10, 19; 17.15). In the epilogue, Job's salvation consists in a return to health and prosperity in this world in his earthly lifetime. The writer was unable to provide a guarantee that Job would possess such blessings for ever.

Yet in the Old Testament hope always goes beyond what people can expect or explain. They were so fully convinced that God is faithful and righteous that they found their hope in him (Psalm 62.1, 2; Job 5.8–16). Again and again the Old Testament provides descriptions of what life would be like one day, when God fulfilled all his purposes. We must take a closer look at the nature of these hopes, asking ourselves, 'What did people expect?' and, 'How would these things happen?'.

Prophetic and Apocalyptic Expectations

Many scholars draw our attention to two forms of hope expressed by the Old Testament writers: the prophetic hope and the apocalyptic hope. The former is closely related to coming events in the history of Israel, when God's purposes would be achieved through the activities of individuals and nations. The latter is based on the belief that God will intervene in history and bring evil to an end by some dramatic action, and establish his rule of righteousness.

We can see the contrast between the two by comparing the writings of Deutero-Isaiah with the second part of the book of Daniel. In the former the coming of Cyrus of Persia would bring in the new day of God's glory (Isaiah 45.1–7), while in the latter the writer sees history as an earthly echo of events in heaven (Daniel 7.1–14). But the contrast between the two types of hope is less than some scholars suggest, for on the one hand we see that God (Isaiah 45.1) has acted in raising up Cyrus, and on the other we notice that 'the saints of the Most High' (Daniel 7.18) are the ones who are represented by the 'one like a son of man' (Daniel 7.14). Both the prophetic and the apocalyptic writings recognize that hope for the future lies in the hands of God, and that he works his purposes out through and for his people.

We should notice a difference of emphasis and a difference in the way the message is presented, but both sorts of writings share the same basic ideas. This explains the difficulty which scholars face in trying to decide how much apocalyptic writing there is in the books of the Old Testament. Some scholars assert that the visions recorded in Daniel are the only true apocalyptic writing in the Old Testament. They believe that the real origin of the apocalyptic kind of writings is in the literature produced in the period between the Old Testament and the New Testament. We can see this literature in the Apocrypha/Deutero-Canonical books in the Common Bible version of the RSV, and also in part in the Apocrypha in some other English translations. Many scholars accept that Isaiah 24—27, Zechariah 9—14 and Daniel 7—12 are apocalyptic writings. Some scholars see many more such passages in the prophetic books of the Old Testament. We should notice that apart from Daniel, all the apocalyptic passages appear in the prophetic books. If there had been a real conflict between the messages of the two sorts of writing, we would have difficulties in seeing how the apocalyptic passages became part of the contrasting prophetic books.

Even the literary styles of the two kinds are less distinctive than some scholars suggest. Let me quote some words from my *History of Israel* concerning apocalyptic writers: They 'usually recorded their teachings in the form of dreams and visions, which they attributed to important men of past ages. They used these famous names to make the Jews take note of what was written. The names of the authors of these books themselves are mostly unknown.'

We can find all these characteristics of apocalyptic writings in one place or another among the passages which scholars accept as prophetic. The books of Amos, Jeremiah, and especially Ezekiel contain dreams and visions. The book of Jonah is a story which has little to do with the actual life of the man called Jonah, just as the book of Daniel is a story which has little to do with the actual life of the man called Daniel. The books of Obadiah and Malachi are probably anonymous. Their titles simply mean 'Servant of the LORD', and 'My Messenger', respectively.

Thus there seems to be plenty of evidence to suggest that the apocalyptic writings were a natural development from the earlier prophetic writings, and that there is a clear relation between the ideas of both concerning hope for the future. This is what we would expect if we accept the belief that God was leading his people stage by stage to a deeper understanding of his purposes. In the second half of this chapter we shall examine the content of Old Testament hope, and how this was to be achieved. We shall see again the close connection between the prophetic and apocalyptic hopes.

> 📖 **Check Your Understanding 23**
>
> 1 The title of this chapter is 'The Ultimate Goal'. Which of the following definitions best explains the word 'goal' in that heading?
>   (a) A score, as in the game of football,
>   (b) The fulfilment and establishment of all that is good.
>   (c) The end of the Israelites' journey in the wilderness.
> 2 All the following words have some connection with the idea of *hope* as people use this word in the English language. Which three of them are *least* useful in explaining the biblical idea of hope?
>
> CONFIDENCE   DESIRE   DREAM
EXPECTATION   OPTIMISM   TRUST

What Did the Israelites Expect?

The Transformation of the Present World

The Jews were realists: they were fully aware of the discomforts and distresses which are part of life in this world. But they expected changes in the future which would remove these sorrows. They looked forward to a time when people would find freedom from them, and would be able to live complete and wholesome lives. Then, as now, droughts, blight and other troubles hindered successful farming and led to hunger. The prophets refused to believe that God intended the righteous to suffer in this way; so they looked forward to a time of rich harvests and plenty of food (Amos 9.13–15; Joel 3.18; Ezekiel 47.12). Trade with foreign countries would bring prosperity, and poverty would disappear from Israel (Isaiah 45.14; 60.11). Troublesome wild animals would be tamed (Isaiah 11.6–8; Hosea 2.18), or driven away (Isaiah 35.9; Ezekiel 34.25; Leviticus 26.6). Ill health and crippling disabilities would be cured (Isaiah 29.18; 35.5, 6). Because people regarded death as a disaster, some writers promised long life in the new age (Isaiah 65.20; Zechariah 8.4), and one even believed that death itself would be destroyed (Isaiah 25.8). All this would be the work of God, 'For behold, I create new heavens, and a new earth . . .' (Isaiah 65.17).

Zion Would Become the Centre of a New Community

The people of Old Testament times came to believe that Zion, another name for Jerusalem, was to be the centre of a new community ruled by God in harmony and understanding, bringing peace to the whole world. We need to see how this belief developed.

Jerusalem remained outside Israelite control until the time of David. An ancient tradition existed that one of the early rulers of the city, Melchizedek, had been 'priest of God Most High' and that he had blessed Abraham (Genesis 14.18–20). But until the time of David the Jebusites lived in Jerusalem as one of the enemies of Israel (Joshua 10.1–5; Judges 1.21). David captured Jerusalem with the help of his own private army (2 Samuel 5.6–10), and it remained his property: the city of David (2 Kings 16.20; 2 Chronicles 32.30). David made full use of the independence of this city, when he made it the capital of Israel and Judah (2 Samuel 5.6–10). None of the tribes involved in his kingdom were able to claim that the city had been their property and that they should have special privileges as a result. He brought the Ark of the Covenant, which contained the stones of the Ten Commandments, to his city (2 Samuel 6.1–2). Craftsmen created golden models of Cherubim, as winged creatures, and set them on the lid of the Ark, creating the mercy seat (Exodus 25.17–22). The Israelites believed that God ruled them by instructing their leaders from above the Ark (2 Samuel 6.2). So Jerusalem became the centre of God's rule. The prophet Nathan told David not to build a temple to house the Ark, and during his reign the Israelites housed it in a tent (2 Samuel 7.5–6). When Solomon built the temple, it became the centre of worship for all his people. When the Babylonians destroyed the temple and took many of the people into exile, a sense of despair filled the hearts of the exiles. They felt unable to worship God adequately in exile (Psalm 137.1–6). As time went by the people born in exile felt a grudge against their ancestors who, they believed, had been responsible for the Exile (Jeremiah 31.29–30; Ezekiel 18.2). But the prophets Ezekiel and Deutero-Isaiah taught the people to look forward to a time when they could return to Jerusalem. The prophet responsible for Deutero-Isaiah rightly believed that Cyrus of Babylon would allow the people to return to Jerusalem, and to worship God there (Isaiah 45.1, 2; compare Ezra 1.1–4). Ezekiel promised that God would be present in the city (Ezekiel 43.1–9), and they would be able to build a new temple and worship him there for ever (Ezekiel 37.26). Judah and Israel would be reunited (Isaiah 11.12, 13; Jeremiah 3.18), and the people would have many children to repopulate the land (Jeremiah 30.18, 19). There are two separate records of one early prophecy which had promised that other nations too would learn to serve the LORD in Jerusalem (Isaiah 2.24; Micah 4.1–3), and this would bring world peace. So Zionism developed among the Jews: the belief that God had a special purpose for Jerusalem in all his work for the salvation of humans. Some Christians today believe that God will yet establish his rule in Zion, the fulfilment of God's purposes for the present Jerusalem, and many Jews look forward to such a time. But the existing State of Israel has failed to provide an adequate fulfilment of Jewish beliefs, and many look for a heavenly Jerusalem.

This is, of course, comparable to New Testament teaching about the New Jerusalem as both part of current Christian experience and vision (Hebrews 12.22–24), and future blessing awaiting fulfilment (Revelation 3.12; 21.2, 10).

How Would God Fulfil this Expectation?

The two ideas which together sum up the Old Testament revelation of how God would achieve his purposes are

- the Day of the LORD, and
- the One who will come.

The Day of the LORD

We noticed the importance of this idea when we were thinking about God's judgement on sinful humans (see page 102). The prophets rejected the idea, which was common among the Israelites, that it would be a day when God's people would be given glorious victories over their enemies. They were sinful people, and they would face judgement and punishment for what they had done. Yet through God's activity on the final great Day he would act in a new way to establish his rule over his people.

God's activity of judgement would make people recognize that all power, authority and glory belong to him. We can find this idea in the earliest prophetic books (see Isaiah 2.10, 19; Amos 8.9, 10; Hosea 2.18–20; Micah 4.6, 7). Look up the word 'know' in a concordance, and you will see that Ezekiel repeated again and again that on that day 'they shall know that I am the LORD'. The people of Israel would know it (Ezekiel 39.22), and so would all other nations (Ezekiel 39.7, 8). Zephaniah took up the idea (Zephaniah 3.9), also Deutero-Isaiah (Isaiah 52.6), and Joel looked forward to the time when the people of Israel 'shall know that I am the LORD your God' (Joel 3.17).

The apocalyptic chapters of the book of Isaiah make full use of the idea (for example, Isaiah 24.14–15; 25.9), and the book of Daniel includes a vision of the reign of 'one that was ancient of days', served by a thousand thousand, and with ten thousand times ten thousand standing before him (Daniel 7.9, 10).

Many of the books we have just quoted describe the Day more fully: the glory of the LORD will be revealed (Isaiah 40.5; compare Isaiah 28.5; Habakkuk 2.14); he will reign in Zion (Isaiah 24.23; 52.7; Micah 4.6–7); his majesty will be known among humans (Isaiah 2.10; 24.14): he shall be exalted (Isaiah 2.11; 30.18); people will sing his praises (Isaiah 12.5; 24.14; Zechariah 2.10; Joel 2.26); 'Out of Zion shall go forth the law, and the word of the LORD from Jerusalem.

He shall judge between the nations and shall decide for many peoples' (Isaiah 2.3, 4); and in the Day 'all who call upon the name of the LORD shall be delivered' (Joel 2.32).

The One Who Will Come

Many passages in the Old Testament illustrate the way people make use of their past experiences of God in order to understand what he will do in the future. They were well aware that God had achieved his purposes in the past by calling people to do his will, and by leading the people of Israel back into his service. So they came to expect that God would send other leaders in the future who would teach them to do God's will, and that God would achieve his purposes for his people through these leaders.

Expected Leaders

A new prophet

The people who prepared the book of Deuteronomy believed that Moses had been a great prophet, speaking to the people in God's name. They expected that God would send other prophets to lead his people (Deuteronomy 18.15–19). They knew from experience that there had been false prophets teaching lies, and they described how readers could distinguish these from those who were sent by God (Deuteronomy 18.20–22). But they knew that none of the prophets had served God as faithfully and effectively as Moses had done (Deuteronomy 34.10). The other prophets who would come would have the example of Moses to follow.

The later writers regarded Elijah as one of the greatest of the prophets who followed Moses, probably because of his bold stand against all that was involved in the worship of the Baalim, the fertility gods worshipped by other peoples in South West Asia. The writers expressed his greatness through the belief that he escaped Sheol and entered heaven (2 Kings 2.11). The prophet Malachi looked back to Elijah, and believed that God would send him again to act as herald at the coming of 'the great and terrible day of the LORD' (Malachi 4.5, 6).

A new king

Many of the Old Testament writers looked back to the time of David and remembered his great triumph over Israel's enemies. They remembered the covenant God had made with David, and they looked forward to a time when a descendant of David would rule in Israel with similar authority and justice. They believed that what God had done once through David, he could do again through the One who would come.

Figure 11. Elijah's greatness was expressed through the belief that he 'escaped Sheol and entered heaven' (p. 156). Even the Egyptians, who believed in life after death for their Pharaohs and other royal leaders, feared that they might miss this blessing if not properly prepared for it. This picture from the tomb of Tutankhamun shows his successor performing the ritual of 'opening the mouth' so that the dead Pharaoh could receive a new body in the other world and establish communion between the living and the dead.

In the meantime, lesser men descended from David would rule over God's people. When evil men gained power as rulers of Judah, the prophets found comfort in looking forward to the time when a righteous ruler would restore justice and peace. The prophet Isaiah spoke of one who would come when Ahaz had been defeated by the Assyrians (Isaiah 7.10–17). The same prophet was probably author of the prophecies about a new king in Israel, which we read in Isaiah 9.6, 7 and 11.1–5. Notice especially the word 'branch' in Isaiah 11.1, because this became an important way of expressing the hope for a new king. Micah made use of similar ideas in writing about the one who would come from Bethlehem, David's home town (Micah 5.2–4).

Jeremiah, who frequently preached about God's judgement on Israel, looked forward to the coming of a new king of the family of David, who would rule in justice and righteousness (Jeremiah 23.5, 6). Ezekiel wrote several times about the one whom God would set in authority over his people (Ezekiel 17.22; 34.23, 24; 37.22, 24). The prophets who worked in Jerusalem soon after the return from exile looked for the righteous ruler of the house of David that the prophets before them had promised so often. Haggai makes a direct reference to Zerubbabel being God's chosen ruler who would rule after the defeat of the major countries of their time (Haggai 2.20–23). The prophet Zechariah was only responsible for the first nine chapters of the book which goes by his name. He at first pointed to two men as those chosen by God: Joshua, a priest, as religious leader (Zechariah 3.1–7) and Zerubbabel as 'the Branch', descendant of King David, God's chosen ruler (Zechariah 3.8–4.10). But something happened to prevent Zerubbabel fulfilling his calling, which led Zechariah to name Joshua as the Branch (Zechariah 6.9–14). The Bible says nothing about the reason for this change. But it probably led to the priests gaining greater authority as leaders of the people in national and political matters as well as their original religious responsibilities.

Nehemiah and Ezra came in turn to rebuild the city walls and to introduce the Torah as the basis for Jewish community life, but nobody regarded these actions as bringing the final fulfilment of God's purposes. Life went on but the promised blessings did not come. The Greeks gained power over many nations eastward of their own land as far as the River Indus, and southward to include Egypt. The Jews were subject to foreign rule like the other peoples known to them. In that period of Jewish history apocalyptic played an important part. Zechariah 9—13 probably belongs to this time. Like all such writings, scholars find great difficulty in knowing how to interpret the various parts of these chapters. They are unable to reach a general agreement as to their significance.

The best known verses are Zechariah 9.9–10, which Jesus chose to enact on Palm Sunday, as Matthew and John recognized in writing their accounts (Matthew 21.5; John 12.15). Clearly the crowds recognized that Jesus was God's chosen leader, since they welcomed him into the city with shouts of 'Blessed be he who comes in the name of the Lord'. The significance of the donkey is clearly that Jesus came to establish peace and, rather than to destroy his enemies, to bring forgiveness and mercy rather than judgement. Jesus also used words from these chapters of Zechariah, when warning his disciples in the garden of Gethsemane of what was to happen: 'I will strike the shepherd and the sheep of the flock will be scattered' (Zechariah 13.7; as quoted in Matthew 26.31; compare Mark 14.27). By the time of Jesus the Jews shared a great hope that the Messiah who was coming would attack and destroy the forces of Rome and establish his own rule over the world, based in Jerusalem. Jesus truly fulfilled the purposes of God in establishing his kingdom on earth, but was reluctant to let the word 'Messiah' be used about himself, because of the disastrously widespread mistaken idea about what the One who was to come would achieve.

Two other books of the Old Testament belong to the time of the Greek Empire: Daniel and Malachi. In Daniel the most significant section is chapter 7, which provides us with a vision of things happening in heaven. Here the writer compares the nations which had ruled over large empires to wild animals, and contrasts them with the new rule that was to be established under one 'like a son of man' (Daniel 7.13). The heavenly court is in session, and the Son of Man is given rule over all nations eternally, never to pass away and never to be destroyed. Jesus seemed to prefer to be called the Son of Man, perhaps because it was open to various meanings, being a phrase commonly used simply to speak of a human, but used here in Daniel to speak of the one who was to rule eternally. This made it necessary for people to judge for themselves which role Jesus was claiming for himself.

As we have seen, Malachi introduced the idea that Elijah would come again to prepare the way for God's rule on earth, which would be fulfilled in the coming of the LORD himself (Malachi 3.1–2; 4.5). In the Gospels we can see that people debated the meaning of this prophecy, and some thought that John the Baptist was the one described as Elijah. But John the Baptist denied it (John 1.21), and Jesus gives a strange answer: 'If you are willing to accept it, he is Elijah who is to come' (Matthew 11.14). He seems to be saying, 'If you find it helpful to think in these terms, then that is all right'. He emphasizes this by saying, 'He who has ears to hear, let him hear' (Matthew 11.15). Our understanding of any new idea depends on our ability to relate it to our previous knowledge and experience. People who really understood Malachi's prophecy could be sure that they understood the role of John the Baptist. Matthew gives a further account of what Jesus said about Elijah in his discussion with his disciples (Matthew 17.10–13). He told them, 'Elijah does come, and he is to restore all things; but I tell you that Elijah has already come, and they did not know him.' The first half of this sentence speaks of a future time when the purposes of God will be reaching their fulfilment. The second half clearly accepts the idea that John the Baptist prepared the way for the coming of Jesus, and adds the warning that just as John had suffered at the hands of Herod, so Jesus himself would suffer. Clearly this failed to lead immediately to the final fulfilment of God's purpose, yet the suffering of Jesus was a vitally important part of the way God was preparing for the final fulfilment which is yet to come.

One final point worth noticing is that the translators of the Old Testament never use the word 'Messiah' to describe the One who was to come. This is simply because the original meaning of the word was *anointed*, and this was thoroughly suitable to interpret the word wherever it was used by Old Testament writers. Only in the New Testament does the word 'Messiah' appear in the RSV, because this had become a widespread term for the One that the people of Jesus' time believed was due to come to release them from foreign rule and to establish God's rule on earth. The title 'Christ' is simply based on the Greek word for 'the anointed'.

A Righteous Group

Some Old Testament writers hoped for the creation of a new community, rather than the coming of a righteous community. There was never a time in the history of Israel when a particular group had provided an example of a perfect society that later writers could use to suggest this future possibility. But the fact remained that God had always worked through human communities, for example the families of the Patriarchs, the tribes in the time of Moses, the faithful remnant in the time of the kings. Even when God's judgement brought defeat and destruction to his people, a few survivors were always left who continued to serve the LORD. So hope for the future was often built around the idea of a community serving the LORD.

We have already seen that we can best understand 'the Servant' described by Deutero-Isaiah as representing the faithful in Israel who were to be an example to the nation and to other peoples of how they should serve God (see page 125). The sufferings of these righteous ones, as they shared in the experiences of the whole of God's people, could serve to bring salvation to the unfaithful by helping them to understand God's purposes and his grace.

This same idea of a righteous community serving the LORD probably underlies the vision of the 'Son of Man' in Daniel 7.13–14. In the earlier part of the chapter the writer uses wild beasts to represent the various kingdoms of the world, and the Son of Man was coming to rule in their place. He used the contrast between the individual beasts and the individual Son of Man to distinguish the new kingdom as founded on justice and peace, in contrast to the disorder and violence of earlier kingdoms. So just as each beast stood for all who shared in the old kingdoms, the Son of Man stood for all those who would share in the kingdom that was to come. In Daniel 7.18 we can read that the new kingdom belonged to the 'saints of the Most High'. This is the community which the writer of Daniel believed would be ruled in God's name.

New Interpretations

As we have seen in part already, the passages we have been studying in this chapter came to be interpreted in new ways in the New Testament. This was inevitable, since Christ's coming into the world brought substantial fresh revelations of God's purposes for his people, and through them for all people. In this chapter we have primarily been concerned to understand the hopes of the Jewish people at the end of the Old Testament period, recognizing that God's work of revelation was still incomplete. Remembering this, we shall find it easier to understand why so many of the Jewish people failed to recognize that the coming of Jesus was itself the most important revelation ever toward the fulfilment of all that God had promised his people in Old Testament times. They had learnt to look forward to a new activity of God among his people, but they were unaware of how it would happen. They believed, and still believe, that God would in some way establish his rule over the whole human race in justice and righteousness. The incarnation of the Son of God was a mystery too deep for the most profound and faithful people to understand, except, as Paul said, 'in a mirror dimly . . . in part' (1 Corinthians 13.12). We will be able to understand this if we remember that we still lack any clear idea of the nature of Christ's Second Coming, and the final completion of all that God has planned from the beginning. What we do know is that our Lord will come with great power, but also with great mercy and love, for that is what was revealed by his death on the cross.

📖 Check Your Understanding 24

1 Which of the following definitions properly expresses the true nature of Zionism? It is the belief that . . .
   (a) . . . the Jews are destined to rule the world in God's name.
   (b) . . . God has a special place for Jerusalem in all his plans for the salvation of humankind.
   (c) . . . all people will learn to worship God in Jerusalem.

2 Which one of the following words best explains the meaning of the word 'kingdom' in the phrase 'the kingdom of God'?

COUNTRY   INHABITANTS   NATIONALITY
POPULATION   RULE   TERRITORY

📖 Study Suggestions

FOR GROUP DISCUSSION

1 What use should we make of the Old Testament idea of the transformation of the present world in our preaching and our faith?

2 What would you say to somebody who says 'God is unchanging. God is merciful. So we need not fear God's judgement, either at the end of our lives or at the end of this present world'?

3 How far is it helpful to try to understand Old Testament ideas in separation from their New Testament interpretation? Do Old Testament passages really have two meanings:
   (a) the meaning they had for the people who wrote and those who read them in Old Testament times, and
   (b) the meaning that Christians can see in them through the great light which shines on God's purposes because of the coming of Jesus?

If so, does this mean that Old Testament writers were unaware of the full significance of what they wrote?

FOR ESSAY WRITING

4 'Many passages in the Old Testament illustrate the way people make use of their past experiences of God in order to understand what he will do in the future' (page 156). Give two or three examples of how your own experiences have affected your beliefs about your future in this world or beyond.

5 What is the most important difference in ideas between prophetic and apocalyptic writings? What is the relationship

between the two sets of ideas? Give examples, and the reasons for your answers.

6 What ideas about the ultimate goal of all things are part of the traditional religion of your own people, or of those you have lived among for a long time? How do these ideas differ from the ideas of Old Testament writers? Which group of ideas provides the most helpful basis for the study of New Testament ideas among your people?

WORK WITH THE BIBLE AND A CONCORDANCE

7 Look closely at the references in the book of Psalms to the LORD's anointed. What type of office does the anointed hold? Do you think that in every example the same individual person is meant? Or are the references true for each person who holds the office?

8 What teachings about the future of Jerusalem do the prophecies of Isaiah 40—66 contain? Remember that 'Zion' is an alternative name for Jerusalem. Do you think these teachings were solely concerned with the immediate future, or are they also about the ultimate future?

9 The word 'exalted' means 'to be lifted up'. It can express the success of people, and contrasts with the failure of others. But if you look the word up in your concordance you will find that it often refers to God. So what does it mean for God to be exalted? What terms do the Old Testament writers use to describe his exaltation?

The Old Testament in the New Testament 10

In many and various ways God spoke of old to our fathers by the prophets; but in these last days he has spoken to us by a Son, whom he
appointed the heir of all things, through whom also he created the
world.

(Hebrews 1.1–2)

A Growing Plant

We can compare the Bible with a growing plant, such as a rose. The
Old Testament is like the root, stem, leaves and calyx. The New Testament is like the blossom, the crowning glory of the plant. The Holy
Spirit is like the sap running through the plant and bringing life to
every part of the flower.

Biblical theology is like botany. It is the study of the nature of the
Bible, just as botany is the study of the nature of the plant. Old Testament theology is like that part of botany which describes the part of
a plant's life that makes its flowering possible. It is an attempt to
describe the knowledge and understanding that came to people in
Old Testament times through God's unceasing work of revelation. It
shows what went before and supports the revelation of God in Christ
Jesus.

Some scholars who study the Old Testament attempt to describe
in detail each stage of its growth from the beginning with Abraham,
showing how understanding of God developed stage by stage. This is
like a botanist describing the development of a flower by starting
from its seed, and following every stage of the plant's development
till it is fully grown and ready to produce its blossom.

We studied the religious ideas and practices of Old Testament religion in this way in the first volume of this *Old Testament Introduction*.
The third section of each chapter of that book describes the religious
activities and customs of God's people as they developed, stage by
stage, throughout the history of Israel. But this was much easier to do
than it is to describe the development of Old Testament theology in
the same way. It is easier to recognize and record the outward forms
of religious practices than the inward realities of theological
thought.

Botanists can see a plant at each stage of its growth and describe its development as it takes place. They would find it more difficult to describe each stage of growth merely by looking at the full-grown plant, though some things would be obvious from the final form to which it developed. The Old Testament, as we know it, is at its final stage of growth, and we have to face similar problems in trying to describe how it grew.

We are unable to go back in time to see how the Old Testament developed, and can only draw our conclusions from the Old Testament in its present form. Even though there is a wide range of books in the Old Testament, recording the thoughts of writers of those times, we are unable to give a final, accurate account of when each was written, or which parts of each book are later additions, containing later ideas. Some things stand out clearly enough, but other things are obscure. Scholars publish their own findings and present their own theories, but even things which a majority of Old Testament scholars have agreed on in one decade can be upset in later decades by the work of other scholars, who gain widespread approval of scholars in their own time. The second volume of this *Old Testament Introduction* attempts to provide as clear a picture as possible of the origins of the various books. But I have indicated some of the uncertainties about their origins. I have also tried to isolate the thinking of the individual writers and editors in the Old Testament but other teachers may disagree, and present their own assessments of the beliefs of the writers.

But beyond this there is the more important need to recognize the full content of God's revelation of himself in the Old Testament, and this has been what I have attempted to provide in this volume. I have tried to present a helpful description of the theology of the Old Testament, and to show the most obvious evidence of development of thought over the centuries as we have dealt with each part of the subject.

In this chapter we could go on to describe the theology of the New Testament, just as a botanist would go on to describe the blossom and the part it plays in the life of the plant. But in order to do this we would need to study the history of the New Testament period and the origin and contents of the books of the New Testament. This would involve such far-ranging study that the chapter would become another book. So we steer clear of any attempt to study New Testament theology in this volume. But Margaret Baxter has provided two volumes for the International Study Guides as *New Testament Introduction: Jesus Christ: his Life and his Church* and *The Formation of the Christian Scriptures*. These help us to understand the basis for New Testament theology. More detailed studies of this subject, or of particular aspects of it, are available from other sources, just as there are other books on Old Testament theology and specific aspects of it.

As a preparation for such studies, the purpose of this chapter is to examine the connections between the Old Testament and the New Testament. This connection is just as important as that between a blossom and the plant on which it grew. A vase of cut flowers may look very beautiful, but the blossoms have ceased to grow and will never produce seeds leading to new life. If the New Testament is to be properly understood and appreciated it must never be cut off from the richness of its association with the Old Testament. God has been revealing his nature and purposes throughout history, and he still makes himself known to us through the whole record of his activities in Israel. If we separate the New Testament from the Old Testament, and study the revelation of God in Christ apart from the whole record of how God has made himself known to men and women, we hinder our understanding of God and the world, and of people and their destiny. What then are the living connections between the two parts of the Bible?

Direct Quotations

We face difficulties when we want to see how Old Testament ideas have affected the thinking of New Testament writers. Apart from Paul, they seldom provide a personal witness about how they became Christians and reached their understanding of God's purposes and God's activities. Since they were Christians the most important influence in all their thinking must have been Jesus Christ himself depending on what they knew about his life, his activities and his teachings. But there is plenty of evidence in the writings of the New Testament to show that they were only able to understand and appreciate the importance of Jesus Christ because they were already aware of all that God had revealed in Old Testament times. This evidence is clearest where the writers quote verses from the Old Testament to help them explain the new revelation that had come in Christ Jesus. They were leading their readers along the same paths towards understanding as they had travelled themselves.

There are several ways in which we can discover these quotations in order to see how the New Testament writers used Old Testament ideas:

1 The RSV and many other modern translations of the Bible print much of the Old Testament in the style of poetry, based on the poetic forms of the Hebrew Writings, as in most of the prophetic writings, Psalms and Proverbs. None of the New Testament books are written mainly in poetry. It only appears from time to time in the middle of prose writing. Sometimes this poetry is a new expression of praise to God, as in Revelation 4.11 and 5.9–10. But

Figure 12. 'If the New Testament is to be properly understood and appreciated, it must never be cut off from the richness of its association with the Old
Testament' (p. 166). The early Christians, following the example of Jesus
Christ, made great use of religious symbols from Old Testament times. This
picture shows part of the carving on a stone sarcophagus (coffin) of the third
century AD. The Good Shepherd is clearly portrayed in the centre, and the
background is part of a grape-harvest scene, reminding us of the important
part played by the vine in biblical thought.

most of the poetry in the New Testament is in fact quoted from the Old Testament. For example, Hebrews 1.5–13 is composed of quotations from six psalms, and from 2 Samuel and Deuteronomy (see the RSV footnotes).

2 The RSV and some other versions include footnotes which draw our attention to quotations from the Old Testament, whether they are poetic in form or plain prose. So this can be another source of information about direct quotations, but you will discover that many of the footnotes draw attention to similar ideas in both parts of the Bible, without using direct quotations.

3 A concordance can help us too, especially as New Testament writers often introduce quotations by such phrases as, 'Have you not read . . .' (as in Matthew 12.3, 5), and 'It is written . . .' (as in Luke 20.17; 24.46). In several instances of this kind the writers describe an event as 'fulfilling' what is written in the Old Testament (as in Matthew 13.14–15; John 19.28).

Some Difficulties for Us to Grasp

You need to be aware of quotations which for one reason or another seem very odd to readers today. There are four different sources of such problems which can help us recognize the significance of quotations which seem strange to us: contrast in wording between the two Testaments; New Testament references which lack specific Old Testament sources; strange comparisons; and stories to which the New Testament writers give different interpretations.

Contrast in wording between the two Testaments

If we make a careful comparison between the English quotations as they stand in the New Testament and the actual verses as they appear in the Old Testament, we find that in many cases the wording differs between the two. For example, Matthew 13.14 reads: 'You shall indeed hear but never understand, and you shall indeed see but never perceive.' This is a quotation of Isaiah 6.9, which reads: 'Hear and hear, but do not understand; see and see, but do not perceive.'

The meaning is similar, but the way the writers express it is different. This comes from the fact that the Old Testament was written in Hebrew and the New Testament in Greek. The New Testament writers seldom used the Hebrew books which became accepted as the Jewish scriptures. They seldom made their own translations of Hebrew into Greek. Instead, they used the Septuagint, which is a Greek translation of all the books we call the Old Testament, which were originally written in Hebrew and included occasional use of Aramaic. The Septuagint also includes additional books, or parts of books which were written from the start in Greek and are included for us in the Apocrypha/Deuterocanonical section of the RSV

Common Bible. The Septuagint had been prepared by Jews who had migrated to other parts of Asia, Europe and North Africa. It was widely used by Jewish communities living outside Palestine, because their ordinary language was Greek. The New Testament writers used this version because it was the best means by which to persuade such Jews that the Christian gospel was directly related to what they knew about God and his purposes from their study of the Septuagint.

The scholars who prepared the RSV New Testament translated directly from the Greek of the New Testament books, and this explains the differences between these quotations and their Old Testament sources. Often the differences are only slight, as in the example already given. But sometimes there is a more significant difference. For example, Matthew 1.23 refers to a 'virgin' who shall conceive. In the Old Testament it is simply a 'young woman' who shall do so (Isaiah 7.14). The Hebrew word simply means a woman of the age to be married, and fails to show whether she is married or single. The Greek word in the Septuagint means a virgin, and never describes a married woman. So this verse has changed in an important way when it reappears in the New Testament. Those who prepared the Septuagint are responsible for the change and have introduced the idea of a miracle to this verse.

New Testament references which lack specific Old Testament sources

Sometimes the Old Testament fails to provide a verse or verses which directly relate to the New Testament passage concerned. Perhaps the most important of these is found in Luke 24.45–47, which quotes Jesus as saying: 'Thus it is written, that the Christ should suffer and on the third day rise from the dead, and that repentance and forgiveness of sins should be preached . . . beginning from Jerusalem.'

The only Old Testament quotation given in the footnotes to this verse in the RSV is Hosea 6.2, which in origin was part of Hosea's appeal to the people of his time to return to God in penitence. Other Bible versions fail to provide any evidence from the Old Testament in their footnotes. Perhaps the truth lies in Luke 24.45, where Jesus points to the teachings of the Old Testament in general. He had done the same for the two men on the Emmaus road (Luke 24.27). Hidden within the Jewish scriptures which we now call the Old Testament were many things that pointed forward to a time when suffering for the sake of others would bring new hope. The Jewish writers were unable to grasp the truth about what God was going to do for the salvation of mankind, and incapable of recognizing the details of what would happen. But Jesus, better than anyone else, could reinterpret the scriptures to show that his coming and his suffering were the natural fulfilment of God's work in preparing the Jews for his incarnation.

Strange comparisons

Other quotations from the Old Testament which the Gospel writers used to explain events during the life, death and resurrection of Jesus seem to modern minds very odd. Take, for example, Matthew 2.18, where the writer quotes Jeremiah 31.15. The prophet was speaking about the Exile, and he imagines the sorrow felt by Rachel in her grave that the people descended from Joseph and Benjamin were in exile instead of in the land God had given them. He follows this with a message of encouragement. Perhaps the writer of Matthew pictured Rachel as weeping again, this time for the children slaughtered by Herod. But we can sensibly ask: How can Jeremiah be said to be prophesying the death of the children in Bethlehem? But this way of associating an Old Testament event with a New Testament happening was common among Christian writers in New Testament times. Scholars give it the name 'typology'. They call an event or circumstance in the Old Testament a 'type' if it helps to explain the significance of something that happened in New Testament times. The comforting message of Jeremiah 31.16–20 is also to be applied to the death of the children of Bethlehem. In both cases God allows suffering, but is working to achieve great things for the salvation of humankind.

New Testament writers give stories unexpected interpretations

Allegory is another way in which New Testament writers at times make use of Old Testament stories. The use of allegory attempts to provide a coded message through a story which seems to have a straightforward meaning. The characters, objects and events in such a story are each given a secret meaning, and help to provide a message relating to something entirely different. In Galatians 4.21–31 Paul wanted to contrast the belief that obedience to the law brings salvation with the gospel he preached that salvation is through faith in Jesus Christ. So he compares the children born to Abraham by Sarah and Hagar. He says that Ishmael was born according to the established customs of slavery, and so his relationship with Abraham is according to the law. Paul then quotes Genesis 21.10 where Sarah tells Abraham to 'Cast out this slave woman with her son; for the son of this slave woman shall not be heir with my son Isaac'. Paul takes this as evidence that salvation by obedience to the Law is excluded from God's plan. Isaac was born of love and free will between Abraham and Sarah, which Paul takes as a sign that those who come willingly to faith in Christ are the children of God. To confirm the issue Paul reminded his readers that Ishmael's descendants still lived in the land which includes Mount Sinai. He recognized that the earthly Jerusalem, centre of Jewish authority, was still maintained under the Law, and failed to be built on faith. He says the heavenly Jerusalem is free: a place where relationships are based on love, instead of regulations. He added, 'Now we, brethren, like Isaac, are children of promise . . . we are not children of the slave but of the free woman' (Galatians 4.28, 31).

The strange comparisons and stories given different interpretations which we discussed above involve ways of thinking about and presenting the Christian message which are unfamiliar to us, and we may have difficulty in understanding them. But people of New Testament days were used to their writers and scholars using such methods to present their message. As we have seen, these writers and scholars used information from the Old Testament in order to provide answers to important questions about God's purposes and how he is working for their fulfilment. Since these ways are unlikely to be familiar to the people we feel ourselves called to guide, we would be wrong to attempt to adopt these methods and to demand that others use such ways of thinking. We may sometimes need to help our people to appreciate the problems, just as I have tried to help you, if they are eager to understand the significance of the passages of Scripture in which the problems occur. But we must avoid thinking that we should reject the idea of the fulfilment of prophecy altogether. We only need to remember that God was preparing his people for the coming of Christ throughout the period of the Old Testament, to realize that there are real and important connections between the two Testaments. We should expect that the Old Testament has things to teach us which will help us to understand the coming of Christ and what he has done for our salvation.

📖 Check Your Understanding 25

1 (a) Which of the following verses in Mark's Gospel possess footnotes providing direct quotations from the Old Testament?

   Mark 1.2; 3.27; 7.6–7; 10.4; 12.19; 15.31

  (b) What are the connections between the remaining verses of Mark's Gospel in this list and their footnotes which refer to the Old Testament?

2 Look closely at the following verses which all contain examples of the problems we have examined in this chapter:

   Matthew 2.6; Matthew 2.15; Mark 9.12; Hebrews 5.6

Write the appropriate title from those we used to head the paragraphs above against each of the verses we have now quoted, to show that you understand which kind of problem is involved in each case.

How New Testament People Used the Old Testament

Now we are ready to examine quotations from the Old Testament in the New Testament in more detail. First we shall consider the way in which Jesus used the Old Testament, then how the Apostle Paul did, and finally the other New Testament writers.

How Jesus Used the Old Testament

The Old Testament had a very important place in the personal life of Jesus. When he described to his disciples his experience of temptation at the beginning of his ministry, he explained it in terms of Old Testament quotations. Both the Devil and Jesus himself referred to the scriptures during that great conflict of their wills (Matthew 4.1–11; Luke 4.1–13). Similarly, at his crucifixion, Jesus found strength to face the suffering through words from the Old Testament. His cry from the cross, 'Why hast thou forsaken me?', is a direct quotation of Psalm 22.1. Many other verses in that psalm can be used to describe the experience of crucifixion, as, for example, 'They have pierced my hands and feet' (verse 16). And the Psalmist's sudden change to confidence in God's power to deliver (verses 22–24) may even have served to reassure Jesus. Certainly his cry at the moment of death was an expression of trust and confidence in God (Luke 23.46), and was a quotation from Psalm 31.5.

Jesus was also concerned that his followers should properly understand and benefit from God's revelation of himself as the Old Testament records it. Some people have suggested that there is a conflict of ideas in Jesus's teaching regarding the relationship between the Old Testament and his ministry. He said on the one hand, 'I have come not to abolish' the Law and the prophets 'but to fulfil them' (Matthew 5.17). Yet on the other hand, he compared his ministry to new cloth which should never be used to mend old cloth, and new wine which should never be used to fill old wine skins (Matthew 9.16–17).

However, the contrast is quite acceptable when we recognize the truth about the relationship between the Testaments. The Old Testament finds its fulfilment in the New Testament. It is incomplete in itself and provides only an incomplete account of God's whole revelation. We must avoid using it to prevent people from recognizing the fuller truth revealed in Christ, but rather use it to help them to understand and appreciate the New Testament revelation.

Jesus made use of all three parts of the Hebrew scriptures in his teachings.

1 He pointed out the two *Laws* which are a basis for understanding all that God requires of his people (Deuteronomy 6.4–5 and

Leviticus 19.18b; see Mark 12.29–31; Matthew 22.37–40). He approved the Ten Commandments as a guide for life (Exodus 20.1–17; Deuteronomy 5.6–21; see Mark 10.19–21), and added his own fuller interpretation to ensure that his disciples understood their real meaning and importance (Matthew 5.21–30, 33–37).

2 He used the *Prophets* to explain the purpose and significance of his own ministry (Luke 4.18–19; compare Isaiah 61.1–2). 'It is written in the prophets, "And they shall all be taught by God" ' (John 6.45; compare Isaiah 54.13). ' "And he was reckoned with transgressors" ' (Luke 22.37; compare Isaiah 53.12).

3 He used the *Psalms*, which are part of the Hebrew Writings, to explain the significance of his own sufferings, ' "He who ate my bread has lifted his heel against me" ' (John 13.18; compare Psalm 41.9), and, ' "They hated me without a cause" ' (John 15.25; compare Psalm 35.19). He claimed to be the stone that the builders had rejected (Luke 20.17; compare Psalm 118.22–23).

Jesus also tried to prepare his disciples for his suffering, by showing them that it was a fulfilment of what was written in all the scriptures (Mark 9.12; Luke 18.31–34). He returned to the same subject at the Last Supper (Mark 14.21), and at his arrest (Matthew 26.54–56). His meaning became clear to his disciples after his resurrection, on the road to Emmaus and in Jerusalem (Luke 24.27, 44).

Paul and the Old Testament

The first Christian writings were the letters of Paul. He had been a Pharisee, and was trained in the Jewish way of understanding what we call the Old Testament. As a Pharisee he had learnt to value the scriptures very highly, so we should expect that he would often mention them in his letters. Wherever he went on his travels he spoke first to the Jews and the proselytes, and only afterwards to the Gentiles. As a result, many of the early converts to Christianity were people who knew the Septuagint very well and could benefit from their knowledge as they heard Paul preach or they read his letters.

Paul's letter to the Romans provides an excellent example of the way in which he used the Old Testament to support what he was saying. Table 1 shows Paul's quotations from the Law, the Prophets and the Writings, set out in the order in which they appear in that letter. The large number of quotations, and the fact that they come from many parts of the Old Testament, show that Paul had an extensive knowledge of the scriptures and could easily find the right words to use as evidence of what God had revealed about himself and his purposes for humankind in Christ Jesus.

Table 1: Paul's use of Old Testament quotations in his Letter to the Romans.

Romans: The Law	Romans: The Prophets	Romans: The Writings
	1.17 Habakkuk 2.4	
2.11 Deuteronomy 10.17	**2.24** Isaiah 52.5	**2.11** 2 Chronicles 19.7
		3.4 Psalm 51.4
		3.10–12 Psalms 14.1–3; 53.1–3
		3.13 Psalms 5.9; 140.3
		3.14 Psalm 10.7
	3.15–17 Isaiah 59.7–8	**3.18** Psalm 36.1
		3.20 Psalm 143.2
4.3 Genesis 15.6		**4.7** Psalm 32.1–2
4.17 Genesis 17.5		
4.18 Genesis 15.5		
7.7 Exodus 20.17 Deuteronomy 5.21		**7.22** Psalm 1.2
		8.21 Psalm 118.6
	8.33 Isaiah 50.8–9	**8.36** Psalm 44.22
9.7 Genesis 21.12		
9.9 Genesis 18.10		
9.12 Genesis 25.23	**9.13** Malachi 1.2–3	**9.14** 2 Chronicles 19.7
9.15 Exodus 33.19		
9.17 Exodus 9.16	**9.20** Isaiah 45.9	
	9.25 Hosea 2.23	
	9.26 Hosea 1.10	
	9.27 Isaiah 10.22–23 Hosea 1.10	
	9.29 Isaiah 1.9	
	9.33 Isaiah 28.16	
10.5 Leviticus 18.5	**10.5** Ezekiel 20.11	**10.5** Nehemiah 9.29
10.6 Deuteronomy 30.12		
10.8 Deuteronomy 30.14	**10.11** Isaiah 28.16	
	10.13 Joel 2.32	
	10.15 Isaiah 52.7	
	10.16 Isaiah 53.1	**10.18** Psalm 19.4
10.19 Deuteronomy 32.21	**10.20–21** Isaiah 65.1–2	
	11.3–4 1 Kings 19.10, 18	
	11.8 Isaiah 29.10	**11.9** Psalm 69.22–23
	11.26 Isaiah 59.20–21	
	11.34 Isaiah 40.13–14	**11.35** Job 41.11
12.19 Deuteronomy 32.35		**12.20** Proverbs 25.21–22
13.9 Exodus 20.13–17 Deuteronomy 5.17–18		

Table 1: *continued*

Romans: The Law	Romans: The Prophets	Romans: The Writings	
Leviticus 19.18			
	14.11 Isaiah 45.23		
		15.3	Psalm 69.9
	15.9 2 Samuel 22.50	**15.9**	Psalm 18.49
15.10 Deuteronomy 32.43		**15.11**	Psalm 117.1
	15.12 Isaiah 11.10		
	15.21 Isaiah 52.15		

When we look more closely at these same quotations, we find that they include all the most important ideas covered by Old Testament theology. They describe the nature of God, and the quality and character of his relationships with humans. God has made himself known to people (Deuteronomy 30.12, 14). He is wise (Isaiah 40.13–14), and just in his dealings with us (Deuteronomy 10.17; 2 Chronicles 19.7; Psalm 51.4). He has the right to be served by every human being (Isaiah 45.23), and his authority is shown even in his relationships with those who are disobedient (Exodus 9.16). His laws help humans to know how they should live (Leviticus 18.5; Ezekiel 20.11; Psalm 1.2). He will judge disobedient people (Isaiah 28.16), and punish their wrongdoing (Deuteronomy 32.35). Yet God is merciful (Exodus 33.19), and works for people's salvation (Isaiah 52.7; Joel 2.32). His goodness to humans has never been bought (Job 41.11); people's hopes spring from God's willingness to forgive (Psalm 32.1–2).

None can stand secure under God's judgement (Psalm 143.2), because all have been disobedient and have sinned (Psalms 5.9; 14.1–3), but God has provided a way of salvation; Abraham was accepted because of his faith (Genesis 15.6), and others can follow the same way (Habakkuk 2.4). God chose the people of Israel (Malachi 1.2–3); but even they rejected his choice of them (Isaiah 45.9) and refused to hear his messengers (1 Kings 19.10). Yet God went on seeking a response from his people (Isaiah 65.1–2), and continually renewed his election of Israel (Isaiah 59.20–21; Hosea 1.10; 2.23). There would be a remnant who would respond to him (1 Kings 19.18; Isaiah 1.9; 10.22–23), and they would be a witness to all people of God's goodness to humankind (Psalm 19.4; Isaiah 11.10; 52.15). Eventually God's promises to Abraham will be fulfilled (Genesis 15.5; 17.5). People will live according to God's will as described in the Ten Commandments (Exodus 20.13–17); they will learn to love their neighbours (Leviticus 19.18), and to show kindness to their enemies (Proverbs 25.21, 22).

Paul addressed his letter to the Romans to the church in Rome, whose members included Jews and Gentile converts to Judaism who had become Christians. Such people would be greatly helped by Paul's use of the Old Testament, which was well known to them all. But we should avoid the mistake of supposing that Paul simply used the Old Testament quotations because his hearers were familiar with them. Paul himself had come to Christian faith after being a student of the Old Testament. Paul's meeting with Christ on the road to Damascus was a completion and fulfilment of all that he had come to know about God through his study of the Law, the Prophets and the Writings. Paul found the use of the Old Testament an important way to express the Christian ideas he held. The Jewish scriptures were deeply involved in his own understanding of the Christian gospel, and he wanted his hearers to share the same benefits that he himself had found in knowing the Old Testament.

Other Writings

In this Study Guide we are unable to examine in detail the work of other writers who contributed to the New Testament. But one or two examples will show how they valued the Old Testament because it provided familiar passages of Scripture which enabled them to express their message about the coming of Christ in ways that would appeal to their readers.

1 The writers of the Gospels made it clear that they found this useful (Luke 3.4–6; John 12.15), and Matthew used a series of quotations to show that the life of Jesus was a fulfilment of prophecy (Matthew 1.22–23; 2.15; 2.23; 8.17; 12.17–21; 13.35; 21.4). Some scholars have suggested that the Early Church had a collection of such texts drawn up as a help in presenting the gospel to the Jews. This may have been necessary for those Christian teachers who were less well acquainted with the Old Testament than Paul showed himself to be.

2 The writer of the letter to the Hebrews used Old Testament ideas of priesthood, sanctuary and sacrifice to express what he believed Jesus had accomplished by his death and resurrection. His letter also refers to the work of Moses and to the New Covenant. Among the New Testament writers, he especially used many quotations from the Old Testament, which the footnotes of the RSV give in detail; most of these stand out from the prose of the letter because of their poetic form.

📖 **Check Your Understanding 26**

1 'I have come not to abolish' the Law 'but to fulfil' it. In which of the following ways did Jesus fulfil the Law?

    (a) He was completely obedient to every law contained in the Old Testament.

    (b) He was able to provide us with a much clearer understanding of what God requires of us.

    (c) He taught his disciples that if they obeyed every law contained in the Old Testament they would win eternal life.

2 'If the New Testament is to be properly understood and appreciated, it must never be cut off from the richness of its association with the Old Testament' (see page 166). Which of the following words best expresses the meaning of 'appreciated' in that sentence?

ASSESSED   CONFIRMED   CRITICIZED

DIGESTED   HONOURED   INCREASED

Other References

People, Places and Customs

We can find many other references to the Old Testament in the books of the New Testament, besides the direct quotations we have already considered. The most obvious examples are references to people, places and customs which we can best understand by studying the Old Testament.

People

The Old Testament mentions about 50 names of people who also appear in the New Testament. Many of these appear in the two lists of Joseph's ancestors (Matthew 1.1–17; Luke 3.23–38). These Gospel writers use these names to express their belief that Jesus was a true successor to people who had led Israel in God's name in earlier times. They show that his coming was a fulfilment of God's activities among his people, in all ages from the time of Abraham. The New Testament mentions other people: some who were famous for their faith (Hebrews 11.4–40) and others who were the founder members of the tribes of Israel (see especially Revelation 7.4–8). The latter references are meant to point to the fulfilment of all that God had planned when he first revealed himself to the Patriarchs, including these children of Jacob. Paul, for example, was proud of the fact that he belonged to the tribe of Benjamin (Romans 11.1; Philippians 3.5).

But the most important of these people are those who are mentioned again and again in the New Testament. They include the following whose number of New Testament references are shown in brackets after their names: Adam (9 times), Noah (8), Abraham (74), Isaac (19), Jacob (25), Joseph (9), Moses (79), David (58), Solomon (12), Elijah (30), Isaiah (21), and Jonah (9).

Those who heard Jesus or one of the apostles preach, and those who read a New Testament letter, or a Gospel, needed to have a sound knowledge of Old Testament history in order to appreciate these references. The early Christian preachers and teachers knew that such knowledge was available to the Jews and proselytes, because they were regularly taught the scriptures in the synagogues in those days. Christians believed that they could make their own message clear to their hearers by referring to these people of past ages, and to what they had experienced of God in their own day. The New Testament preachers and writers used the sound educational principle of taking the existing knowledge of their hearers and building on it fresh understanding and new knowledge of God's ways.

Places

The events of the New Testament happened in much the same part of the world as those recorded in the Old Testament. Palestine was at the centre and the background of both histories: its towns and villages are mentioned in both parts of the Bible. Well-trained Jews would remember Old Testament stories about places which were in the news in their own time because of the activities of Jesus and his followers. For example, Jerusalem would always be thought of as the City of David, and the news that one of David's descendants was active there would rouse interest in any Jewish heart.

The fact that this descendant of David was rejected and crucified there by some of the Jewish people would cause horror and despair to those who believed that Jesus was sent by God, because God's people had turned against the LORD's Anointed. The Jewish Christians would remember other members of their race who had suffered there as a result of the disloyalty of God's people, for example, Jeremiah and the Maccabees. Christ's warnings about the coming destruction of Jerusalem would remind them of Isaiah's assurance that Jerusalem would never be destroyed, and of the dismay caused by Jeremiah's later certainty that it would, and by the fact that it *had* in fact been destroyed before. If God could reject the Jews so completely in the time of Jeremiah, then it certainly could happen again, as Jesus was predicting. In the minds of the Jews in New Testament times, the background of Old Testament experience and thought was firmly associated with the places involved in the story of the life and ministry of Jesus. The

New Testament writers made full use of these associations in presenting their message to the people of their day.

Here are a few other examples: Bethlehem had been important, and would be again (Matthew 2.3–6). Nowhere in all the journey back from exile was there greater need for valleys to be lifted up, and mountains made low, than in the Jordan valley (Isaiah 40.3–5), and it was here that John the Baptist preached about another new beginning for God's people and claimed to be the voice crying in the wilderness (Matthew 3.1–3; John 1.23).

Samaria had been capital of the Northern Kingdom, as well as the source of opposition to the re-establishment of God's people in Jerusalem after the Exile. If God's rule was to be established, the people of Samaria must be won to the service of God (John 4.39–42; Acts 8.4–8).

Galilee had been a remote part of the kingdom of Israel, easily conquered (2 Kings 15.29), and had even been given away in a trade agreement (1 Kings 9.11). But Isaiah believed that it would have an important part in God's plans for all his people (Isaiah 9.1). The fact that a great part of Jesus's ministry was exercised in Galilee should have caused little surprise to anybody who knew the scriptures, because it was simply what they had expected for the place (Matthew 4.12–17).

Customs

The customs observed by the Jewish people in New Testament times had developed over the long period of their history from the time of Abraham to the time of Christ. The various stages of this development are recorded in the Old Testament, and the New Testament writers refer to many of these customs as they record the life and teaching of Jesus, or describe the growth of the Christian Church and its relations with the Jewish community.

The most obvious example is that of circumcision. The Jerusalem Council recorded in Acts 15 and Paul's letter to the Galatians were largely concerned with whether Gentiles should be circumcised before they could be accepted as Christian converts, or whether circumcision was simply part of Jewish custom. The answer they gave is a matter for New Testament theology, and we are only concerned here to notice the Old Testament background to the dispute. Circumcision for the Jews began in the time of Abraham (Genesis 17.9–14), and became a sign for those who shared in God's covenant with Israel. Jesus himself was circumcised (Luke 2.21), and Paul expressed the pride felt by all Jews in belonging to those who were circumcised (Philippians 3.5). But even in Old Testament times, the Jews recognized that the outward sign was pointless unless it was made significant as an expression of an attitude of heart and mind (Jeremiah 4.4; 9.25–26). When circumcision was eventually declared unnecessary for Gentiles, this was a natural sequel to this development of ideas. The truly circumcised are those 'who worship God in spirit, and glory in Christ Jesus, and put no confidence in the flesh' (Philippians 3.3).

Other religious customs described in the New Testament, which depend for their explanation and significance on the Old Testament, include: the appointment of priests (Matthew 8.4); the observance of the Sabbath (Matthew 12.2), fasts (Matthew 6.16) and annual feasts (Luke 2.41); the giving of tithes (Matthew 23.23), and making of sacrifices (Luke 2.24); teaching in the synagogues (Matthew 4.23); and the wearing of phylacteries (Matthew 23.5). We can only understand these references when we know the origin and purpose of the customs involved. This knowledge comes to us from the study of the Old Testament.

Themes

The most important influence of the Old Testament on the writings of the New Testament is seen in the way in which theological themes are taken up and used afresh in presenting the gospel message. The whole purpose of God's revelation in the Old Testament was that people should learn about him and enter into fellowship with him. Those who knew the LORD were eager to share their experiences with others, so that they might experience the same joy.

In passing on their knowledge of God to others, the Old Testament writers built up a vocabulary of special words and phrases which their hearers would find helpful in trying to understand their message. These same words and phrases were used by Jesus, and by other people of his time, to express the truth of God's new revelation of himself in Christ. We can easily find examples of the way in which the Old Testament vocabulary was used to present the New Testament message. They can be found on every page of the New Testament. Simply as an example, a few of these references are given in Table 2. You must guard against thinking that the table gives a complete list of Old Testament themes, and that the New Testament verses quoted are the complete collection of appropriate verses.

Careful study of these examples will show you that the New Testament writers were doing more than use the Old Testament ideas in their original form. Although they used the same words and phrases, the message which they expressed through them was different. The writers developed their thinking further as a result of the revelation brought by Christ Jesus. What he had been and said and done enriched and transformed people's understanding of God and his purposes.

The Old Testament vocabulary came to have new meanings as a result. To take one example, for Christians the idea of the unity of

Table 2: Examples of Old Testament themes referred to in the New Testament.

Chapter in Guide	O.T. Themes	Quotations from the Synoptic Gospels, John, Paul and the other writers of the New Testament
1. The Word of God	The Word of God	Luke 4.21; John 5.39; Romans 1.1–4; James 1.22–23
	Inspiration	Luke 2.27; 1 Corinthians 12.6; 2 Timothy 3.16;
	Revelation	Matthew 16.17; John 1.31; Romans 1.16–17; 1 Peter 1.3–5
2. God	Holiness	Luke 1.75; John 20.22; 2 Corinthians 1.12; Hebrews 12.10
	Glory	Mark 8.38; John 1.14; Romans 5.2; Revelation 14.7
	Eternal	Matthew 19.16; John 3.14–15; Romans 2.7; Hebrews 9.15
	Everywhere	Matthew 25.34; John 3.16–17; Romans 1.20; Revelation 11.15
	All authority	Matthew 28.18; John 5.26–29; 1 Timothy 1.17; Revelation 4.11
	All knowing	Matthew 11.25; John 16.13; Colossians 2.1–3; Hebrews 4.12
3. Our God is with us	Present with us	Matthew 28.20b; John 1.14; Romans 8.37–39; Revelation 3.20
	in creation	Mark 10.6; John 1.3; Colossians 1.16; Hebrews 11.3
	in history	Mark 1.15; John 8.56; Ephesians 3.8–12; 1 Peter 1.5
	in morality	Matthew 6.33; John 16.8 Romans 3.21–26; 1 Peter 2.24
4. Other Spiritual Beings	Angels	Luke 1.26; John 20.12; 2 Thessalonians 1.7; Revelation 8.2
	Satan	Mark 1.13, John 13.27; Romans 16.20; Revelation 12.9
5. Humanity	Image of God	Only in Paul; 1 Corinthians 11.7; Colossians 3.9–10; etc.
	Flesh	Matthew 26.41; John 1.14; Romans 8.3; 1 Peter 3.18
	Soul	Matthew 10.28; John 12.27; 2 Corinthians 15.4–5; James 1.21
	Spirit	Matthew 26.41; John 4.23; Romans 8.16–17; Hebrews 4.12
	Resurrection	Matthew 22.29–31; John 11.24–26; Romans 6.5; 1 Peter 1.3–4

Table 2: *continued.*

Chapter in Guide	O.T. Themes	Quotations from the Synoptic Gospels, John, Paul and the other writers of the New Testament
6. Human Failure	Temptation	Luke 4.1–2; 1 Corinthians 10.13; Hebrews 2.18
	Sin	Luke 15.18, 21; John 8.11; Romans 2.12; James 1.15
	Wrath	Matthew 3.7; John 3.36; Romans 1.18; Revelation 6.15–17
	Judgement	Matthew 25.45–46; John 3.17–18; Romans 2.1–2; James 2.12–13
7. Salvation	Steadfast Love	Matthew 6.30; John 3.16; Ephesians 2.4, 5; 1 John 4.10–11
	Covenant	Mark 14.24; 2 Corinthians 3.4–6; Hebrews 12.18–24
	Sacrifice	Mark 12.33; Ephesians 5.1–2; Hebrews 9.23–28
8. The New Life	Fear of God	Matthew 10.28; John 12.15; Colossians 3.22; Revelation 14.7
	Faith in God	Mark 11.22; John 20.28; Romans 4.5; Hebrews 11.6
	Love of God	Matthew 22.37; John 14.21; Romans 8.28; 1 John 4.19
	Love for others	Matthew 5.43–45; John 13.34; Romans 13.8; 1 John 4.7
9. The Ultimate Goal	Transformation of the World	Acts 1.7–8; John 17.3; Romans 8.19–21; Revelation 21.1–4
	New Community	Matthew 6.10; John 13.34; Colossians 1.18; Revelation 7.9–12
	Day of the Lord	Matthew 11.22–24; John 6.40; 1 Corinthians 1.7–8; Hebrews 10.25
	Son of Man	Matthew 2.10; John 3.13, 14 (only used in Jesus' life time)

God came to include the existence of Father and Son together as One (John 10.30; 17.22). We are unable to study all such changes, nor can we study the whole range of new understanding which resulted from the coming of Christ. This is the study of New Testament theology. But without the Old Testament vocabulary, Christian teachers would have been unable to express the truth in terms that their hearers knew and understood. And we still use some of that vocabulary today.

We can understand the pages of the New Testament only because we possess information about the experiences and thoughts which the Old Testament records. The New Testament writers were fully aware of their dependence on the Old Testament in trying to express God's new revelation in Jesus Christ in ways that people could understand and appreciate. Jesus himself made full use of the Old Testament revelation, because he knew that all through their history God had been preparing his people's minds and hearts for the time of his coming. 'When the time had fully come, God sent his Son' (Galatians 4.4). In every generation Christians must come to grips with all that God revealed in Old Testament times, if they are to understand the full significance of Christ's coming.

 Study Suggestions

FOR GROUP DISCUSSION

1 Paul's letter to the Philippians lacks any footnotes which refer to the Old Testament. Can you suggest a reason for this? Does it make any difference to the belief that Paul found it necessary to use Old Testament quotations in order to express New Testament theology?

2 Joseph lacked any part in the conception of the baby Jesus. Can you suggest why Matthew 1.1–17 and Luke 3.23–38 provide lists of the ancestors of this man, rather than of Mary? What is the significance of the fact that the two lists fail to provide exactly the same details?

3 How would you answer somebody who said to you 'The study of Old Testament theology is a serious waste of time which could better be spent on studying the teachings of the New Testament'? Give reasons for your answer.

FOR ESSAY WRITING

4 Why did New Testament writers make use of the Septuagint rather than the Hebrew Scriptures? Where can you find Aramaic quotations and their interpretation in the New Testament? Who used the Aramaic language, and why do you think they did this?

5 What was the Old Testament background to the dispute about circumcision in the time of the Early Church? Was there any reason why those who supported circumcision for Gentiles should suppose that they were being obedient to Old Testament revelation?

6 The writer to the Hebrews makes use of a story from Genesis to explain the nature of Christ's priesthood. See Genesis 14.17–20 and Hebrews 6.20—7.10. To what extent does the writer of Hebrews add to the original story as we find it in Genesis in order to make a basis on which to build his account of the priesthood of Jesus?

WORK WITH THE BIBLE AND A CONCORDANCE

7 We have left out many of the references to the Old Testament in the RSV footnotes to Paul's letter to the Romans from the chart on pages 174–5 because they lack the form of direct quotations. What is the significance of these other references? To show the accuracy of your answer, choose three good examples and set the New Testament verses side by side with the Old Testament.

8 Examine the New Testament references to Jonah, and describe how Jesus used the story of this prophet.

9 Look closely at the verses in Mark's Gospel which contain the words 'it is written'. Compare these verses with those in the Old Testament that they are quoting. Summarize the teachings about Jesus and about what he said to others which these examples provide. Are there any such quotations which lack an Old Testament verse to support them? Can you suggest an explanation for this?

Postscript: Many Theologies

Very many writers and editors contributed to the production of the Old Testament in the Hebrew form that scholars know today and that we recognize in many different translations in our own and in other people's languages. There are, of course, 39 books in the Old Testament, but we must avoid thinking of 39 authors. Editors worked on most of the books at various times right through to the format that is familiar to us. In some ways this was easy to achieve, because every book had to be written out by hand, and the copyists were keen to present the contents in the form that would make most sense to their readers. Some of the alterations were attempts to put right errors made by earlier copyists, but others were to take account of the current theology at the time people made the copy. The first five books of the Old Testament only reached their present form when priests had gathered together information from earlier writings and traditions, and had added their own comments during and after the Exile. The traditions came from various sources, some of which were in conflict in the accounts they gave. For example, let me remind you of the contrast between the two separate accounts of creation (Genesis 1.1—2.4a and 2.4b–24). The priests also included the contents of several different codes of Law which had been developed over a period of many years, which again at times conflict in their rulings. For example, the book of Deuteronomy includes the ruling that true worship can only take place in Jerusalem, although earlier codes lack any such instructions. Another obvious example of books having multiple writers is the book of Psalms, which contains psalms from many different times, just as modern hymnbooks contain hymns from various periods in the history of the Church.

So we are unable to count the total number of people who contributed to the Hebrew scriptures which the Church adopted as the Old Testament Scripture, recognizing how closely it related to the coming of Christ and the development of the Church. Each writer had his own understanding of God and God's purposes in creation. They undertook the work of preparing written records because they wanted their readers to share in knowledge of the things they believed God was teaching his people. They were people of their own generation and shared many of the ideas that were inherited from the past, but also developed their own insights for the benefit of their readers. God inspired them to understand and to express more clearly the truth that he was revealing to his people as they learnt to live under his rule. Often their experience of revelation enabled them to offer new ideas for the acceptance of others of their time, and so passed on to later generations as part of their inherited knowledge.

There is a sense in which the Old Testament contains a whole range of theologies which are the teachings available to successive generations. But for us today we need to be aware of the difference between half-formed ideas and the developments which brought fuller understanding. Take, for example, the early widespread belief that sickness and suffering were fair punishment for wrongs that those who experienced them deserved. Only after the Exile did writers challenge this belief by the contributions they made to the on-going debate in the books of Job and Ecclesiastes. Job's friends were absolutely convinced that Job must have done something very serious indeed to deserve the loss of all his possessions and the death of all his children. Job, for his part, tried to defend his innocence and was accused of pride as a result. In the end, God came to him and reminded him that humans are unable to possess a mastery of all knowledge. They must ultimately trust God in spite of their troubles. By his presence, God made this possible for Job, and God told Job's friends that he was truly innocent and they had been unfair to him. This is still an issue in the life of the Church today, where many still believe the things the writers of Job challenged. The writer of Ecclesiastes expressed his doubts about the beliefs which were current in his time about the significance of human life, encouraging people to look for something more, as the writer of Daniel did (Daniel 12.2–3). The Christian confidence in eternal life springs out of the revelation of Jesus Christ and Paul's teaching that through faith we shall know resurrection to eternal life.

Because the Old Testament contains the truth revealed by God through the teachings of a wide variety of writers, many people with knowledge of the Old Testament have made their own attempts to discover its underlying and essential truths. This book that you have been studying is one example, which many colleges and courses have chosen as a helpful introduction to this part of Old Testament study. I have tried my best to share with you the way in which the Old Testament has made sense to me. Probably at times you have wanted to disagree with my ideas and to look at the issues in different ways. I would be unreasonable if I insist that I have got everything right. You must look for what makes sense to you and benefit from it so that you in turn can help others to understand God's revelation in the Old Testament, and the crowning revelation in Christ.

If you have access to a theological library, you may find it helpful to look at any other books that have the same or a similar title to this book: *Theology of the Old Testament*. There are many such books, and as a result a secondary type of book has taken form which tries to present to readers outlines of the different approaches of the various writers. Of course these latter books lack the presentation of all the Old Testament themes, since they are simply concerned to summarize the methods used by individual scholars to obtain their results recorded in their books. I am unable to provide you with the sort of information that these technical books contain, but what I can do is to briefly outline some of the approaches to the Old Testament that Christians have used and use today.

Approaches to the Old Testament

Choosing Favourite Texts

The easiest approach for everyday Christians is to collect a range of texts which express for us the faith by which we try to live, and then to ignore anything else. Many of us already have favourite texts which have helped us in times of crisis, reassuring us that God is with us in the situation we face. For example, 'Be still, and know that I am God' (Psalm 46.10). Some people prefer to use devotional books which clearly choose such passages, rather than struggle with understanding the Old Testament itself. The Early Church in and beyond New Testament days probably used a list of texts which could help to convince Jews and proselytes of the truth of the gospel of Jesus Christ. Many people continue this use of proof texts, but it depends on them first accepting the truth of the scriptures and then, as a result, recognizing the truth of particular verses. You should be glad if you live in a country where many people recognize the importance of the gospel and want to be helped to understand the Christian message. But many countries lack this advantage because they face opposition from followers of other religions, and some people suffer severe persecution if they dare to accept Christ. In Britain there are many who reject the faith because they have a mistaken idea of what Christians believe, or because they are content with life as they know it and are unable to see any need for Christ. The widespread violence and suffering recorded in the Old Testament puts people off. They need to realize that the Old Testament deals with life as it truly exists and to recognize that it deals in large measure with things which are still part of life today because wrong-doing is still so widespread, with its troublesome results.

Studying the Religion of Israel

Sometimes scholars have chosen to write about the religion of Israel, rather than the theology of the Old Testament. But most scholars today accept that a major difference exists between the two. The former covers the customs and practices of worshippers which were adopted as a way of expressing the relationship between Israel and their God. But the religion of Israel is largely only of historical interest to us because the sacrificial systems and festivals of Old Testament times were replaced by Christian ways of worship from the time of Christ. Often the motives behind their religious customs are echoed in the practices of churches, but greatly transformed by our knowledge of the work of Christ on our behalf and our need to respond to what he has done for us.

Selecting Supportive Texts for Christian Doctrine

This is really an extension of 'Choosing Favourite Texts' above, but Christians have made it a widely-used method of studying Old Testament theology over the centuries. Christians have taken the creeds as providing a clear picture of the basic truths of their faith. Obviously the creeds contain much about the place and work of Christ and of the Holy Spirit, but themes which occur in the Old Testament include God, creation, humanity, sin and judgement, and salvation. People have selected material from the Old Testament to support each of the main themes, and used it as a basis for teaching the faith. But this method fails to take account of all that made up the faith of Israel. So people have tried a variety of other ways to present a fuller picture.

The Historical Approach

Many scholars recognize the way in which Israelite faith developed through the Old Testament period and believe that they should provide a series of chapters presenting a very clear picture of what people believed in each succeeding age. So they write about the time of the Patriarchs, Moses and the Exodus, the Judges, the kingdoms of Judah and Israel, the Exile and the Return. At each stage they search out evidence for what people believed and present it in as clear a fashion as possible for their readers. This method has the great advantage of highlighting the development of Israelite faith over the centuries. It looks for a consistent account of what people believed at each stage. But the trouble is that the dating of biblical passages is often difficult, and so we are unable to be sure about the beliefs of each era in the development of the Old Testament. We can give some Old Testament books and parts of books a reasonably clear context in

Israel's history, but other sections are still under debate with little evidence to provide a date. The continual process of editing done by the copyists of manuscripts adds to this problem. We are often unable to say for sure what the original traditions or writers affirmed.

The Study of Vocabulary

Many scholars choose to attempt to summarize the whole teachings of the Old Testament. To do this they group together words which relate to each of the main themes that they wish to present to their readers. As they write about each aspect of a theme, they offer such details as they can of the way in which words changed in meaning and ideas developed over the centuries. This does take account of the development of ideas, but relies on dealing with individual words and ideas in isolation from the whole range of ideas at each stage in the development. Often scholars can only assess what a writer or an editor meant by the words he used by seeing what he actually wrote. The context in which a writer uses words is important if we are to discover the meaning he intended to convey to his readers.

Finding an Appropriate Central Theme

The need to present a study of Israelite belief, without relating it to the use of the creeds, has led some writers to attempt to discover a central theme from all the teachings of the Old Testament. For example, one scholar chose to use the idea of covenant as the basis for his studies. This clearly is an important theme in the Old Testament, and is missing from the creeds. The Jews today still see themselves as sharing a unique covenant relationship with God. The scholar produced two volumes. The first of these provided a good study of all that could be naturally related to the covenant, but a critic commented that the second volume was made up of things which had very little relationship to that theme. So again the method is far from satisfactory.

Selected Themes

Because of the difficulty in finding a satisfactory way of presenting Old Testament theology that includes all the aspects of this vast subject, there came a time when scholars began to regard the task of producing such books as really impossible. So they began to concentrate on particular themes, and to produce books which dealt in detail with one major subject. This faces similar problems on a smaller scale to that involved in writing a complete Old Testament theology. But people have written some very good books. In theory, at least, it should be possible to amalgamate the work of the individuals into a united account of the whole subject, but of course different writers have their own way of understanding and presenting their books, and there would then be a diversity of approaches. However, the production of books on single themes has led to writers dealing with many new subjects which had been lacking in the complete volumes. Now some scholars have returned to writing their own full accounts of Old Testament theology.

I am quite unable to tell you what books you will find in your college library, or be able to borrow from fellow Christians. If you live in Africa you will probably find that a majority of the books have been donated by people who recognize the importance of a good library, and are willing to help by offering some of their own books to a theological college. Money for books is in many places hard to find, and in consequence there are likely to be very few recently published books. Some will be vastly different in approach from my book, and others will take an approach rather like my own. So what has been my approach?

You can read what I have said in Chapter 1 of this volume about God the good teacher. For me that is a basic starting-point, since it allows for the process of development in understanding of God and his purposes throughout the Old Testament. It recognizes that the people involved will have differing views on matters of importance, partly because some lived at a time when Israelite faith was less developed and others lived when understanding was more developed, but also because people of the same generation varied in their understanding of God and his purpose. It also relates to the personal experience of most readers, because God is still our teacher today. Through the course of our lives he can lead us to deeper insights and rich knowledge through our experiences, the witness of others and the challenge of those who reject our beliefs. If you doubt this, try the following experiment. Sit down and write out a list of the things that you find important in what the Church teaches, and then keep it safe for later reference. After a year or two make a fresh list, and then compare it with what you listed originally. You will find that you have changed some of your beliefs and added new knowledge of God and his purposes.

When the publishers invited me to prepare an *Old Testament Introduction* and I reached the stage where I needed to write on Old Testament theology, I already accepted that God is a good teacher, but needed to know what themes to include in my book. So I examined a variety of existing books on the subject, and made a list of what their authors seemed generally to accept. This became the outline of the first edition. When this was published, there were many reviews in Christian newspapers and magazines, and from these I recognized other themes that I have now incorporated in this revised edition.

References and Further Reading

What books should I recommend for further study? Students in universities and degree colleges are the most likely to use the more academic volumes available, but they will have tutors who are sure to want to make their own recommendations. So I have decided in this list to give emphasis to books which are most helpful for diploma and certificate students. These will also be of value to church Bible Study groups and people studying privately with little or no support from other sources. The major Old Testament theology writers such as W. Eichrodt, G. Von Rad, E. Jacob and G. A. F. Knight have published academic works which assume a knowledge of the history and literature of Old Testament times. Such books demand close attention over a long period of study and are of most use to people who possess a basic knowledge of current scholarly research and beliefs. Ordinary readers will more readily understand the books I recommend here. They can be divided into three groups as shown below. There are many more books that could have been included because, 'of making many books there is no end!' (Ecclesiastes 12.12)!

Study of the Stages by which Old Testament Faith Developed

Such books look at the biblical books which belong to each stage of Israel's history, or else take each book in canonical order and draw out what it teaches.

McKeating, H. (1990), *Studying the Old Testament*, Epworth Press.
Zuck, R. B. (1991), *A Biblical Theology of the Old Testament*, Moody.

Study by Selecting Several Themes which Relate to Each Other

Such books do not attempt to be complete accounts of Old Testament theology, but provide fresh insights into biblical beliefs and their relationship. Often these books present different aspects of the nature of God.

Phillips, A. (1977), *God B.C.*, Oxford University Press.
Westermann, C. (1979), *What Does the Old Testament Say about God?*, SPCK.
Westermann, C. (1982), *Elements of Old Testament Theology*, John Knox.

Study of Individual Themes From the Old Testament

Such books can often cover subjects which the major books on Old Testament theology leave out. They often involve study of the New Testament as well. This kind of book is particularly useful where the basis of the curriculum is a selection of themes rather than an attempt at a fuller study.

Brueggemann, W. (1978),*The Land*, Fortress Press.
Crenshaw, J. L. (1984), *A Whirlpool of Suffering*, Fortress Press.
Davidson, R. (1983), *The Courage to Doubt*, SCM Press.
Fretheim, T. E. (1984), *The Suffering of God*, Fortress Press.
Hyers, C. (1984), *Meaning of Creation*, John Knox.
Longman, T. and Reid, D. G. (1995), *God is a Warrior*, Paternoster Press.
Trible, Phyllis (1984), *Texts of Terror*, Fortress Press.
von Rad, G. (1972), *Wisdom in Israel*, SCM Press.
Wolff, H. W. (1974), *The Anthropology of the Old Testament*, SCM Press.
Zimmerli, W. (1971), *Man and his Hope in the Old Testament*, SCM Press.

Answers to Check Your Understanding Questions

PLEASE NOTE: the purpose of putting Self-Test Questions at the end of each section of a chapter is to help you check whether you have understood what you have read in the previous pages. You will lose all help from them if you look up the answers before attempting the questions! You will find that you will gain the greatest benefit if you write down what you believe to be the answer before looking at the answers given here. Answer both parts of each test before checking their answers. If you find that any of your answers are wrong, think about the given answer to try to see why it is correct. Where a question asks you to choose appropriate words from a list and you have made the wrong choice, look up all the words in a dictionary to discover why other words in the list are the ones you should have written.

Check Your Understanding 1
(1) Communication, promise
(2) (c) God has given me insight into his purposes and I am now trying to share this insight with you.

Check Your Understanding 2
(1) Encouragement, prompting, stimulus
(2) The law-givers, the kings, the priests, the prophets and the collectors of wisdom.

Check Your Understanding 3
(1) Knowledge, relationship, understanding
(2) God: make known, teach, uncover.
Man: discover, learn, recognize.

Check Your Understanding 4
(1) (a) Jehovah is a mistaken interpretation of a name for God found in the Hebrew text of the Old Testament, which actually consists of consonants from one word, and vowels from another.
(b) LORD is the way in which this special name is translated in modern versions of the English Old Testament.
(c) YAHWEH is the accepted way in which the Hebrew of the special name is put into English lettering.
(2) Misunderstanding.

Check Your Understanding 5	(1) Identifiable, outstanding, unique (2) Syncretism.
Check Your Understanding 6	(1) Ageless, constant, everlasting (2) Omnipotent expresses 'God is all powerful'; Omnipresent expresses 'God is everywhere'; Omniscient expresses 'God knows and understands all things'.
Check Your Understanding 7	(1) To generate, to produce (2) (b) The outcome of our sinful behaviour, and (d) a mysterious source we are unable to understand.
Check Your Understanding 8	(1) Originating, prompting (2) Direction, outcome
Check Your Understanding 9	(1) (b) A way of life that is appropriate to the purpose of life both for the individual and the individual's group. (2) Directions.
Check Your Understanding 10	(1) Distinct beings, recognizable individuals (2) (b) Sharing a common purpose, and working together to achieve it.
Check Your Understanding 11	(1) Immanent means for Christians that God is near to us and responds to our prayers. Immanent means for Hindus that we are each of us an aspect of God as is all the created world. Immanuel can be used to teach Hindus about God's immanence. Transcendent means for Christians that God is mysterious and wonderful beyond our human understanding. (2) Reject them as nonsense.
Check Your Understanding 12	(1) Elohim is a word used for a variety of spiritual beings: God himself, other gods, angels and powerful humans. (2) Immanence: available, helpful, loving, near, personal. Transcendence: almighty, creator, eternal, perfect, separate.
Check Your Understanding 13	(1) The person's child, since this is the only personal comparison. (2) (a) A goal to be reached, a final event to be worked for.

Check Your ***Understanding 14***	(1) Component, integral (2) A person's physical heart, the source of appetite, the centre of emotions, the place of thought, understanding and memory, the source of human will, and basis of character.
Check Your ***Understanding 15***	(1) Character, part (2) (c) God endowed people with gifts at the time of their conception, and inspired them to make full use of these gifts when he called them.
Check Your ***Understanding 16***	(1) Enticement, lure, seduction (2) (c) Turns to a different way.
Check Your ***Understanding 17***	(1) (a) For example: Did you attend worship at Trinity Church last Sunday?; Were you present at Trinity Church last Sunday? She gave us a wonderful present when we married; Do you want the nurse to attend to your wounds now? (b) Ask a friend to check whether you have written a good answer to this part of the question. (2) Rebelliousness, unkindness. These are attitudes of mind, while the others are evil actions.
Check Your ***Understanding 18***	(1) Disappointment, pain (2) (a) Affection, devotion, sympathy (b) Affection: friendliness and goodwill; devotion: commitment and constancy; sympathy: compassion and understanding. (c) Admiration: respect and amazement; appetite: hunger for and sense of need; need: dependence and inadequacy.
Check Your ***Understanding 19***	(1) Agreement, promise (2) (b) Association and behaviour between people.
Check Your ***Understanding 20***	(1) (a) The Exile. (b) After the return from Exile. (c) The Patriarchs. (d) The Kings. (e) The Exodus. (f) Independent Tribes.

(2) (a) Dedication, obedience. The Old Testament regards both as providing a means of reconciliation with God.

Check Your Understanding 21

(1) Respect, reverence
(2) Believable, dependable, faithful, loveable and reliable or words of similar meaning to each of these.

Check Your Understanding 22

(1) Friendship
(2) (a) Abortion: destroying a living foetus; euthanasia: providing a means of dying for people whose lives are spoilt by severe and incurable mental or physical illness; execution: ending the life of a person who has committed a very serious crime, usually murder; manslaughter: the unintentional and accidental killing of a human being; murder: the deliberate killing of a person for evil reasons.
(b) Manslaughter.
(c) This varies according to the culture and laws of the country in which you live, so ask a knowledgeable person what the laws cover. Christians should always act with loving concern for everybody their actions can influence.

Check Your Understanding 23

(1) (b) The fulfilment, and establishment of all that is good.
(2) Desire, dream, optimism

Check Your Understanding 24

(1) (b) It is the belief that God has a special place for Jerusalem in all his plans for the salvation of humankind.
(2) Rule.

Check Your Understanding 25

(1) (a) Mark 1.2 contains a direct quotation of Malachi 3.1 (strangely, Mark wrote that it came from Isaiah, which is true of Mark 1.3. Maybe a copyist added verse 2, to the proper quotation of 1.3). Mark 7.6–7 is a direct quotation.
(b) Isaiah 49.4–5 contains similar ideas to Mark 3.27; and Psalm 22.7–8 gives a similar idea to Mark 15.31. Deuteronomy 24.1–4 gives in full the law

referred to in Mark 10.4, and
Deuteronomy 25.5 does the same for
Mark 12.19.
(2) Matthew 2.6 is an example of 'contrast
in wording between the two Testaments'.
See Micah 5.2. Matthew 2.15 is an
example of 'strange comparisons'. The
reference is to Hosea 11.1b which in fact
refers to wayward Israel in the time of
Hosea, but Matthew refers to it as a
prophecy of the return from being
refugees of Joseph, Mary and the baby
Jesus. Mark 9.12 is an example of 'New
Testament references which lack
specific Old Testament sources'. Jesus is
referring to evidence that suffering
individuals can bring blessing to humankind. Hebrews 5.6 is a 'direct quotation'
from Psalm 110.4, but both these verses
give new interpretation to the story of
Abraham's encounter with Melchizedek,
which lacks any question about the
source of authority for this priest of God
Most High (Genesis 14.18–19).

Check Your
Understanding 26

(1) (b) He was able to provide us with a
much clearer understanding of what God
requires of us.
(2) Digested, in the sense of gaining a full
understanding of something. Ideas need
to nourish our thinking as food nourishes
our bodies.

Subject Index

Scripture Index

This index contains almost 1,500 references to the Old and New Testament books, which have helped us in the study of Old Testament Theology. They consist of single verses, groups of verses and occasionally whole chapters. When this book has used two sets of verses from the same chapter, these are given separately in order to place every reference its rightful place in the sequence of verses.

You may find this index helpful simply to discover the whereabouts of a particular quotation in the book. If you are a preacher you should check the things that are said about the verses on which you wish to preach. This will help you to start thinking about detailed aspects of what you intend to say. You can then be sure that you have understood what the Old Testament has to say about the subject you have chosen.